Ahn's Latin Vocabulary For Beginners

—

AHN'S

LATIN VOCABULARY

FOR BEGINNERS.

BY

Dr. P. HENN.

NEW YORK:

E. STEIGER & CO.

STEIGER's Latin Series.

FⁱˢᶜᵏAHN'S

LATIN VOCABULARY

FOR BEGINNERS,

METHODICAL AND ETYMOLOGICAL.

WITH A

COLLECTION OF LATIN PROVERBS AND QUOTATIONS.

BY

Dr. P. HENN.

NEW YORK:

E. STEIGER.

1879.

REQUEST.

The undersigned, in his efforts to secure the greatest possible correctness in his educational publications, will feel obliged for the suggestion of improvements.

E. Steiger, *Publisher.*

Press of
E. Steiger, N. Y.

PREFACE.

We are bound to be practical....

This *Latin Vocabulary for Beginners* is the result of many years' practical teaching, and has been undertaken with the view of improving the present methods of instruction in Latin. Experienced examiners can not have failed to observe how few even of those who have studied the language for years, are competent to translate with moderate facility a Latin passage which they have not previously seen. That the results obtained are so meager, is, however, not surprising. The traditional treatment of theoretical grammar, with a sentence now and then for illustration, on the one hand, and the abstractions and complications of grammatical analysis, on the other, can not possibly insure the pupil's ability to read an author of average difficulty accurately as well as rapidly, without a lexicon and other helps. To accomplish a practical purpose like this, we are bound to be practical; we must first have, beyond question, a sufficient knowledge of forms and syntax, to distinguish the case, person, tense, etc., and to connect the words properly — and in this regard, there seems to be a general desire among thinking teachers for a clearer and simpler method of teaching Latin grammar, than that in common use — and secondly, we must have a carefully selected stock of words, sufficient in quantity, and competent in matter, that is, an efficient vocabulary. To provide the learner with the latter, is the main object of the present volume.

The First, or **Methodical Part** is an attempt to bring home to the pupil at an age when the memory is much more active and developed than the reasoning faculties, those words and expressions of every-day life which are of prime importance for easy reading. These are arranged on a simple and natural plan, under appropriate headings for the sake of reference, and in such a way, as to be easy of remembrance. The collection of adjectives and abstract nouns with their opposites will be found especially framed to guide the pupil to a clear and discriminating use of these words. This part of the *Vocabulary* should be used with the *First Latin Book.*

In the Second, or **Etymological Part** the words derived from the same root are classed together. They will accordingly become more interesting and lively, and the knowledge of them more intelligent and fruitful. To bring this part into substantial harmony with the *Second Latin Book,* with which it is intended to be used, the primitive verbs of the four conjugations, regular as well as irregular, have been laid down as **ground-forms** or **key-words** for the grouping of derivatives, so as to associate their meanings. As a rule, only the leading, or principal meaning of each word has been given; at the same time, however, care has been taken to choose this meaning so as to allow its being easily traced to the etymological force of the key-word. By this means the fundamental idea from which the other meanings and shades of meaning naturally proceed, is presented with peculiar distinctness, and the surest of all aids supplied to a clear and effective study of the Latin language, which enters so largely into the formation of the English.

As supplementary to the *Vocabulary* a Collection of **Latin Proverbs and Quotations**, with their English translation, has been added. These short passages have been selected on account of their beauty and forcibleness, and by committing only one of them to memory each day, the pupil will gradually acquire a stock of elegant Latin expressions for school, and likewise a treasure of useful precepts for life.

While AHN-HENN's *Latin Vocabulary* has been specially prepared as a part of STEIGER's *Latin Series*, it will be found a useful companion to all other Latin text-books.

TABLE of CONTENTS.

METHODICAL PART.

1. Hŏmŏ. *Man.*

Fīgūră et membră. *Form and Members.*

hŏmŏ, -ĭnĭs (m.), *a human being, man**
corpŭs, -ŏrĭs (n.), *the body*
membrŭm, -ī (n.), *a member*
artŭs, -ŭŭm (m. pl.), *the limbs*
artĭcŭlŭs, -ī (m.), *a joint*
căpŭt, -ĭtĭs (n.), *the head*
occĭpŭt, -ĭtĭs (n.), *the hinder part of the head*
vertex, -ĭcĭs (m.), *the crown of the head*
cĕrĕbrŭm, -ī (n.), *the brain*
crīnĭs, - (m.), *the hair*
barbă, -ae (f.), *the beard*
făcĭēs, -ēī (f.), *the face*
frons, -tĭs (f.), *the forehead, brow*
sŭpercĭlĭŭm, -ī (n.), *an eyebrow*
ŏcŭlŭs, -ī (m.), *an eye*
palpĕbrae, -ārŭm (f. pl.), *the eyelids*
tempŏră, -ŭm (n. pl.), *the temples*

aurĭs, - (f.), *an ear*
aurĭcŭlă, -ae (f.), *the earlap*
nāsŭs, -ī (m.), *the nose*
gĕnă, -ae (f.), *a cheek*
maxillă, -ae (f.), *the jaw*
ōs, ōrĭs (n.), *the mouth*
ŏs, ossĭs (n.), *a bone*
lăbrŭm, -ī (n.), *a lip*
dens, -tĭs (m.), *a tooth*
linguă, -ae (f.), *the tongue*
mentŭm, -ī (n.), *the chin*
guttŭr, -ĭs (n.), *the throat*
jŭgŭlŭm, -ī (n.), *the collar-bone*
collŭm, -ī (n.), *the neck*
cervīcēs, -ŭm (f. pl.), *the nape*
hŭmĕrŭs, -ī (m.), *a shoulder*
bracchĭŭm, -ī (n.), *the lower arm*
lăcertŭs, -ī (m.), *the upper arm*
cŭbĭtŭs, -ī (m.), *the elbow*
mănŭs, -ŭs (f.), *a hand*
dĭgĭtŭs, -ī (m.), *a finger; a toe*
index, -ĭcĭs (m.), *the index finger*

---

* Note. Changeable parts of words are printed in **bold-faced** type, so as to indicate the manner of forming the genitive and the gender endings, and to show the infinitive endings.

The - simply added to a noun indicates that the genitive is like the nominative.

(m.), (f.), (n.), (pl.) mean: masculine, feminine, neuter, plural, respectively.

The signs of quantity are given, unless the syllable is long by position or contains a diphthong.

pollex, -ĭcĭs (m.), *the thumb; the great toe*
pugnŭs, -ĭ (m.), *a fist*
unguĭs, - (m.), *a nail*
tergŭm, -ĭ (n.), *the back*
pectŭs, -ŏrĭs (n.), *the breast*
ventĕr, -rĭs (m.), *the belly*
lātŭs, -ĕrĭs (n.), *the side*
fēmŭr, -ŏrĭs (n.), *the thigh*
gĕnŭ, -ŭs (n.), *the knee*
pŏplĕs, -ĭtĭs (m.), *the hough*
crūs, -rĭs (n.), *the leg*
pēs, pĕdĭs (m.), *a foot*
plantă, -ae (f.), *the sole of the foot*

calx, -cĭs (f.), *the heel*
stŏmăchŭs, -ĭ (m.), *the stomach*
viscĕră, -ŭm (n. pl.), *the bowels*
cor, cordĭs (n.), *the heart*
jĕcŭr, -ŏrĭs, -ĭnŏrĭs (n.) ⎫ *the*
hēpăr, -ătĭs (n.) ⎭ *liver*
pulmŏ, -ōnĭs (m.), *a lung*
vēnă, -ae (f.), *a vein*
sanguĭs, -ĭnĭs (m.), *blood*
nervŭs, -ĭ (m.), *a sinew*
cŭtĭs, - (f.), *the skin*
cărŏ, carnĭs (f.), *flesh*
fĭgūră, -ae (f.), *the form*
truncŭs, -ĭ (m.), *the trunk*

Corpŏrĭs affectĭōnēs. Affections of the Body.

affectĭŏ, -ōnĭs (f.), *an affection*
vītă, -ae (f.), *life*
spīrĭtŭs, -ŭs (m.), *a breathing*
ănĭmă, -ae (f.), *the breath*
vōx, -cĭs (f.), *the voice*
lăcrĭmă, -ae (f.), *a tear*
vultŭs, -ŭs (m.), *the mien*
rīsŭs, -ŭs (m.), *laughter*
gestŭs, -ŭs (m.), *gesture*
incessŭs, -ŭs (m.), *the gait*
sensŭs, -ŭs (m.), *sense*
vīsŭs, -ŭs (m.), *sight*
audītŭs, -ŭs (m.), *hearing*
olfactŭs, -ŭs (m.), *smell*
tactŭs, -ŭs (m.), *touch*
gustŭs, -ŭs (m.), *taste*
vĭgĭlĭă, -ae (f.), *waking*
somnŭs, -ĭ (m.), *sleep*

somnĭŭm, -ĭ (n.), *a dream*
fămēs, -ĭs (f.), *hunger*
sĭtĭs, - (f.), *thirst*
vălētūdŏ, -ĭnĭs (f.), *state of health*
sănĭtās, -ătĭs (f.), *health*
aegrōtătĭŏ, -ōnĭs (f.), *state of disease*
morbŭs, -ĭ (m.), *a disease*
fĕbrĭs, - (f.), *a fever*
tussĭs, - (f.), *a cough*
răvĭs, - (f.), *hoarseness*
pītūĭtă, -ae (f.), *phlegm*
tŭbĕr, -ĭs (n.), *a tumor*
ulcŭs, -ĕrĭs (n.), *an ulcer*
vulnŭs, -ĕrĭs (n.), *a wound*
cĭcătrĭx, -ĭcĭs (f.), *a scar*
mors, -tĭs (f.), *death*
cădăvĕr, -ĭs (n.), *a corpse*

Anĭmŭs ĕjusquĕ affectĭōnēs. The Mind and its Affections.

ănĭmŭs, -ĭ (m.), *the soul, mind*
ingĕnĭŭm,-ĭ(n.),*natural capacity*
mens, -tĭs (f.), *the mind*

rătĭŏ, -ōnĭs (f.), *reason*
mĕmŏrĭă, -ae (f.), *memory*
indŏlēs, -ĭs (f.), *disposition*

affectŭs, -ŭs (m.), *affect*
perturbătiŏ, -ŏnĭs (f.), *passion*
mōtŭs, -ŭs (m.), *emotion*
cŭpĭdĭtăs, -ătĭs (f.) *a desire*
lĭbĭdŏ, -ĭnĭs (f.), *lust*
vŏluntăs, -ătĭs (f.), *will*
vŏluptăs, -ătĭs (f.), *pleasure*
gaudĭŭm, -ĭ (n.), *joy*
taedĭŭm, -ĭ (n.), *loathing*
admīrātĭŏ, -ŏnĭs (f.), *admiration*
dŏlŏr, -ōrĭs (m.), *pain*
aegrĭtŭdŏ, -ĭnĭs (f.), *grief*
spēs, spĕĭ (f.), *hope*
tĭmŏr, -ōrĭs (m.), *fear*
mĕtŭs, -ŭs (m.), *dread*
Ĭră, -ae (f.), *anger*

Īrăcundĭă, -ae (f.), *wrath*
suspĭcĭŏ, -ŏnĭs (f.), *suspicion*
fĭdŭcĭă, -ae (f.), *trust*
laetĭtĭă, -ae (f.), *gladness*
sollĭcĭtŭdŏ, -ĭnĭs (f.), *solicitude*
scĭentĭă, -ae (f.), *knowledge*
cognĭtĭŏ, -ŏnĭs (f.), *an inquiry*
intellĕgentĭă, -ae (f.), *intelligence*
intellectŭs, -ŭs (m.), *understanding*
inscĭtĭă, -ae (f.), *unskillfulness*
inscĭentĭă, -ae (f.), *ignorance*
ŏpĭnĭŏ, -ŏnĭs (f.), *an opinion*
errŏr, -ōrĭs (m.), *a mistake*
insănĭă, -ae (f.), *insanity*
fŭrŏr, -ōrĭs (m.), *fury*
poenĭtentĭă, -ae (f.), *repentance*

Aetātēs et sexūs.   Ages and sexes.

Ĭnfans, -tĭs (m. & f.), *an infant, a babe*
pŭĕr, -ĭ (m.), *a boy*
pŭĕrŭlŭs, -ĭ (m.), *a little boy*
ădŭlescens, -tĭs (m.) ⎫ *a youth, young man*
jŭvĕnĭs,- (m.) ⎭
sĕnex, sĕnĭs (m.), *an old man*
vĭr, -ĭ (m.), *a man*
sexŭs, -ŭs (m.), *sex*
fēmĭnă, -ae (f.), *a woman*
mŭlĭĕr, -ĭs (f.), *a wife*

pŭellă, -ae (f.), *a girl*
virgŏ, -ĭnĭs (f.), *a maid, virgin*
mătrōnă, -ae (f.), *a lady*
ănŭs, -ŭs (f.), *an old lady*
aetăs, -ătĭs (f.), *age*
infantĭă, -ae (f.), *infancy*
pŭĕrĭtĭă, -ae (f.), *boyhood, childhood*
ădŭlescentĭă, -ae (f.) ⎫ *youth*
jŭventŭs, -ŭtĭs (f.) ⎭
sĕnectŭs, -ŭtĭs (f.), *old age*

2. Dŏmŭs.   The House.

dŏmŭs, -ŭs (f.), *a house*
fundămentŭm, -ĭ (n.), *a foundation*
līmĕn, -ĭnĭs (n.), *a threshold*
portă, -ae (f.), *a gate*
jănŭă, -ae (f.), *a door*
valvă, -ae (f.), *a valve;* valvae,
  -ārŭm (f. pl.), *a folding-door*

rēpăgŭlă, -ōrŭm (n. pl.), *a bolt*
claustră, -ōrŭm (n. pl.), *a lock*
clăvĭs, - (f.), *a key*
postĭs, - (m.), *a door post*
cardŏ, -ĭnĭs (m.), *the hinge (of a door)*
fēnestră, -ae (f.), *a window*
mūrŭs, -ĭ (m.), *a wall*

părĭĕs, -ĕtĭs (m.), *a wall*
pīlă, -ae (f.), *a pillar*
cŏlumnă, -ae (f.), *a column*
scālae, -ārŭm (f. pl.), *the stairs*
grădŭs, -ūs (m.), *a step*
tăbŭlātŭm, -ī (n.), *a floor, story*
conclāvĕ, -ĭs (n.), *a room*
cŭbĭcŭlŭm, -ī (n.), *a bedroom*
coenācŭlŭm, -ī (n.) ⎱ *a dining-*
trĭclīnĭŭm,-ī (n.) ⎰ *room*
vestĭbŭlŭm, -ī (n.), *a vestibule*
ătrĭŭm, -ī (n.), *the entrance-hall*

balnĕŭm, -ī (n.), *a bath*
implŭvĭŭm, -ī (n.), *the yard*
pŭtĕŭs, -ī (m.), *a well*
cellă, -ae (f.), *a chamber, store-room*
cŭlīnă, -ae (f.), *a kitchen*
fŏcŭs, -ī (m.), *a hearth*
fornax, -ācĭs (f.), *a furnace*
sŏlŭm, -ī (n.), *the floor*
păvīmentŭm, -ī (n.), *a pavement*
lăcūnăr, -ārĭs (n.), *a ceiling*
tectŭm, -ī (n.), *a roof*
tēgŭlă, -ae (f.), *a tile*

3. Vestītŭs. *Clothing.*

pannŭs, -ī (m.), *a cloth*
lānă, -ae (f.), *wool*
lintĕŭm, -ī (n.), *linen*
vestĭs, - (f.), *a dress*
vestīmentŭm, -ī (n.), *a garment*
vestītŭs,-ūs (m.), *clothing, clothes*
ămictŭs, -ūs (m.), *a mantle*
tŭnĭcă, -ae (f.), *the tunic, an undergarment*
tŏgă, -ae (f.), *the toga*
pallĭŭm, -ī (n.), *a cloak*
paenŭlă, -ae (f.), *a traveling-cloak, rain-cloak*
pallă, -ae (f.), *a robe*

trăbĕă, -ae (f.), *a robe of state*
stŏlă, -ae (f.), *a stole*
cingŭlŭs, -ī (m.), *a belt*
brācae, -ārŭm (f. pl.), *breeches*
calcĕŭs, -ī (m.), *a shoe*
crĕpĭdă, -ae (f.), *a sandal*
pīlĕŭs, -ī (m.), *a hat*
ornāmentŭm, -ī (n.), *an ornament*
torquĕs, -ĭs (f.), *a neck chain*
ănŭlŭs, -ī (m.), *a finger-ring*
armillă, -ae (f.), *a bracelet*
vēlŭm, -ī (n.), *a veil*
vittă, -ae (f.), *a head-band*

4. Sŭpellex. *Household Utensils.*

sŭpellex, -ectĭlĭs (f.), *household utensils, furniture*
mensă, -ae (f.), *a table*
scrīnĭŭm, -ī (n.), *a chest, press*
hŏrŏlŏgĭŭm, -ī (n.), *a clock*
plŭtĕŭs, -ī (m.), *a book-case*
scamnŭm, -ī (n.), *a bench*

scăbellŭm, -ī (n.), *a footstool*
sellă, -ae (f.), *a chair*
subsellĭŭm, -ī (n.), *a seat*
tŏrŭs, -ī (m.), *a couch*
lectŭs, -ī (m.), *a sofa*
lectĭcă, -ae (f.), *a litter*
pulvīnŭs, -ī (m.), *a cushion*

pulvīnăr, -ārīs (n.), *a cushioned seat*
strāgŭlŭm, -Ī (n.), *a carpet*
cūbĭlĕ, -Īs (n.), *a bed*
cūnābŭlă, -ōrŭm (n. pl.), *a cradle*
pătĕră, -ae (f.), *a bowl*
pătĭnă, -ae (f.), *a pan*
văs, -Īs, (n.), *a vessel*
ollă, -ae (f.), *a pot*
lanx, -cĭs (f.), *a dish*
mappă, -ae (f.), *a napkin*

sălīnŭm, -Ī (n.), *a salt-cellar*
cȳăthŭs, -Ī (m.), *a cup*
pōcŭlŭm, -Ī (n.), *a goblet*
ampullă, -ae (f.), *a bottle*
cădŭs, -Ī (m.), *a jug*
amphŏră, -ae (f.), *an amphora (a jar with two handles)*
crătĕră, -ae (f.), *a mixing vessel*
spĕcŭlŭm, -Ī (n.), *a mirror*
pectĕn, -Ĭnĭs (m.), *a comb*
scōpae, -ārŭm (f. pl.), *a broom*

5. Victŭs. *Victuals.*

victŭs, -ūs (m.), *victuals, provisions*
ălĭmentŭm, -Ī (n.), *nourishment*
cĭbŭs, -Ī (m.), *food*
pōtŭs, -ūs (m.), *a drink*
pōtĭŏ, -ōnĭs (f.), *a drinking*
haustŭs, -ūs (m.), *a draught*
frustŭm, -Ī (n.), *a bit*
pānĭs, - (m.), *bread*
cărŏ, carnĭs (f.), *meat*
ŏlŭs, -ĕrĭs (n.), *vegetables*
sāl, sălĭs (m.), *salt*

obsōnĭŭm, -Ī (n.), *viands*
fercŭlŭm, -Ī (n.), *a course (of a meal)*
pĕnŭs, -ūs (m.), *provisions*
jentācŭlŭm, -Ī (n.), *breakfast*
praudĭŭm, -Ī (n.), *luncheon*
coenă, -ae (f.), *dinner*
ĕpŭlŭm, -Ī (n.), *a banquet*
ĕpŭlae, -ārŭm (f. pl.), *sumptuous dishes*
convīvĭŭm, -Ī (n.), *a dinner-party*

6. Fămĭlĭă. *The Family.*

fămĭlĭă, -ae (f.), *a family*
pătĕr, -rĭs (m.), *a father*
mătĕr, -rĭs (f.), *a mother*
părentĕs,-ŭm (m. pl.), *the parents*
lĭbĕrĭ, -ōrŭm (m. pl.), *the children*
fĭlĭŭs, -Ī (m.), *a son*
fĭlĭă, -ae (f.), *a daughter*
frătĕr, -rĭs (m.), *a brother*
sŏrŏr, -ōrĭs (f.), *a sister*
lēvĭr, -Ī (m.), *a brother-in-law*
glōs, -ōrĭs (f.), *a sister-in-law*

gĕmĭnĭ, -ōrŭm (m. pl.), *twins*
vĭtrĭcŭs, -Ī (m.), *a step-father*
nŏvercă, -ae (f.), *a step-mother*
prīvignŭs, -Ī (m.), *a step-son*
prīvignă, -ae (f.), *a step-daughter*
pătrŭŭs, -Ī (m.), *a paternal uncle*
ămĭtă, -ae (f.), *a paternal aunt*
ăvuncŭlŭs, -Ī (m.), *a maternal uncle*
mătertĕră, -ae (f.), *a maternal aunt*

— 6 —

påtrŭělĭs, - (m.), *a father's brother's son (a cousin)*
consōbrīnŭs, -ī (m.), *a mother's
brother's son (a cousin)*
cŏnsōbrīnī, -ōrŭm (m. pl.), *cous-
ins german*
ăvŭs, -ī (m.), *a grandfather*
ăvĭă, -ae (f.), *a grandmother*
prŏăvŭs, -ī (m.), *a great grandfather*
prŏăvĭă, -ae (f.), *a great grandmother*
nĕpōs, -ōtĭs (m.), *a grandson;
a nephew*
neptĭs, - (f.), *a granddaughter; a
niece*
prŏnĕpōs, -ōtĭs (m.), *a great
grandson*
mātrĭmōnĭŭm, -ī (n.), *matrimony*
conjŭgĭŭm, -ī (n.), *a marriage*
conjux, -ŭgĭs (m.), *a husband*
uxŏr, -ōrĭs (f.), *a wife* [*ding*
nuptĭae, -ārŭm (f. pl.), *a wed-
nātălĭs, - (m.), *a birthday*
prŏcŭs, -ī (m.), *a suitor*
sponsŭs, -ī (m.), *a bridegroom*
sponsă, -ae (f.), *a bride*

vĭdŭă, -ae (f.), *a widow*
tūtŏr, -ōrĭs (m.), *a guardian*
pūpillŭs, -ī (m.) } *a ward*
pūpillă, -ae (f.) }
prŏpinquŭs, -ī (m.), *a relative*
cognātŭs, -ī (m.) } *a kins-*
consangnĭnĕŭs, -ī (m.) } *man*
affĭnĭs, - (m. & f.), *a relation by
marriage*
sŏcĕr, -ī (m.), *a father-in-law*
sŏcrŭs, -ūs (f.), *a mother-in-law*
gĕnĕr, -ī (m.), *a son-in-law*
nŭrŭs, -ūs (f.), *a daughter-in-law*
prŏgĕnĭēs, -ēī (f.), *the lineage*
gens, -tĭs (f.), *a clan*
stirps, -ĭs (f.), *a stem, stock*
mājōrēs, -ŭm (m. pl.), *ancestors*
prōlēs, -ĭs (f.), *offspring*
postĕrī, -ōrŭm (m. pl.), *descend-
ants*
hĕrŭs, -ī (m.), *the master* } *of the*
hĕră, -ae (f.), *the mistress* } *house*
fămŭlŭs, -ī (m.), *a servant*
servŭs, -ī (m.), *a slave*
ancillă, -ae (f.), *a maid-servant*
vernă, -ae (m. & f.), *a home-born
slave*

7. Commercĭŭm. *Commercial Intercourse.*

commercĭŭm, -ī (n.), *trade, commerce*
sŏcĭŭs, -ī (m.), *a partner*
sŏcĭĕtās, -ātĭs (f.), *partnership*
merx, -cĭs (f.), *ware*
mercātŭs, -ūs (m.), *a market*
mercātūră, -ae (f.), *trade, traffic*
mercātŏr, -ōrĭs (m.), *a merchant*
prĕtĭŭm, -ī (n.), *price*
pĕcūnĭă, -ae (f.), *money;* pĕcūnĭă
praesens, *ready money*

nummŭs, -ī (m.), *a coin*
emptŏr, -ōrĭs (m.), *a buyer*
vendĭtŏr, -ōrĭs (m.), *a seller*
quaestŭs, -ūs (m.), *acquisition*
lŭcrŭm, -ī (n.), *profit*
damnŭm, -ī (n.), *loss*
nĕgōtĭŭm, -ī (n.), *business*
nĕgōtĭātŏr, -ōrĭs (m.), *a trader*
tăbernă, -ae (f.), *a shop*
lībră, -ae (f.), *a pair of scales; a
pound*

argentārīŭs, -ī (m.), *a banker*
mensūră, -ae (f.), *a measure*
pondŭs, -ĕrīs (n.), *a weight*
ēmŏlŭmentŭm, -ī (n.), *advantage*
dētrīmentŭm, -ī (n.), *damage*
pondō (n. indecl.), *a pound in weight*
căpŭt, -ĭtīs (n.) } *the principal*
sors, -tīs (f.) } *sum*

faenŭs, -ŏrīs (n.), *interest*
faenĕrātŏr,-ŏrīs (m.), *a capitalist*
dēbītŏr, -ŏrīs (m.), *a debtor*
crēdītŏr, -ŏrīs (m.), *a creditor*
pignŭs, -ŏrīs (n.), *a pawn, mortgage*
aes ălīēnŭm, aerīs -ī (n.), *a debt, debts*
auctĭō, -ōnīs (f.), *an auction*

8. Nĕgōtĭŭm. *Business.*

nĕgōtĭŭm, -ī (n.), *business, occupation*
ŏpĕrārīŭs, -ī (m.), *a workman*
ŏpīfex, -ĭcīs (m.), *a mechanic*
făbĕr, -rī (m.), *a worker in hard materials;* făbĕr ferrārīŭs, *a smith;* făbĕr tignārīŭs, *a carpenter*
pistŏr, -ŏrīs (m.), *a baker*
vestītŏr, -ŏrīs (m.), *a tailor*
sartŏr, -ŏrīs (m.), *a botcher*
sūtŏr, -ŏrīs (m.), *a shoemaker*
textŏr, -ŏrīs (m.), *a weaver*
fullō, -ōnīs (m.), *a fuller*
cŏrīārīŭs, -ī (m.), *a currier*
fīgŭlŭs, -ī (m.), *a potter*
tonsŏr, -ŏrīs (m.), *a barber*
aurifex, -ĭcīs (m.), *a goldsmith*
lăpĭcīdă, -ae (m.), *a stone-cutter*

piscātŏr, -ŏrīs (m.), *a fisherman*
auceps, -ŭpīs (m.), *a bird-catcher*
vēnātŏr, -ŏrīs (m.), *a hunter*
lănĭŭs, -ī (m.), *a butcher*
cŏquŭs, -ī (m.), *a cook*
mercātŏr,-ŏrīs (m.), *a merchant*
nĕgōtĭātŏr, -ŏrīs (m.), *a trader*
emptŏr, -ŏrīs (m.), *a buyer*
vendĭtŏr, -ŏrīs (m.), *a seller*
rĕdemptŏr, -ŏrīs (m.), *a contractor*
archĭtectŭs, -ī (m.), *an architect*
vĭātŏr, -ŏrīs (m.), *a traveler*
aurīgă, -ae (m.), *a coachman*
naută, -ae (m.), *a sailor*
bājŭlŭs, -ī (m.), *a porter*
mercēnārīŭs, -ī (m.), *a hired servant*

9. Instrūmentă. *Tools.*

instrŭmentŭm, -ī (n.), *a tool, instrument*
ăcŭs, -ūs (f.), *a needle*
forfex,-ĭcīs (f.), *a pair of scissors*
fīlŭm, -ī (n.), *a thread*
nŏvăcŭlă, -ae (f.), *a razor*

sĕcūrīs, - (f.), *an axe, a hatchet*
asciă, -ae (f.) } *an axe*
dŏlābră, -ae (f.) }
līmă, -ae (f.), *a file*
tĕrĕbră, -ae (f.), *a borer*
caelŭm, -ī (n.), *a chisel*

serră, -ae (f.), *a saw*
mallĕŭs, -ĭ (m.), *a hammer*
cultĕr, -rĭ (m.), *a knife*
scalpellŭm, -ĭ (n.), *a lancet*
cōs, cōtĭs (f.), *a grindstone*
incūs, -ūdĭs (f.), *an anvil*
follĭs, – (m.), *a pair of bellows*

vectĭs, – (m.), *a lever*
prēlŭm, -ĭ (n.), *a press*
furnŭs, -ĭ (m.), *an oven*
forceps -ĭpĭs (f.), *a pair of tongs*
offĭcīnă, -ae (f.) }
făbrĭcă, -ae (f.) } *a workshop*

10. Lūdŭs. *Play.*

lūdŭs, -ĭ (m.), *a play, game*
pĭlă, -ae (f.), *a ball*
ălĕă, -ae (f.), *a game at dice*
tălŭs, -ĭ (m.) }
tessĕră,-ae (f.) } *a die*
ălĕātŏr, -ōrĭs (m.), *a gambler*
turbŏ, -ĭnĭs (m.), *a spinning top*
lūdicrŭm, -ĭ (n.) }
spectăcŭlŭm, -ĭ (n.) } *a stage play*
scēnă, -ae (f.), *the stage*
aulaeŭm, -ĭ (n.), *the curtain*
spectātŏr, -ōrĭs (m.), *a spectator*
căvĕă, -ae (f.), *the spectators' seats*
făbŭlă, -ae (f.), *a play*
cōmoedĭă, -ae (f.), *a comedy*
trᴵ.goedĭă, -ae (f.), *a tragedy*
actŭs, -ūs (m.), *an act*

actŏr, -ōrĭs (m.) } *an actor, a*
histrĭŏ, -ōnĭs (m.) } *stage-player*
persōnă, -ae (f.), *a mask*
partēs, -ĭŭm (f. pl.), *the part*
grex, grĕgĭs (m.), *a company*
praestĭgĭae, -ārŭm (f. pl.), *jugglers' tricks*
praestĭgĭātŏr, -ōrĭs (m.), *a juggler*
glădĭātŏr, -ōrĭs (m.), *a gladiator*
circŭs, -ĭ (m.), *a circus*
cancellī, -ōrŭm (m. pl.), *the railings*
stădĭŭm, -ĭ (n.), *a race-course*
pŭgĭl, -ĭs (m.), *a pugilist*
pŭgĭlātĭŏ, -ōnĭs (f.), *boxing*
luctātŏr, -ōrĭs (m.), *a wrestler*
luctātĭŏ, -ōnĭs (f.), *wrestling*

11. Schŏlă. *The School.*

schŏlă, -ae (f.), *a school*
tīrŏ, -ōnĭs (m.), *a beginner*
paedăgōgŭs, -ĭ (m.), *a pedagogue*
ălumnŭs, -ĭ (m.), *a pupil*
discĭpŭlŭs, -ĭ (m.), *a scholar*
condĭscĭpŭlŭs, -ĭ (m.), *a schoolmate*
praeceptŏr,-ōrĭs (m.) }
doctŏr, -ōrĭs (m.) } *a teacher*

magistĕr, -rĭ (m.), *a master*
căthĕdră, -ae (f.), *a professor's chair*
subsellĭŭm, -ĭ (n.), *a bench*
tăbŭlă, -ae (f.) }
tăbellă, -ae (f.) } *a slate*
crētă, -ae (f.), *chalk*
lŏcŭlī, -ōrŭm (m. pl.), *a box*
classĭs, – (f.), *a class*

audītōrĭŭm, -ī (n.), *a lecture room*
doctrīnă, -ae (f.), *teaching*
disciplīnă, -ae (f.), *instruction*
instītūtĭŏ, -ōnĭs (f.), *education*
interprētătĭŏ, -ōnĭs (f.), *a translation*
praeceptŭm, -ī (n.), *a precept*
auctōrĭtās, -ātĭs (f.), *authority*
ŏboedĭentĭă, -ae (f.) }
obsĕquĭŭm, -ī (n.) } *obedience*

pětŭlantĭă, -ae (f.), *wantonness*
intentĭŏ, -ōnĭs (f.), *attention*
prōgressŭs, -ŭs (m.), *progress*
dīlĭgentĭă, -ae (f.), *diligence*
explōrătĭŏ, -ōnĭs (f.), *an examination*
laus, -dĭs (f.), *praise*
vĭtŭpěrătĭŏ, -ōnĭs (f.), *censure*
pĭgrĭtĭă, -ae (f.), *idleness*
castīgătĭŏ, -ōnĭs (f.), *a correction, chastisement*

12. Lībĕr. *The Book.*

lībĕr, -rī (m.), *a book*
littĕră, -ae (f.), *a letter*
littĕrae, -ārŭm (f. pl.), *a letter, epistle*
syllăbă, -ae (f.), *a syllable*
verbŭm, -ī (n.), *a word*
chartă, -ae (f.), *paper*
membrānă, -ae (f.), *parchment*
cōdex, -ĭcĭs (m.), *a copy-book*
versŭs, -ŭs (m.), *a line*
fōlĭŭm, -ī (n.), *a leaf*
păgīnă, -ae (f.), *a page*
vōlŭmĕn, -ĭnĭs (n.), *a volume*

margŏ, -ĭnĭs (m.), *a margin*
bĭblĭōpōlă, -ac (m.), *a bookseller*
lībrārĭŭs, -ī (m.), *a copyist*
prēlŭm, -ī (n.), *a press*
bĭblĭōthēcă, -ae (f.), *a library*
scrīptŏr, -ōrĭs (m.), *a writer*
auctŏr, -ōrĭs (m.), *an author*
scrībă, -ae (m.), *a clerk*
scrīptūră, -ae (f.), *writing*
lectĭŏ, -ōnĭs (f.), *reading*
ātrāmentŭm, -ī (n.), *ink*
stĭlŭs, -ī (m.), *a pencil*
invōlūcrŭm, -ī (n.), *a wrapper*

13. Urbs. *The City.*

urbs, -ĭs (f.), *a city*
urbānŭs, -ī (m.), *a city-man*
cīvĭs, - (m.), *a citizen*
cīvĭtās, -ātĭs (f.), *a community*
oppĭdŭm, -ī (n.), *a town*
oppĭdānŭs, -ī (m.), *a townsman*
oppĭdŭlŭm, -ī (n.), *a small town*
vīcŭs, -ī (m.), *a village*
căsă, -ae (f.), *a cottage*

dōmŭs, -ŭs (f.) }
aedēs, -ĭŭm (f. pl.) } *a house*
hăbĭtătĭŏ, -ōnĭs (f.), *a dwelling*
plătĕă, -ae (f.), *a street*
angĭportŭs, -ŭs (m.), *a lane*
fōrŭm, -ī (n.), *the market place*
cūrĭă, -ae (f.), *the senate house, city hall*
dēversōrĭŭm, -ī (n.), *an inn*

— 10 —

caupōnă, -ae (f.), *a tavern*
thĕātrŭm, -ī (n.), *a theater*
custōdīă, -ae (f.) } *a prison*
carcĕr, -Is (m.) }
mūrŭs, -ī (m.), *a wall*

moenīă, -Iŭm (n. pl.), *city walls*
prōpugnācŭlŭm, -ī(n.), *a bulwark*
turrīs, - (f.), *a tower*
portă, -ae (f.), *a gate*
sŭbŭrbiŭm, -ī (n.), *a suburb*

14. Rēs pūblĭcă. *The Commonwealth, State.*

rēs pūblĭcă, rĕī -ae (f.), *the commonwealth, republic, state*
praesĕs, -Idīs (m.), *a president*
rex, rēgĭs (m.), *a king*
rēgīnă, -ae (f.), *a queen*
princeps, -Ipĭs (m.), *a chief*
princĭpātŭs, -ūs (m.), *sovereignty*
măgistrātŭs,-ūs(m.), *a magistrate*
collēgă, -ae (m.), *a colleague*
pŏpŭlŭs, -ī (m.), *the people*
nātĭŏ, -ōnĭs (f.), *a nation*
plēbs, -īs (f.), *the commonalty*
praefectŭs, -ī (m.), *a prefect*
nōbĭlĭs, - (m.), *a nobleman*
vulgŭs, -ī (n.), *the rabble*
indĭgĕnă, -ae (m.), *a native*
pĕrĕgrīnŭs, -ī (m.), *a stranger*
servŭs, -ī (m.), *a slave*
mancĭpĭŭm, -ī (n.), *a bond slave*
dŏmĭnŭs, -ī (m.), *a master*
pŏtestās, -ātĭs (f.), *official power*
pŏtentĭă, -ae (f.), *might pire*
impĕrĭŭm, -ī (n.), *dominion, em-*
regnŭm, -ī (n.),*a reign, kingdom*
rŏgātĭŏ, -ōnĭs (f.), *a bill, draft of a law*

lex, lēgĭs (f.), *a law*
mūnŭs, -ĕrĭs (n.), *an office*
concĭlĭŭm, -ī (n.), *an assembly*
consĭlĭŭm, -ī (n.), *a council*
contĭŏ, -ōnĭs (f.), *a meeting*
cŏmĭtĭă, -ōrŭm (n. pl.), *the comitia (assembly for electing magistrates)*
candĭdātŭs, -ī (m.), *a candidate for office*
sŏlĭŭm, -ī (n.), *a throne*
dĭadēmă, -tĭs (n.), *a diadem, crown*
sceptrŭm, -ī (n.), *a sceptre*
aulă, -ae (f.), *the court*
aulĭcŭs, -ī (m.), *a courtier*
pălātĭŭm, -ī (n.), *a palace*
aerārĭŭm, -ī (n.), *the treasury*
censŭs, -ūs (m.), *a census*
vectĭgăl, -ālĭs (n.), *a toll*
trĭbūtŭm, -ī (n.), *a contribution*
stĭpendĭŭm, -ī (n.), *a tax*
rēdĭtŭs, -ŭŭm (m. pl.), *income*
lēgātŭs, -ī (m.), *an ambassador*
lēgā⁺ĭŏ, -ōnĭs (f.), *an embassy*
foedŭs, -ĕrĭs (n.), *a treaty*

15. Ars. *Art.*

ars, -tĭs (f.), *art*
artĭfex, -Icĭs (m.), *an artist*
artĭfĭcĭŭm, -ī (n.), *the occupation of an artist*

mătĕrĭă, -ae (f.), *matter*
rhētŏrĭcă, -ae (f.), *rhetoric*
fācundĭă, -ae (f.), *readiness of speech*

ēlŏquentĭā, -ae (f.), *eloquence*
ŏrātŏr, -ōrĭs (m.), *a speaker, an orator*
ŏrātĭŏ, -ōnĭs (f.), *a speech, an oration*
pŏĕtĭcă, -ae (f.), *the poetic art*
carmĕn, -ĭnĭs (n.), *a song*
pŏēmă, -tĭs (n.), *a poem*
pŏētă, -ae (m.), *a poet*
mĕtrŭm, -ī (n.), *a meter*
nŭmĕrŭs, -ī (m.), *rhythm*
mūsĭcŭs, -ī (m.), *a musician*
mūsĭcă, -ōrŭm (n. pl.), *music*
cantŭs, -ūs (m.), *singing*
cantŏr, -ōrĭs (m.), *a singer*
mŏdŭs, -ī (m.), *melody*
concentŭs, -ūs (m.), *harmony*
testŭdŏ, -ĭnĭs (f.), *a lute*
lȳră, -ae (f.), *a lyre*
fĭdēs, -ĭŭm (f. pl.), *a stringed instrument, lute*
fĭdĭcĕn, -ĭnĭs (m.), *a lute-player, minstrel*
nervŭs, -ī (m.) ⎫ *a string*
chordă, -ae (f.) ⎭

tībĭă, -ae (f.), *a flute*
tībĭcĕn, -ĭnĭs (m.), *a flute-player*
fĭstūlă, -ae (f.), *a shepherd's pipe*
tūbă, -ae (f.), *a trumpet*
tūbĭcĕn, -ĭnĭs (m.), *a trumpeter*
lĭtŭŭs, -ī (m.), *a cornet*
tympănŭm, -ī (n.), *a kettle-drum*
pictūră, -ae (f.), *painting*
pictŏr, -ōrĭs (m.), *a painter*
tăbūlă (pictă), -ae -ae (f.), *a picture*
cŏlŏr, -ōrĭs (m.), *color*
pēnĭcillŭs, -ī (m.), *a painter's brush*
effĭgĭēs, -ēī (f.), *a likeness*
ĭmāgŏ, -ĭnĭs (f.) ⎫ *an image*
sĭmŭlăcrŭm, -ī (n.) ⎭
stătŭă, -ae (f.) ⎫ *a statue*
signŭm, -ī (n.) ⎭
stătŭārĭă, -ae (f.), *statuary*
stătŭārĭŭs, -ī (m.), *a statuary*
sculptūră, -ae (f.), *sculpture*
sculptŏr, -ōrĭs (m.), *a sculptor*
archĭtectūră, -ae (f.), *architecture*
archĭtectŭs, -ī (m.), *an architect*

16. Mălĕfĭcĭŭm. Evil Deed.

mălĕfĭcĭŭm, -ī (n.), *an evil deed, misdeed*
fraus, -dĭs (f.), *a fraud*
dŏlŭs, -ī (m.), *evil intent*
injūrĭă, -ae (f.), *injury*
culpă, -ae (f.), *fault*
nĕfās (n. indecl.), *an impious deed*
scĕlŭs, -ĕrĭs (n.), *a crime*
dēlictŭm, -ī (n.), *an offense*
flāgĭtĭŭm, -ī (n.), *a shameful act*
caedēs, -ĭs (f.), *murder*
parrĭcĭdĭŭm, -ī (n.), *parricide*
conjūrātĭŏ, -ōnĭs (f.), *a conspiracy*

perdŭellĭŏ, -ōnĭs (f.), *high treason*
rĕbellĭŏ, -ōnĭs (f.), *a rebellion*
parrĭcĭdă, -ae (m.), *a parricide*
percussŏr, -ōrĭs (m.), *a murderer*
sĭcārĭŭs, -ī (m.), *an assassin*
lătrŏ, -ōnĭs (m.), *a highwayman*
lătrŏcĭnĭŭm, -ī (n.), *highway robbery*
praedŏ, -ōnĭs (m.), *a robber*
pīrătă, -ae (m.), *a sea-robber, pirate*
fūr, -ĭs (m.), *a thief*
furtŭm, -ī (n.), *theft*

săcrĭlĕgŭs, -ĭ (m.), *a sacrilegist*
săcrĭlĕgĭŭm, -ĭ (n.), *sacrilege*
perjŭrŭs, -ĭ (m.), *a perjurer*
perjŭrĭŭm, -ĭ (n.), *perjury*

pĕcūlātŭs, -ŭs (m.), *peculation*
pĕcūlātŏr, -ōrĭs (m.), *a peculator*
infāmĭă, -ac (f.), *infamy*

17. Jūdĭcĭŭm. *The Court.*

jŭdĭcĭŭm, -ĭ (n.) } *a court of*
fŏrŭm, -ĭ (n.) } *justice.*
jūs, jūrĭs (n.), *right, law*
lĭs, lītĭs (f.), *a lawsuit*
causă, -ae (f.), *a cause in law*
contrōversĭă, -ae (f.), *a dispute*
crĭmĕn, -ĭnĭs (n.), *a charge*
arbĭtĕr, -rĭ (m.), *an arbiter*
jŭdex, -ĭcĭs (m.), *a judge*
trĭbūnăl, -ālĭs (n.), *a judgment seat, tribunal*
practŏr, -ōrĭs (m.), *the president of the court*
advŏcātŭs, -ĭ (m.), *a counselor*
actŏr, -ōrĭs (m.), *a plaintiff*
rĕŭs, -ĭ (m.), *a defendant*
pătrōnŭs, -ĭ (m.), *an advocate*
accūsātŏr, -ōrĭs (m.), *an accuser*
dēlātŏr, -ōrĭs (m.), *an informer*
adversārĭŭs, -ĭ (m.), *an opponent*
nŏcens, -tĭs (m. & f.), *a guilty person*
lictŏr, -ōrĭs (m.), *a lictor* [son
văs, vădĭs (m.), *a bail, security*

vădĭmōnĭŭm, -ĭ (n.), *bail*
praes, -dĭs (m.), *a bondsman*
testĭs, - (m. & f.), *a witness*
jūsjūrandŭm, jūrisjūrandĭ (n.), *an oath*
testĭmōnĭŭm, -ĭ (n.), *testimony*
argūmentŭm, -ĭ (n.), *a proof*
quaestĭŏ, -ōnĭs (f.), *an inquisition*
tormentŭm, -ĭ (n.), *torture*
sententĭă, -ae (f.), *a decision*
absŏlūtĭŏ, -ōnĭs (f.), *an acquittal*
damnātĭŏ, -ōnĭs (f.), *a condemnation*
vincŭlă, -ōrŭm (n. pl.), *fetters*
exĭlĭŭm, -ĭ (n.), *exile*
poenă, -ae (f.), *punishment*
multă, -ae (f.), *a fine*
carnĭfex, -ĭcĭs (m.), *an executioner*
supplĭcĭŭm, -ĭ (n.), *capital punishment*
pătĭbŭlŭm, -ĭ (n.), *a gibbet*

18. Vectūră. *Conveyance.*

vectūră, -ae (f.), *conveyance, transportation by carriage or by ship*
vĕhĭcŭlŭm, -ĭ (n.), *a vehicle*
currŭs, -ŭs (m.), *a chariot*
plaustrŭm, -ĭ (n.), *a wagon*
carpentŭm, -ĭ (n.), *a carriage*

bĭgae, -ārŭm (f. pl.), *a pair of horses*
quadrĭgae, -ārŭm (f. pl.), *a team of four*
cărrŭs, -ĭ (m.), *a cart*
tēmŏ, -ōnĭs (m.), *the tongue of a cart*

rōtā, -ae (f.), *a wheel*
jūgŭm, -ī (n.), *a yoke*
axĭs, - (m.), *an axle-tree*
aurīgā, -ae (m.), *a coachman*
nāvĭgĭŭm, -ī (n.), *a vessel*
nāvĭs, - (f.), *a ship*
rătĭs, - (f.), *a raft*
lintĕr, -rĭs (f.), *a boat*
scăphā, -ae (f.), *a skiff*
trĭrēmĭs, - (f.), *a trireme*
quădrĭrēmĭs, - (f.), *a quadrireme*
rēmŭs, -ī (m.), *an oar*
vectōr, -ōrĭs (m.), *a passenger*
nauarchŭs, -ī (m.), *the master of a vessel*
nautā, -ae (m.), *a sailor*
rēmex, -ĭgĭs (m.), *an oarsman*

gŭbernātŏr, -ōrĭs (m.), *a pilot*
gŭbernācŭlŭm, -ī (n.), *a helm, rudder*
prōrā, -ae (f.), *the prow*
puppĭs, - (f.), *the stern, poop*
alvĕŭs, -ī (m.), *the hold*
mālŭs, -ī (m.), *a mast*
antennā, -ae (f.), *a sail-yard*
ōrā, -ae (f.), *the board; a cable*
fūnĭs, - (m.) }
rūdens, -tĭs (m.) } *a rope*
vēlŭm, -ī (n.), *a sail*
rostrŭm, -ī (n.), *a ship's beak*
ancŏrā, -ae (f.), *an anchor*
naufrăgĭŭm, -ī (n.), *a shipwreck*
portŭs, -ūs (m.), *a port*
nāvālĭā, -ĭŭm (n. pl.), *a dock*

19. Équěs. The Horseman.

ĕquěs, -ĭtĭs (m.), *a horseman, rider*
ĕquŭs, -ī (m.), *a horse*
ĕquā, -ae (f.), *a mare*
frēnā, -ōrŭm (n. pl.), *a bridle*
hăbēnā, -ae (f.), *a halter, rein*
calcăr, -ārĭs (n.), *a spur*
ĕphippĭŭm, -ī (n.), *a horse-cloth*

phălěrae, -ārŭm (f.pl.), *trappings*
clītellae, -ārŭm (f. pl.), *a saddle*
lōrā, -ōrŭm (n. pl.), *a whip*
ăgāsŏ, -ōnĭs (m.), *a hostler*
călŏ, -ōnĭs (m.), *a groom*
stăbŭlŭm -ī (n.), *a stable*
praesaepĕ, -ĭs (n.), *a manger*
pābŭlŭm, -ī (n.), *fodder*

20. Mīlěs. The Soldier.

mīlěs, -ĭtĭs (m.), *a soldier*
pěděs, -ĭtĭs (m.), *a foot-soldier*
ĕquěs, -ĭtĭs (m.), *a horseman*
tīrŏ, -ōnĭs (m.), *a recruit*
vŏlŏ, -ōnĭs (m.), *a volunteer*
commīlĭtŏ, -ōnĭs (m.), *a fellow-soldier, comrade*
větěrānŭs, -ī (m.), *a veteran*

praefectŭs, -ī (m.), *an officer*
děcŭrĭŏ, -ōnĭs (m.), *a decurion*
centŭrĭŏ, -ōnĭs (m.), *a captain*
dux, dŭcĭs (m.), *a leader*
lēgātŭs, -ī (m.), *a lieutenant-general*
impěrātŏr, -ōrĭs (m.), *a commander-in-chief*

trĭbūnŭs, -ī (m.), *a colonel*
hastâtī, -ōrŭm (m. pl.), *spearmen*
scûtâtī, -ōrŭm (m. pl.), *troops bearing shields*
săgittârĭŭs, -ī (m.), *an archer*
fundĭtŏr, -ōrĭs (m.), *a slinger*
antēsignânŭs, -ī (m.), *a soldier fighting before the colors*

vēlĕs, -ĭtĭs (m.), *a skirmisher*
classĭârĭŭs, -ī (m.), *a marine*
signĭfĕr, -ī (m.), *an ensign*
lixă, -ae (m.), *a sutler*
spĕcŭlâtŏr, -ōrĭs (m.), *a spy*
dēsertŏr, -ōrĭs (m.), *a deserter*
perfŭgă, -ae (m.) ⎰ *a trans-*
transfŭgă, -ae (m.) ⎱ *fuge*

21. Armă. *Arms.*

armă, -ōrŭm (n. pl.), *arms (of defense)*
tēlă, -ōrŭm (n. pl.), *arms (of offense)*
armâtûră, -ae (f.), *armor* [*er*]
gălĕă,-ae (f.),*a helmet (of leath-cassĭs, -ĭdĭs (f.), a helmet (of metal)*
cristă, -ae (f.), *a crest, plume*
lōrīcă, -ae (f.), *a leather cuirass*
thōrax, -âcĭs (m.), *a breast-plate (of iron)*
scûtŭm, -ī (n.), *a buckler*
clĭpĕŭs, -ī (m.), *a round shield*
parmă, -ae (f.), *a target*
ŏcrĕă, -ae (f.), *a legging*
tēlŭm,-ī (n.), *a missile*
glădĭŭs, -ī (m.) ⎰
ferrŭm, -ī (n.) ⎱ *a sword*
ensĭs, - (m.), *a broad sword*
rûdĭs, - (f.), *a foil*

âcĭnâcēs, -ĭs (m.), *a short sabre*
pûgĭŏ, -ōnĭs (m.), *a dagger*
mûcrŏ, -ōnĭs (m.), *the sword's*
căpŭlŭs, -ī (m.), *the hilt* [*point*
vâgīnă, -ae (f.), *a sheath*
baltĕŭs, -ī (m.), *a sword-belt*
bĭpennĭs, - (f.), *a battle-axe*
hastă, -ae (f.), *a lance, spear*
hastīlĕ, -ĭs (n.), *a shaft*
pīlŭm, -ī (n.), *a heavy javelin*
săgittă, -ae (f.), *an arrow*
spīcŭlŭm, -ī (n.) ⎰ *a point*
cuspĭs, -ĭdĭs (f.) ⎱
arcŭs, -ûs (m.), *a bow*
phărētră, -ae (f.), *a quiver*
fundă, -ae (f.), *a sling*
armâmentârĭŭm, -ī (n.), *an armory*
săgŭm, -ī (n.), *a military cloak*
pălûdâmentŭm, -ī (n.), *a general's cloak*

22. Exercĭtŭs. *The Army.*

exercĭtŭs, -ûs (m.), *an army*
ĕquĭtâtŭs, -ûs (m.), *cavalry*
pĕdĭtâtŭs, -ûs (m.), *infantry*
cōpĭae, -ârŭm (f. pl.), *troops*
auxĭlĭă, -ōrŭm (n. pl.) ⎰ *auxiliary*
auxĭlĭârēs,-ĭŭm(m.pl.) ⎱ *troops*

subsĭdĭă,-ōrŭm (n.pl.), *a reserve*
lēgĭŏ, -ōnĭs (f.), *a legion*
cŏhors, -tĭs (f.), *a battalion*
mănĭpŭlŭs, -ī (m.), *a company*
ordŏ, -ĭnĭs (m.), *a rank*
turmă, -ae (f.), *a squadron*

ālă, -ae (f.), *a regiment of horse*
agmĕn, -ĭnĭs (n.), *an army on the march, a column*
ĭtĕr, ĭtĭnĕrĭs (n.), *a march*
signŭm, -ī (n.), *the colors*
vexillŭm, -ī (n.), *a banner*
stĭpendĭŭm, -ī (n.), *pay*

insignĭă, -ĭŭm (n. pl.), *a decoration*
praemĭŭm, -ī (n.), *a reward*
sarcĭnă, -ae (f.), *a knapsack*
impĕdĭmentă, -ōrŭm (n. pl.), *the baggage (of an army)*
expĕdītĭō, -ōnĭs (f.), *a campaign*

23. Castră. *The Camp.*

castrŭm, -ī (n.), *a castle*
castră, -ōrŭm (n. pl.), *a camp*
aestīvă, -ōrŭm (n. pl.), *a summer camp*
hĭbernă, -ōrŭm (n. pl.), *winter quarters*
stătīvă, -ōrŭm (n. pl.), *a stationary camp*
vallŭm, -ī (n.), *a rampart*
vallŭs, -ī (m.), *a pallisade*
tăbernăcŭlŭm, -ī (n.) } *a tent*
tentōrĭŭm, -ī (n.) }

fossă, -ae (f.), *a ditch*
contŭbernĭŭm, -ī (n.), *tent companionship*
contŭbernālĭs,- (m.), *a comrade*
praetōrĭŭm, -ī (n.), *a general's tent*
vĭgĭlĭae, -ārŭm (f. pl.), *the watch (sentinels)*
excūbĭae, -ārŭm (f. pl.), *a guard*
stătĭō, -ōnĭs (f.), *a post*
tessĕră, -ae (f.), *parole*
classĭcŭm, -ī (n.), *a field-signal*

24. Bellŭm. *War.*

bellŭm, -ī (n.), *a war*
hostĭs, - (m.), *an enemy*
sŏcĭŭs, -ī (m.), *an ally*
proelĭŭm, -ī (n.), *a battle*
pugnă, -ae (f.), *a combat*
ăcĭēs, -ēī (f.), *battle array*
frons, -tĭs (f.), *the front*
cornū, -ūs (n.), *the wing*
tergŭm, -ī (n.), *the rear*
cŭnĕŭs, -ī (m.), *a wedge*
orbĭs, - (m.), *an orb (a body of troops drawn up in a circle)*
impĕtŭs, -ūs (m.), *an attack*
incursĭō, -ōnĭs (f.), *an incursion*
insĭdĭae,-ārŭm (f.pl.),*an ambush*
rĕceptŭs, -ūs,(m.), *a retreat*

caedēs, -ĭs (f.), *a slaughter*
strāgēs, -ĭs (f.), *a massacre*
clādēs, -ĭs (f.), *a defeat*
fūgă, -ae (f.), *a flight*
victōrĭă, -ae (f.), *a victory*
victŏr, -ōrĭs (m.), *a conqueror*
captīvŭs, -ī (m.), *a prisoner*
obsĕs, -ĭdĭs (m.), *a hostage*
praedă, -ae (f.), *booty*
spŏlĭă, -ōrŭm (n. pl.), *spoils*
indūtĭae, -ārŭm (f. pl.), *a truce*
pax, păcĭs (f.), *peace*
trŏpaeŭm, -ī (n.), *a trophy*
trĭumphŭs, -ī (m.), *a triumph*
trĭumphātŏr, -ōrĭs (m.), *a triumpher*

25. Obsĭdĭŏ. *The Siege.*

obsĭdĭŏ, -ōnĭs (f.), *a siege, blockade*
castellŭm, -ī (n.), *a castle*
praesĭdĭŭm, -ī (n.), *a garrison*
dēfensĭŏ, -ōnĭs (f.), *a defense*
obsessĭŏ, -ōnĭs (f.), *a blockade*
oppugnātĭŏ,-ōnĭs (f.), *an assault*
expugnātĭŏ, -ōnĭs (f.), *a capture*
aggĕr, -ĭs (m.), *a mound*
crătēs, -ĭŭm (f. pl.), *fascines*
ărĭēs, -ĕtĭs (m.), *a battering ram*
vīnĕă, -ae (f.), *a mantlet for sheltering besiegers*

testūdŏ, -ĭnĭs (f.), *a tortoise (for protection against missiles)*
tormentŭm, -ī (n.), *a shot*
cŭnĭcŭlŭs, -ī (m.), *a mine*
plŭtĕŭs, -ī (m.), *a parapet*
ballistă, -ae (f.), *an engine for throwing stones*
cătăpultă, -ae (f.), *an engine for throwing arrows*
excursĭŏ, -ōnĭs (f.), *a sally*
dēdĭtĭŏ, -ōnĭs (f.), *a surrender*
excĭdĭŭm, -ī (n.), *destruction*

26. Rēs săcrae. *Divine Service.*

rēs săcrae, rērŭm -ārŭm (f. pl.), *divine service*
Dĕŭs, -ī (m.), *God*
dĕă, -ae (f.), *a goddess*
nūmĕn, -ĭnĭs (n.), *godhead*
dīvīnĭtās, -ātĭs (f.), *divinity*
pĭĕtās, -ātĭs (f.), *piety*
impĭĕtās, -ātĭs (f.), *impiety*
rĕlĭgĭŏ, -ōnĭs (f.), *fear of God*
templŭm, -ī (n.), *a temple*
aedēs, -ĭs (f.), *a dwelling of the gods, a temple*
săcellŭm, -ī (n.), *a chapel*
săcrārĭŭm, -ī (n.), *a shrine*
ără, -ae (f.) }
altărĕ, -ĭs (n.) } *an altar*
săcrĭfĭcĭŭm, -ī (n.), *a sacrifice*
săcrĭfĭcātĭŏ,-ōnĭs (f.) } *a sacri-*
immŏlătĭŏ, -ōnĭs (f.) } *ficing*

tūs, tūrĭs (n.), *incense*
cultŭs, -ŭs (m.), *veneration*
caerĭmōnĭă, -ae (f.), *a religious ceremony*
vĕrēcundĭă, -ae (f.), *awe*
implōrātĭŏ, -ōnĭs (f.), *an imploring*
ădōrātĭŏ, -ōnĭs (f.), *worship*
prēcēs, -ŭm (f. pl.), *prayer*
supplĭcātĭŏ, -ōnĭs (f.), *a supplication*
vōtŭm, -ī (n.), *a vow*
consĕcrātĭŏ, -ōnĭs (f.), *a consecration*
exsĕcrātĭŏ, -ōnĭs (f.), *an execration*
săcerdōs, -ōtĭs (m.) } *a priest*
pontĭfex, -ĭcĭs (m.) }
Vestālĭs,- (f.),*a priestess of Vesta*

27. Caelŭm. *Heaven.*

caelŭm,-ī (n.),*the heavens,Heaven*
astrŭm, -ī (n.) } *a star*
stellă, -ae (f.) }

sĭdŭs, -ĕrĭs (n.), *a constellation*
plănētă, -ae (m.) } *a*
stellă errans, -ae -tĭs (f.) } *planet*

cōmētēs, -ae (m.), *a comet*
sōl, -ĭs (m.), *the sun*
lūnă, -ae (f.), *the moon*
rădĭŭs, -ī (m.), *a ray*
lux, lūcĭs (f.), *daylight*
lūmĕn, -ĭnĭs (n.), *light*
tĕnĕbrae,-ārŭm (f.pl.), *darkness*
dīlūcŭlŭm, -ī (n.), *daybreak*

aurōră, -ae (f.), *the morning, dawn*
crĕpuscŭlŭm,-ī(n.),*twilight, dusk*
ōrĭens, -tĭs (m.), *the east*
occĭdens, -tĭs (m.), *the west*
septentrĭōnēs, -ŭm (m. pl.), *the north*
mĕrĭdĭēs, -ēī (m.), *the south*

28. Āēr. *Air.*

āĕr, āĕrĭs (m.), *the (lower) air, atmosphere*
aethēr, -ĕrĭs (m.), *the upper air, ether*
pōlŭs, -ī (m.), *the pole*
aură, -ae (f.), *a breeze*
ventŭs, -ī (m.), *wind*
prŏcellă, -ae (f.), *a storm*
turbŏ, -ĭnĭs (m.), *a whirlwind*
eurŭs,-ī(m.), *the east wind*
caurŭs,-ī(m.),*the north-west wind*
zĕphўrŭs, -ī (m.),
făvōnĭŭs, -ī (m.) } *the west wind*
austĕr, -rī (m.), *the south wind*
āquĭlŏ,-ōnĭs (m.)
bŏrĕās, -ae (m.) } *the north wind*
nūbēs, -ĭs (f.), *a cloud*
nĕbŭlă, -ae (f.), *mist*

văpōr, -ōrĭs (m.), *a vapor*
imbĕr, -rĭs (m.), *a shower*
plŭvĭă, -ae, (f.), *rain*
grandŏ, -ĭnĭs (f.), *hail*
nix, nĭvĭs (f.), *snow*
glăcĭēs, -ēī (f.), *ice*
rōs, rōrĭs (m.), *dew*
prŭĭnă, -ae (f.), *hoar frost*
tempestās, -ātĭs (f.), *weather*
tŏnĭtrŭs, -ŭs (m.), *thunder*
fulgŭr, -ĭs (n.), *lightning*
fulmĕn, -ĭnĭs (n.), *a thunderbolt*
călŏr, -ōrĭs (m.), *warmth, heat*
aestŭs, -ŭs (m.), *heat*
ardŏr, -ōrĭs (m.), *burning heat*
frīgŭs, -ōrĭs (n.), *cold*
tĕpŏr, -ōrĭs (m.), *tepidity*

29. Tempŭs. *Time.*

tempŭs, -ōrĭs (n.), *time, a season*
annŭs, -ī (m.), *a year*
vēr, -ĭs (n.), *spring*
aestās, -ātĭs (f.), *summer*
auctumnŭs, -ī (m.), *autumn*
hĭems, hĭĕmĭs (f.), *winter*
brŭmă, -ae (f.), *the shortest day*
aevŭm, -ī (n.), *lifetime*
saecŭlŭm, -ī (n.), *a century*
bĭennĭŭm, -ī (n.), *two years*

trĭennĭŭm, -ī (n.), *three years*
mensĭs, - (m.), *a month*
dĭēs, -ēī (m. & f.), *a day*
bīdŭŭm, -ī (n.), *two days*
trīdŭŭm, -ī (n.), *three days*
prīmă lūx, -ae -cĭs (f.), *day-break*
aurōră, -ae (f.), *the morning, dawn*
māně, *in the morning*

— 18 —

mĕrĭdĭēs, –ēī (m.), *noon*
vespĕr, –ī (m.), *evening*
nox, noctĭs (f.), *night*
vĭgĭlĭă,–ae (f.), *a watch (a fourth part of a night)*

mĕdĭă nox, –ae –ctĭs (f.), *midnight*
hōră, –ae (f.), *an hour*
mōmentŭm, –ī (n.), *a moment*
aeternĭtās, –ātĭs (f.), *eternity*

30. Spătĭŭm. *Space.*

spătĭŭm, –ī (n.), *space*
amplĭtūdŏ, –ĭnĭs (f.), *the width*
ambĭtŭs, –ūs (m.), *the circumference*
sŭperfĭcĭēs, –ēī (f.), *the surface*
longĭtūdŏ, –ĭnĭs (f.), *length*
lātĭtūdŏ, –ĭnĭs (f.), *breadth*
altĭtūdŏ, –ĭnĭs (f.), *height, depth*
fĭnĭs, – (m.), *a boundary;* fĭnēs, –ĭŭm (m. pl.), *territory*
lĭmĕs, –ĭtĭs (m.), *a limit*
intervallŭm, –ī (n.), *an interval*
vĭă, –ae (f.), *a road, way*
ĭtĕr, ĭtĭnĕrĭs (n.), *a way*
trāmĕs, –ĭtĭs (m.), *a cross-way*
dĕvertĭcŭlŭm, –ī (n.), *a by-way*
trĭvĭŭm, –ī (n.), *a cross-road*
mĭlĭărĭŭm, –ī (n.), *a mile-stone*

lŏcŭs, –ī (m.), *a place*
rĕgĭŏ, –ōnĭs (f.) } *a region*
plăgă, –ae (f.)
pāgŭs, –ī (m.), *a district*
prōvincĭă, –ae (f.), *a province*
angustĭae, –ārŭm (f. pl.), *a narrow place*
lĭnĕă, –ae (f.), *a line*
punctŭm, –ī (n.), *a point*
orbĭs, – (m.), *a circle;* orbĭs terrārŭm, *the whole earth*
circŭlŭs, –ī (m.), *a circular figure*
centrŭm, –ī (n.), *a center*
glŏbŭs, –ī (m.), *a globe* [ner
angŭlŭs, –ī (m.), *an angle*, *a cor-*
trĭangŭlŭm, –ī (n.), *a triangle*
quădrătŭm, –ī (n.), *a square*

31. Ignĭs. *Fire.*

ignĭs, – (m.), *fire*
scintĭllă, –ae (f.), *a spark*
fōmĕs, –ĭtĭs (m.), *tinder*
sulfŭr, –ĭs (n.), *sulphur*
lignŭm, –ī (n.), *wood*
flammă, –ae (f.), *a flame*
incendĭŭm, –ī (n.), *a fire, conflagration*
fŭlĭgŏ, –ĭnĭs (f.), *soot*
tĭtĭŏ, –ōnĭs (m.) } *a firebrand*
torrĭs, – (m.)
taedă, –ae (f.), *a torch*

fax, făcĭs (f.), *a link*
cĭnĭs, –ĕrĭs (m.), *ashes*
făvillă, –ae (f.), *glowing ashes*
fŭmŭs, –ī (m.), *smoke*
cămĭnŭs, –ī (m.), *a fire-place*
carbŏ, –ōnĭs (m.), *coal*
lūmĕn, –ĭnĭs (n.), *light*
candēlă, –ae (f.), *a candle*
candēlābrŭm, –ī (n.), *a candlestick*
lŭcernă, –ae (f.), *a lamp*
lanternă, –ae (f.), *a lantern*

32. Terrā. The Earth.

terrā, -ae (f.), the earth; a land
campūs, -ī (m.), a field, land
agĕr, -rī (m.), a field
glēbā, -ae (f.), a clod
plānĭtĭēs, -ēī (f.), a plain
fundūs, -ī (m.), a piece of land
praedĭūm, -ī (n.), an estate
rūs, rūrĭs (n.), the country; a farm
prātūm, -ī (n.), a meadow
hortūs, -ī (m.), a garden
mons, -tĭs (m.), a mountain
prōmontōrĭūm, -ī (n.), a promcollĭs, - (m.), a hill   [ontory
rūpēs, -ĭs (f.), a rock
căcūmĕn, -ĭnĭs (n.), a summit
vallĭs, - (f.), a valley

silvā, -ae (f.), a wood
saltūs, -ūs (m.), a woodland
nĕmūs, -ŏrĭs (n.), a grove
contĭnens,-tĭs (f.), the main land, continent
insūlā, -ae (f.), an island
pĕninsūlā, -ae (f.), a peninsula
sĭnūs, -ūs (m.), a bay
aestūārĭūm, -ī (n.), an inlet
spēluncā, -ae (f.)) a cave, den
spēcūs, -ūs (m.))
faucēs, -ĭūm (f. pl.), a pass
rīpā, -ae (f.), the bank of a stream
lĭtūs, -ŏrĭs (n.), the sea shore
ōrā, -ae (f.), the sea coast
scŏpūlūs, -ī (m.), a cliff

33. Ănĭmālĭā. Animals.

Gĕnĕrālĭā. General Items.

ănĭmăl, -ālĭs (n.), an animal
bestĭā, -ae (f.), a beast
bēlŭā, -ae (f.), a beast, monster
amphĭbĭūm, -ī (n.)) an
bestĭā quāsī anceps, }amphibious
-ae -ĭpĭtĭs (f.)) animal
piscĭs, - (m.), a fish
pĕcūs, -ŏrĭs (n.), small cattle
armentūm, -ī (n.), cattle for plowing
jūmentūm, -ī (n.), draught cattle
pullūs, -ī (m.)) a young anicătūlūs, -ī (m.)) mal
stăbūlūm, -ī (n.), a stable
nīdūs, -ī (m.), a nest
păbūlūm, -ī (n.), fodder
săgĭnā, -ae (f.), fattening
pascŭūm -ī (n.), a pasture

pastŏr, -ōrĭs (m.), a herdsman
fĕrā, -ae (f.), a wild beast
vēnātŏr, -ōrĭs (m.), a hunter
vēnātĭŏ, -ōnĭs (f.), hunting
pellĭs, - (f.), a skin
cŏrĭūm, -ī (n.), leather
pĭlūs, -ī (m.), a hair
villūs, -ī (m.), a tuft of hair
sētā, -ae (f.), a bristle
lānā, -ae (f.), wool
cornŭ, -ūs (n.), a horn
ungŭlā, -ae (f.), a claw, hoof
jūbā, -ae (f.), a mane
prōboscĭs, -ĭdĭs (f.), a trunk, proboscis
caudā, -ae (f.), a tail
ăcūlĕūs, -ī (m.), a sting
rostrūm, -ī (n.), a beak

plūmă, -ae (f.), *a feather (down)*
pennă, ae (f.), *a feather (of the*
ālă, -ae (f.), *a wing* [*wing)*
ŏvŭm, -ī (n.), *an egg*
testă, -ae (f.), *a shell*

squămă, -ae (f.), *a scale of a fish*
pinnă, -ae (f.), *a fin*
spīnă, -ae (f.), *a fish-bone*
branchĭae, -ārŭm (f. pl.), *the*
gills (of fish)

Quădrŭpĕdēs. *Quadrupeds.*

quădrŭpēs,-ĕdĭs (m. & f.),*a quad-*
cănĭs, - (m.), *a dog* [*ruped*
fēlĭs, - (f.), *a cat*
mūs, mūrĭs (m.), *a mouse*
glĭs, glīrĭs (m.), *a dormouse*
sīmĭă, -ae (f.), *an ape*
sŭs, sŭĭs (f.) ⎫ *a swine*
porcŭs, -ī (m.) ⎭
bōs, bŏvĭs (m.), *an ox*
vaccă, -ae (f.), *a cow*
vītŭlŭs, -ī (m.), *a calf*
taurŭs, -ī (m.), *a bull*
ŏvĭs, - (f.), *a sheep*
ārĭēs, -ĕtĭs (m.), *a ram*
agnŭs, -ī (m.), *a lamb*
vervex, -ĕcĭs (m.), *a wether*
căpĕr, -rī (m.) ⎫ *a he-goat*
hircŭs, -ī (m.) ⎭
căpră, -ae (f.), *a she-goat*
haedŭs, -ī (m.), *a kid*
ăsĭnŭs, -ī (m.), *an ass*

mūlŭs, -ī (m.), *a mule*
ĕquŭs, -ī (m.), *a horse*
ĕquă, -ae (f.), *a mare*
ĕlĕphantŭs, -ī (m.) ⎫ *an*
ĕlĕphās, -antĭs (m.) ⎭ *elephant*
cămēlŭs, -ī (m.), *a camel*
rhīnŏcĕrōs, -ōtĭs (m.), *a rhinoc-*
cervŭs, -ī (m.), *a stag* [*eros*
căprĕă, -ae (f.), *a roe*
lĕpŭs, -ŏrĭs (m.), *a hare;* lĕpŭs
cŭnĭcŭlŭs, -ŏrĭs -ī (m.), *a rab-*
ăpĕr, -rī (m.), *a wild boar* [*bit*
lŭpŭs, -ī (m.), *a wolf*
lŭpă, -ae (f.), *a she-wolf*
vulpēs, -ĭs (f.), *a fox*
lĕō, -ōnĭs (m.), *a lion*
lĕaenă, -ae (f.), *a lioness*
tĭgrĭs, - (m.), *a tiger*
ursŭs, -ī (m.), *a bear*
ursă, -ae (f.), *a she-bear*
lynx -cĭs (f.), *a lynx*

Ăvēs. *Birds.*

ăvĭs, - (f.), *a bird*
gallŭs, -ī (m.), *a cock*
gallīnă, -ae (f.), *a hen*
cŏlumbă, -ae (f.), *a dove*
cĭcōnĭă, -ae (f.), *a stork*
hĭrundŏ, -ĭnĭs (f.), *a swallow*
passĕr, -ĭs (m.), *a sparrow*
luscĭnĭă, -ae (f.), *a nightingale*
ălaudă, -ae (f.), *a lark*

cŏturnix, -ĭcĭs (f.), *a quail*
pīcŭs, -ī (m.), *a woodpecker*
pīcă, -ae (f.), *a magpie*
perdix, -ĭcĭs (f.), *a partridge*
păvō, -ōnĭs (m.), *a peacock*
păvă, -ae (f.), *a peahen*
grūs, -ŭĭs (f.), *a crane*
cornix, -ĭcĭs (f.), *a crow*
corvŭs, -ī (m.), *a raven*

grācŭlŭs, -ī (m.), *a jackdaw*
strŭthīŏcămēlŭs, -ī (m.), *an ostrich*
ăqŭīlă, -ae (f.), *an eagle*
vultŭr, -īs (m.), *a vulture*

turtŭr, -īs (m.), *a turtle-dove*
accĭpītĕr, -rīs (m.), *a hawk*
cycnŭs, -ī (m.), *a swan*
ansĕr, -īs (m.), *a goose*
ănăs, -ătīs (f.), *a duck*

Insectă et bestĭae quāsĭ ancĭpītēs. *Insects and Amphibious Animals.*

insectŭm, -ī (n.), *an insect*
ăpīs, - (f.), *a bee*
fūcŭs, -ī (m.), *a drone*
vespă, -ae (f.), *a wasp*
muscă, -ae (f.), *a fly*
cŭlex, -īcīs (m.), *a gnat*
pūlex, -īcīs (m.), *a flea*
scărăbaeŭs, -ī (m.), *a beetle*
cĭcădă, -ae (f.), *a tree-cricket*
lŏcustă, -ae (f.), *a locust*
blattă, -ae (f.), *a moth*
formīcă, -ae (f.), *an ant*

ērŭcă, -ae (f.), *a caterpillar*
păpīlĭŏ, -ōnīs (m.), *a butterfly*
ărănĕă, -ae (f.), *a spider*
hīrŭdŏ, -ĭnīs (f.), *a leech*
cŏchlĕă, -ae (f.), *a snail*
cancĕr, -rī (m.), *a crab*
angŭīs, - (m.) ⎫ *a snake, serpens*, -tīs (f.) ⎭ *pent*
vīpĕră, -ae (f.), *a viper*
vermīs, - (m.), *a worm*
lăcertă, -ae (f.), *a lizard*
rānă, -ae (f.), *a frog*

34. Arbŏrēs. *Trees.*

arbŏr, -īs (f.), *a tree*
arbustŭm, -ī (n.), *a plantation of trees*
frŭtex, -īcīs (m.), *a shrub*
virgultŭm, -ī (n.), *a shrubbery*
rādix, -īcīs (f.), *a root*
lignŭm, -ī (n.), *wood*
cortex, -īcīs (m.), *bark*
stirps, -īs (f.), *a stem*
flŏs, -ōrīs (m.), *a blossom*
caudex, -īcīs (m.), *a block (of wood)*
rāmŭs, -ī (m.), *a branch*
virgă, -ae (f.), *a twig*
frons, -dīs (f.), *foliage*
căcūmĕn, -ĭnīs (n.), *the top*
pŏmŭs, -ī (f.), *a fruit-tree*

pōmŭm, -ī (n.), *fruit*
mālŭs, -ī (f.), *an apple-tree*
mālŭm, -ī (n.), *an apple*
pīrŭs, -ī (f.), *a pear-tree*
pīrŭm, -ī (n.), *a pear*
fīcŭs, -ūs or -ī (f.), *a fig-tree; a fig*
prŭnŭs, -ī (f.), *a plum-tree*
prŭnŭm, -ī (n.), *a plum*
cĕrăsŭs, -ī (f.), *a cherry-tree*
cĕrăsŭm, -ī (n.), *a cherry*
persĭcŭs, -ī (f.), *a peach-tree*
persĭcŭm, -ī (n.), *a peach*
myrrhă, -ae (f.), *a myrrh-tree*
myrtŭs, -ī (f.), *a myrtle-tree*
ŏlīvă, -ae (f.) ⎫ *an olive-tree*
ŏlĕă, -ae (f.) ⎭
ăbĭēs, -ĕtīs (f.), *a silver fir*

cŭpressŭs, -ī (f.), *a cypress*
fāgŭs, -ī (f.), *a beech-tree*
fraxīnŭs, -ī (f.), *an ash-tree*
sălix, -ĭcĭs (f.), *a willow-tree*
tĭlĭă, -ae (f.), *a lime-tree*
pīnŭs, -ī (f.), *a fir-tree*
quercŭs, -ūs (f.), *an oak-tree*
glans, -dĭs (f.), *an acorn*
bācă, -ae (f.), *a berry*
nux, nŭcĭs (f.), *a nut; a nut-tree*
jūglans, -dĭs (f.), *a walnut; a walnut-tree*
laurŭs, -ī or -ūs (f.), *a laurel-tree*
pōpŭlŭs, -ī (f.), *a poplar*

ulmŭs, -ī (f.), *an elm-tree*
hĕdĕră, -ae (f.), *ivy*
pōmārĭŭm, -ī (n.), *an orchard*
vītĭs, - (f.), *a vine*
ūvă, -ae (f.), *a grape*
pampīnŭs, -ī (m. & f.), *a tendril of a vine*
vīnĕă, -ae (f.), *an arbor of vine*
vīnētŭm, -ī (n.), *a vineyard*
vīnĭtŏr, -ōrĭs (m.), *a vine-dresser*
vindēmĭă, -ae (f.), *a vintage*
vīnŭm, -ī (n.), *wine*
torcŭlăr, -ārĭs (n.), *a wine-press*
cellă vīnārĭă, -ae -ae (f.), *a wine-cellar*

35. Flōrēs. *Flowers.*

flōs, -ōrĭs (m.), *a flower*
vĭŏlă, -ae (f.), *a violet*
hўăcinthŭs, -ī (m.), *the hyacinth*
rŏsă, -ae (f.), *a rose*
ămărantŭs, -ī (m.), *amaranth*
rōs mărīnŭs, -ōrĭs -ī (m.), *rosemary*
mentă, -ae (f.), *mint*
lilĭŭm, -ī (n.), *a lily* [*flower*
cўănŭs, -ī (m.), *the blue corn-*

urtīcă, -ae (f.), *a nettle*
narcissŭs, -ī (m.), *the narcissus*
crŏcŭs, -ī (m.), *saffron*
păpāvĕr, -ĭs (n.), *poppy*
sertŭm, -ī (n.), *a nosegay*
cŏrōnă, -ae (f.), *a garland*
caulĭs, - (m.), *a stalk*
călix, -ĭcĭs (f.), *a calyx*
fŏlĭŭm, -ī (n.), *a leaf*
floscŭlŭs, -ī (m.), *a little flower*

36. Ăgrĭcultūră. *Agriculture.*

ăgrĭcultūră, -ae (f.), *agriculture*
villă, -ae (f.), *a country-seat*
jūgĕrŭm, -ī (n.), *an acre*
ăgrĭcŏlă, -ae (m.), *a farmer*
rustĭcŭs, -ī (m.), *a countryman*
ărătŏr, -ōrĭs (m.), *a plowman*
villĭcŭs, -ī (m.), *an overseer of a*
ărătrŭm, -ī (n.), *a plow* [*farm*
vōmĭs, -ĕrĭs (m.), *a plowshare*

sulcŭs, -ī (m.), *a furrow*
rastrŭm, -ī (n.), *a prong hoe*
lĭgŏ, -ōnĭs (m.), *a mattock*
stercŭs, -ōrĭs (n.), *manure*
sătŏr, -ōrĭs (m.), *a sower*
sēmĕn, -ĭnĭs (n.), *seed*
sēmentĭs, - (f.), *a seeding*
sĕgĕs, -ĕtĭs (f.), *a crop*
fructŭs, -ūs (m.), *product*

frūgēs, -ŭm (f. pl.), *fruits of the earth*
frūmentŭm, -ĭ (n.), *corn*
spīcă, -ae (f.), *an ear*
cālămŭs, -ĭ (m.) } *a straw of*
culmŭs, -ĭ (m.) } *grain*
herbă, -ae (f.), *an herb*
grāmēn, -ĭnĭs (n.), *grass*
falx, -cĭs (f.), *a sickle*
furcă, -ae (f.), *a fork*
pălĕă, -ae (f.), *chaff*
strāmentŭm, -ĭ (n.), *straw*
foenŭm, -ĭ (n.), *hay*
ăvēnă, -ae (f.), *oats*
hordĕŭm, -ĭ (n.), *barley*
ădŏr, -ĭs (n.), *spelt*
fār, farrĭs (n.), *spelt, corn, grain*
trītĭcŭm, -ĭ (n.), *wheat*
mergēs, -ĭtĭs (f.), *a sheaf*

ārĕă, -ae (f.), *a threshing-floor*
flăgellŭm, -ĭ (n.), *a threshing-flail*
trībŭlŭm, -ĭ (n.), *a threshing-sledge*
grānŭm, -ĭ (n.), *a grain*
fārīnă, -ae (f.), *flour*
lĕgūmĭnă, -ŭm (n. pl.), *leguminous plants*
lens, -tĭs (f.), *a lentil*
pīsŭm, -ĭ (n.) *a pea*
cīcĕr, -ĭs (n.), *a chick-pea*
făbă, -ae (f.), *a bean*
răpă, -ae (f.) } *a turnip*
răpŭm, -ĭ (n.) }
cŭcŭmĭs, -ĕrĭs (m.), *a cucumber*
lūpīnŭs, -ĭ (m.), *a lupine*
messŏr, -ōrĭs (m.), *a reaper*
messĭs, - (f.), *a harvest*

37. Mĕtallă. *Minerals.*

mĕtallŭm, -ĭ (n.), *a mine; a metal; a mineral*
aes, aerĭs (n.), *copper, bronze*
cŭprŭm, -ĭ (n.), *copper*
plumbŭm, -ĭ (n.), *lead*
ferrŭm, -ĭ (n.), *iron*
chălybs, -ўbĭs (m.), *steel*
argentŭm, -ĭ (n.), *silver; argentūm vīvŭm, quicksilver*
aurŭm, -ĭ (n.), *gold*
lăpĭs, -ĭdĭs (m.), *a stone*
saxŭm, -ĭ (n.), *a rock*
marmŏr, -ĭs (n.), *marble*

ăchātēs, -ae (m.), *the agate*
gemmă, -ae (f.), *a precious stone*
ădămās, -antĭs (m.), *a diamond*
ūnĭŏ, -ōnĭs (m.) } *a pearl*
margărītă, -ae (f.) }
conchă, -ae (f.), *a mussel, shell*
sĭlex, -ĭcĭs (m.), *a pebble*
ărēnă, -ae (f.), *sand*
argillă, -ae (f.), *clay*
lūtŭm, -ĭ (n.), *loam*
pūmex, -ĭcĭs (m.), *a pumice-stone*
calx, -cĭs (f.), *limestone*
caementŭm, -ĭ(n.), *a quarry stone*

38. Äquă. *Water.*

ăquă, -ae (f.), *water*
fons, -tĭs (m.), *a spring*
guttă, -ae (f.), *a drop*

spūmă, -ae (f.), *foam*
torrens, -tĭs (m.), *a torrent*
rīvŭs, -ĭ (m.), *a brook*

flūmĕn, -ĭnĭs (n.) }
flŭvĭŭs, -ī (m.) } a river
amnĭs, -(m.), a large river
stagnŭm, -ī (n.), a pond
lăcŭs, -ūs (m.), a lake
pălūs, -ūdĭs (f.), a swamp, bog
vertex, -ĭcĭs (m.), an eddy
gurgĕs, -ĭtĭs (m.), a whirlpool
frĕtŭm, -ī (n.), a strait
mărĕ, -ĭs (n.), the sea
aequŏr, -ĭs (n.), the (calm) sea

fluctŭs, -ūs (m.), a flood
undă, -ae (f.), a wave
vădŭm, -ī (n.), a ford
fundŭs, -ī (m.), the bottom
pons, -tĭs (m.), a bridge
alvĕŭs, -ī (m.), a river-bed
ostĭŭm, -ī (n.), the mouth of a river
aggĕr, -ĭs (m.), a dike
aestŭs, -ūs (m.), the surge, aestūs, -ŭŭm (m. pl.), the tide

39. Virtūtēs et vĭtĭă. Good and Bad Qualities.

abstĭnentĭă,-ae (f.), self-restraint
aequĭtās, -ātĭs (f.), equity
ămĭcĭtĭă, -ae (f.), friendship

ămŏr, -ōrĭs (m.), love

assĭdŭĭtās, -ātĭs (f.), assiduity, constant application
audācĭă, -ae (f.), audacity
bĕnĕvŏlentĭă, -ae (f.), good-will
bĕnignĭtās, -ātĭs (f.), kindness

bŏnĭtās, -ātĭs (f.), goodness
cărĭtās, -ātĭs (f.), esteem
clēmentĭă, -ae (f.), mildness
cōmĭtās, -ātĭs (f.), gentleness
concordĭă, -ae (f.), concord
consĭdĕrātĭŏ, -ōnĭs (f.), consideration
contĭnentĭă, -ae (f.), continence

constantĭă, -ae (f.), constancy
cūră, -ae (f.), carefulness

dĕcŭs, -ŏrĭs (n.), honor

dĭlĭgentĭă, -ae (f.), diligence
fĭdēs, -ĕī (f.), trust

ăvărĭtĭă, -ae (f.), covetousness
ĭnĭquĭtās, -ātĭs (f.), unfairness
ĭnĭmĭcĭtĭae, -ārŭm (f. pl.), enmity
{ ŏdĭŭm, -ī (n.), hatred
{ invĭdĭă, -ae (f.), envy
dēsĭdĭă, -ae (f.), inactivity

tĕmĕrĭtās, -ātĭs (f.), temerity
mălĕvŏlentĭă, -ae (f.), ill-will
ĭnhūmānĭtās, -ātĭs (f.), unkindness
mălĭtĭă, -ae (f.), malice
dēspĭcĭentĭă, -ae (f.), contempt
saevĭtĭă, -ae (f.), severity
aspĕrĭtās, -ātĭs (f.), harshness
discordĭă, -ae (f.), discord
ĭnconsĭdĕrantĭă, -ae (f.), inconsiderateness
incontĭnentĭă, -ae (f.), incontinency
mōbĭlĭtās, -ātĭs (f.), inconstancy
incūrĭă, -ae (f.), carelessness
{ dēdĕcŭs, -ŏrĭs (n.) }
{ ignōmĭnĭă, -ae (f.) } dishonor
nĕglĕgentĭă, -ae (f.), negligence
perfĭdĭă, -ae (f.), perfidy

fīdūcĭă, -ae (f.), *confidence*
fortĭtūdŏ, -ĭnĭs (f.), *bravery*
glōrĭă, -ae (f.), *renown*
grăvĭtās, -ātĭs (f.), *seriousness*
hŏnestās, -ātĭs (f.), *honesty*
hūmānĭtās, -ātĭs (f.), *humanity*

industrĭă, -ae (f.), *industry*
justĭtĭă, -ae (f.), *justice*
laus, -dĭs (f.), *praise*
lēnĭtās, -ātĭs (f.), *gentleness*
lībĕrālĭtās, -ātĭs (f.), *liberality*
mĭsĕrĭcordĭă, -ae (f.), *pity*
mŏdĕrātĭŏ, -ōnĭs (f.), *moderateness*
mŏdestĭă, -ae (f.), *modesty*
parsĭmōnĭă, -ae (f.), *parsimony*
pătĭentĭă, -ae (f.), *patience*
pĭĕtās, -ātĭs (f.), *piety*
prŏbĭtās, -ātĭs (f.), *honesty*
prŏvĭdentĭă, -ae (f.), *providence*

prūdentĭă, -ae (f.), *prudence*
săpĭentĭă, -ae (f.), *wisdom*
sĕvērĭtās, -ātĭs (f.), *strictness*
stŭdĭŭm, -ĭ (n.), *zeal*
tempĕrantĭă, -ae (f.), *temperance*

vĕrēcundĭă, -ae (f.), *bashfulness*

vērĭtās, -ātĭs (f.), *truthfulness*

dēspērātĭŏ, -ōnĭs (f.), *despair*
ignāvĭă, -ae (f.), *cowardice*
infāmĭă, -ae (f.), *infamy*
lĕvĭtās, -ātĭs (f.), *levity*
turpĭtūdŏ, -ĭnĭs (f.), *baseness*
immānĭtās, -ātĭs (f.), *inhumanity*
sēgnĭtĭă, -ae (f.), *sluggishness*
injustĭtĭă, -ae (f.), *injustice*
vĭtŭpĕrātĭŏ, -ōnĭs (f.), *censure*
ăcerbĭtās, -ātĭs (f.), *severity*
largĭtĭŏ, -ōnĭs (f.), *profusion*
crūdēlĭtās, -ātĭs (f.), *cruelty*
lĭcentĭă, -ae (f.), *license*

immŏdestĭă, -ae (f.), *immodesty*
luxŭrĭă, -ae (f.), *luxury*
impătĭentĭă, -ae (f.), *impatience*
implĕtās, -ātĭs (f.), *impiety*
imprŏbĭtās, -ātĭs (f.), *dishonesty*
imprūdentĭă, -ae (f.), *imprudence*
stultĭtĭă, -ae (f.), *foolishness*
insĭpĭentĭă, -ae (f.), *folly*
crūdēlĭtās, -ātĭs (f.), *cruelty*
sŏcordĭă, -ae (f.), *indolence*
intempĕrantĭă, -ae (f.), *intemperance*
importūnĭtās, -ātĭs (f.) *impoliteness*
{ fraus, -dĭs (f.), *cheating*
{ mendācĭŭm, -ĭ (n.), *falsehood*

---

abstĭnens, -tĭs, *abstinent*
acceptŭs, -ă, -ŭm, *agreeable*
ăcĕr, -rĭs, -rĕ, *sharp*
aequŭs, -ă, -ŭm, *fair*
ălăcĕr, -rĭs, -rĕ, *gay*
ămīcŭs, -ă, -ŭm, *friendly*

cŭpĭdŭs, -ă, -ŭm, *greedy*
mŏlestŭs, -ă, -ŭm, *annoying*
hĕbĕs, -ētĭs, *dull*
Inĭquŭs, -ă, -ŭm, *unfair*
dēmissŭs, -ă, -ŭm, *downcast*
{ Inĭmĭcŭs, -ă, -ŭm, *inimical*
{ infestŭs, -ă, -ŭm, *unfriendly*

aptŭs, -ă, -ŭm, *fit*

assĭdŭŭs, -ă, -ŭm, *assiduous*

attentŭs, -ă, -ŭm, *attentive*

bĕătŭs, -ă, -ŭm, *blessed*

bellĭcōsŭs, -ă, -ŭm, *warlike*

bĕnĕvŏlŭs, -ă, -ŭm, *benevolent*

bĕnignŭs, -ă, -ŭm, *beneficent*

blandŭs, -ă, -ŭm, *flattering*

bŏnŭs, -ă, -ŭm, *good*

callĭdŭs, -ă, -ŭm, *skillful*

candĭdŭs, -ă, -ŭm, *clear, white*

cārŭs, -ă, -ŭm, *dear*

cautŭs, -ă, -ŭm, *cautious*

cĕlĕbĕr, -rĭs, -rĕ, *celebrated, famous*

certŭs, -ă, -ŭm, *fixed, certain*

cĭcŭr, -ĭs, *tame*

clārŭs, -ă, -ŭm, *bright*

clēmens, -tĭs, *mild*

cōmĭs, -ĕ, *kind, gentle*

commŏdŭs, -ă, -ŭm, *comfortable*

concors, -dĭs, *harmonious*

dĕcōrŭs, -ă, -ŭm, *becoming*

dignŭs, -ă, -ŭm, *worthy*

dĭlĭgens, -tĭs, *careful*

dīvĕs, -ĭtĭs, *rich*

dŏcĭlĭs, -ĕ, *docile*

doctŭs, -ă, -ŭm, *educated*

dulcĭs, -ĕ, *sweet*

dūrŭs, -ă, -ŭm, *hardy*

ēgrĕgĭŭs, -ă, -ŭm, *excellent*

ēlātŭs, -ă, -ŭm, *exalted*

ēlĕgans, -tĭs, *elegant*

ēmendātŭs, -ă, -ŭm, *faultless*

făcētŭs, -ă, -ŭm, *facetious, witty*

fĕrox, -ōcĭs, *courageous*

fertĭlĭs, -ĕ, *fertile*

fīdēlĭs, -ĕ, *faithful*

fīdŭs, -ă, -ŭm, *trusty*

firmŭs, -ă, -ŭm, *firm*

{ ĭneptŭs, -ă, -ŭm
{ ăllēnŭs, -ă, -ŭm } *not suited*

segnĭs, -ĕ, *sluggish*

rĕmissŭs, -ă, -ŭm, *relaxed*

mĭsĕr, -ă, -ŭm, *wretched*

imbellĭs, -ĕ, *imbellic, peaceful*

mălĕvŏlŭs, -ă, -ŭm, *malevolent*

mălignŭs, -ă, -ŭm, *malicious*

austērŭs, -ă, -ŭm, *austere*

mălŭs, -ă, -ŭm, *bad*

stŏlĭdŭs, -ă, -ŭm, *stupid*

nĭgĕr, -ră, -rŭm, *black*

invīsŭs, -ă, -ŭm, *hated*

incautŭs, -ă, -ŭm, *incautious*

dēsertŭs, -ă, -ŭm, *solitary*

{ incertŭs, -ă, -ŭm, *uncertain*
{ ambĭgŭŭs, -ă, -ŭm, *ambiguous*

fĕrŭs, -ă, -ŭm, *wild, untamed*

obscūrŭs, -ă, -ŭm, *obscure*

saevŭs, -ă, -ŭm, *fierce, severe*

importūnŭs, -ă, -ŭm, *uncivil*

incommŏdŭs, -ă, -ŭm, *troublesome*

discors, -dĭs, *discordant*

indēcōrŭs, -ă, -ŭm, *unbecoming*

indignŭs, -ă, -ŭm, *unworthy*

nĕglĕgens, -tĭs, *careless*

paupĕr, -ĭs, *poor*

indŏcĭlĭs, -ĕ, *indocile*

ăgrestĭs, -ĕ, *uncultivated*

ămārŭs, -ă, -ŭm, *bitter*

dēlĭcātŭs, -ă, -ŭm, *delicate*

vulgārĭs, -ĕ, *ordinary*

sŭperbŭs, -ă, -ŭm, *proud*

vīlĭs, -ĕ, *mean*

vītĭōsŭs, -ă, -ŭm, *faulty*

pinguĭs, -ĕ, *dull*

păvĭdŭs, -ă, -ŭm, *timorous*

stĕrĭlĭs, -ĕ, *barren*

perfĭdŭs, -ă, -ŭm, *treacherous*

infĭdŭs, -ă, -ŭm, *faithless*

imbēcillŭs, -ă, -ŭm, *feeble*

formōsŭs, -ă, -ŭm, *finely formed*
fortĭs, -ĕ, *brave*
frŭgālĭs, -ĕ, *thrifty*,
gĕnĕrōsŭs, -ă,-ŭm, *of noble birth*
glōrīōsŭs, -ă, -ŭm, *glorious*
gnārŭs, -ă, -ŭm, *knowing*
grātŭs, -ă, -ŭm, *beloved*
hĭlărĭs, -ĕ, *cheerful*
hŏnestŭs, -ă, -ŭm, *honest*
hŭmānŭs, -ă, -ŭm, *humane*
hŭmĭdŭs, -ă, -ŭm, *moist*
immensŭs, -ă, -ŭm, *measureless*
impĭgĕr, -ră, -rŭm, *active*
indulgens, -tĭs, *indulgent*
innŏcens, -tĭs, *innocent*
intĕgĕr, -ră, -rŭm, *uninjured*
jūcundŭs, -ă, -ŭm, *pleasant*
justŭs, -ă, -ŭm, *just*
laetŭs, -ă, -ŭm, *gay*
largŭs, -ă, -ŭm, *liberal*
lēvĭs, -ĕ, *smooth*
lĕvĭs, -ĕ, *light*
lĭbĕr, -ă, -ŭm, *free*
lĭbĕrālĭs, -ĕ, *noble-minded*
lŏcŭplēs, -ĕtĭs, *wealthy*
mansŭĕtŭs, -ă,-ŭm, *tamed, gentle*
mātūrŭs, -ă, -ŭm, *ripe*
mŏdĕrātŭs, -ă, -ŭm, *moderate*
mŏdestŭs, -ă, -ŭm, *modest*
mundŭs, -ă, -ŭm, *clean*
nĭtĭdŭs, -ă, -ŭm, *neat*
opportūnŭs, -ă, -ŭm, *opportune*
ŏpŭlentŭs, -ă, -ŭm, *opulent*
officĭōsŭs, -ă, -ŭm, *obliging*
pĕrītŭs, -ă, -ŭm, *experienced*

pĭŭs, -ă, -ŭm, *pious*
plăcĭdŭs, -ă, -ŭm, *calm*
prŏbŭs, -ă, -ŭm, *upright*
promptŭs, -ă, -ŭm, *prompt*
prōvĭdŭs, -ă, -ŭm, *cautious*

pūrŭs, -ă, -ŭm, *pure*

dēformĭs, -ĕ, *deformed*
ignāvŭs, -ă, -ŭm, *coward*
luxŭrīōsŭs, -ă, -ŭm, *wanton*
hŭmĭlĭs, -ĕ, *low*   [*ious*
ignōmĭnĭōsŭs, -ă,-ŭm, *ignomin-*
ignārŭs, -ă, -ŭm, *unaware*
ingrātŭs, -ă, -ŭm, *not acceptable*
tristĭs, -ĕ, *sad*
turpĭs, -ĕ, *base*
immānĭs, -ĕ, *inhuman*
siccŭs, -ă, -ŭm, *dry*
exĭgŭŭs, -ă, -ŭm, *scanty*
pĭgĕr, -ră, -rŭm, *lazy*
crūdēlĭs, -ĕ, *cruel*
nŏcens, -tĭs, *guilty*   [*inated*
contămĭnātŭs, -ă, -ŭm, *contam-*
tĕtĕr, -ră, -rŭm, *shocking*
injustŭs, -ă, -ŭm, *unjust*
maestŭs, -ă, -ŭm, *sorrowful*
ăvārŭs, -ă, -ŭm, *avaricious*
aspĕr, -ă, -ŭm, *rough*
grăvĭs, -ĕ, *heavy*
captīvŭs, -ă,-ŭm, *captive, caught*
illĭbĕrālĭs, -ĕ, *mean*
ĕgens, -tĭs, *needy*
fĕrŭs, -ă, -ŭm, *wild*
immātūrŭs, -ă, -ŭm, *unripe*
tĕmĕrārĭŭs, -ă, -ŭm, *thoughtless*
pĕtŭlans, -tĭs, *petulant*
squālĭdŭs, -ă, -ŭm, *dirty*
sordĭdŭs, -ă, -ŭm, *sordid*   [*ient*
importūnŭs, -ă, -ŭm, *inconven-*
indĭgens, -tĭs, *needy*
inhŭmānŭs, -ă, -ŭm, *uncivil*
impĕrītŭs, -ă, -ŭm, *unexper-*
                                        ienced
nĕfārĭŭs, -ă, -ŭm, *nefarious*
ăcerbŭs, -ă, -ŭm, *harsh*
scĕlestŭs, -ă, -ŭm, *wicked*
dŭbĭŭs, -ă, -ŭm, *doubtful*
imprōvĭdŭs, -ă, -ŭm, *improvi-*
                                        dent
măcŭlōsŭs, -ă, -ŭm, *spotted*

quĭĕtŭs, -ă, -ŭm, *quiet*
rectŭs, -ă, -ŭm, *right*
rĕlĭgĭōsŭs, -ă, -ŭm, *religious*

rōbustŭs, -ă, -ŭm, *robust,strong*
săgax, -ācĭs, *sagacious*
sălūtārĭs, -ĕ, *beneficial*
sanctŭs, -ă, -ŭm, *holy*
sānŭs, -ă, -ŭm, *sound*
săpĭens, -tĭs, *wise*
simplex, -ĭcĭs, *sincere*
sōbrĭŭs, -ă, -ŭm, *sober*
sollers, -tĭs, *skillful*
stăbĭlĭs, -ĕ, *steadfast*
strēnŭŭs, -ă, -ŭm, *vigorous*
stŭdĭōsŭs, -ă, -ŭm, *zealous*
sŭblīmĭs, -ĕ, *sublime*
tranquillŭs, -ă, -ŭm, *tranquil*
ūtĭlĭs, -ĕ, *useful*
vălĭdŭs, -ă,-ŭm, *healthy, strong*
vĕnustŭs, -ă, -ŭm, *charming*
vērax, -ācĭs, *truthful*
vērŭs, -ă, -ŭm, *true*

pugnax, -ācĭs, *contentious*
prăvŭs, -ă, -ŭm, *wrong*
sŭperstĭtĭōsŭs, -ă, -ŭm, *super-
stitious*
infirmŭs, -ă, -ŭm, *weak*
ĭneptŭs, -ă, -ŭm, *foolish*
dīrŭs, -ă, -ŭm, *awful*
abjectŭs, -ă, -ŭm, *abject*
aegrōtŭs, -ă, -ŭm, *ill*
dēmens, -tĭs, *foolish*
astūtŭs, -ă, -ŭm, *shrewd*
ēbrĭŭs, -ă, -ŭm, *drunk*
ĭners, -tĭs, *unskilled*
fūgax, -ācĭs, *fleeting*
languĭdŭs, -ă, -ŭm, *faint*
lassŭs, -ă, -ŭm, *weary*
summissŭs, -ă, -ŭm, *low*
anxĭŭs, -ă, -ŭm, *anxious*
pernĭcĭōsŭs, -ă,-ŭm, *destructive*
dēbĭlĭs, -ĕ, *weak*
foedŭs, -ă, -ŭm, *ugly*
mendax, -ācĭs, *lying*
falsŭs, -ă, -ŭm, *false*

40. Adjectīvă oppŏsĭtă. *Opposite Adjectives.*

aequālĭs, -ĕ, *equal*
aestīvŭs, -ă, -ŭm, *belonging to
summer*
albŭs, -ă, -ŭm, *white*
altŭs, -ă, -ŭm, *high*
amplŭs, -ă, -ŭm, *roomy*
antīquŭs, -ă, -ŭm, *old*
ārĭdŭs, -ă, -ŭm, *dry*
călĭdŭs, -ă, -ŭm, *warm, hot*
cĕlĕr, -ĭs, -ĕ, *swift*
cīvīlĭs, -ĕ, *civil*
commūnĭs, -ĕ, *common*
conscĭŭs, -ă, -ŭm, *conscious*
cōpĭōsŭs, -ă, -ŭm, *plenty*
crassŭs, -ă, -ŭm, *thick*
crēbĕr, -ră, -rŭm, *frequent*

ĭnaequālĭs, -ĕ, *unequal*
hĭbernŭs, -ă, -ŭm, *wintry, belonging to winter*
ătĕr, -ră, -rŭm, *black*
hŭmĭlĭs, -ĕ, *low*   [*row*
angustŭs, -ă, -ŭm, *strait, nar-
nŏvŭs, -ă, -ŭm, *new*
hŭmĭdŭs, -ă, -ŭm, *moist*
frīgĭdŭs, -ă, -ŭm, *cold*
tardŭs, -ă, -ŭm, *slow*
mīlĭtārĭs, -ĕ, *military*
singŭlārĭs, -ĕ, *singular*
inscĭŭs, -ă, -ŭm, *ignorant*
parcŭs, -ă, -ŭm, *sparing*
tĕnŭĭs, -ĕ, *thin, slender*
insŏlens, -tĭs, *unusual*

crēdĭbĭlĭs, -ĕ, *credible*
densŭs, -ă, -ŭm, *dense*
dextĕr, -ă, -ŭm
dextĕr, -ră, -rŭm } *right*
dīrectŭs, -ă, -ŭm, *straight*
dĭurnŭs, -ă, -ŭm, *in the day-time*
dīvīnŭs, -ă, -ŭm, *divine*
dŏmestĭcŭs, -ă, -ŭm, *domestic*
făcĭlĭs, -ĕ, *easy*
fēlix, -īcĭs, *happy*
frēquens, -tĭs, *much frequented*
jŭvĕnĭlĭs, -ĕ, *youthful*
lentŭs, -ă, -ŭm, *slow*
longŭs, -ă, -ŭm, *long*   [*big*
magnŭs, -ă, -ŭm, *great, large*,
mĕmŏr, -ĭs, *mindful*
mīrŭs, -ă, -ŭm, *wonderful*
mītĭs, -ĕ, *mild*
mollĭs, -ĕ, *soft*
montānŭs, -ă,-ŭm,*mountainous*
mortālĭs, -ĕ, *mortal*
multĭplex, -ĭcĭs, *manifold*
multŭs, -ă, -ŭm, *much, many*
nōbĭlĭs, -ĕ, *noble*
occŭpātŭs, -ă, -ŭm, *busy*
pār, părĭs, *even*
partĭceps, -ĭpĭs, *sharing*
perpĕtŭŭs, -ă,-ŭm, *everlasting*
pervĭŭs, -ă, -ŭm, *passable*
plēnŭs, -ă, -ŭm, *full*
pŏtens, -tĭs, *able, potent*
praesens, -tĭs, *present*
prētĭōsŭs, -ă, -ŭm, *costly*
prīvātŭs, -ă, -ŭm, *private*
prōpensŭs, -ă, -ŭm, *disposed*
prōpinquŭs, -ă, -ŭm, *near*
rĕcens, -tĭs, *recent*
rēgĭŭs, -ă, -ŭm
rēgālĭs, -ĕ } *kingly*
săcĕr, -ră, -rŭm, *sacred*
salvŭs, -ă, -ŭm, *safe*
sătŭr, -ă, -ŭm, *sated*
sērēnŭs, -ă, -ŭm, *clear, bright*

incrēdĭbĭlĭs, -ĕ, *incredible*
rārŭs, -ă, -ŭm, *rare, single*
sĭnistĕr, -ră, -rŭm } *left*
laevŭs, -ă, -ŭm
oblīquŭs, -ă, -ŭm, *oblique*
nocturnŭs, -ă, -ŭm, *by night*
hŭmānŭs, -ă, -ŭm, *human*
externŭs, -ă, -ŭm, *strange*
diffĭcĭlĭs, -ĕ, *difficult*
infēlix, -īcĭs, *unhappy*
dēsertŭs, -ă, -ŭm, *desert*
sĕnĭlĭs, -ĕ, *aged, senile*
răpĭdŭs, -ă, -ŭm, *swift, rapid*
brĕvĭs, -ĕ, *short*
parvŭs, -ă, -ŭm, *little, small*
immĕmŏr, -ĭs, *unmindful*
sōlĭtŭs, -ă, -ŭm, *ordinary*
sĕvērŭs, -ă, -ŭm, *severe*
rĭgĭdŭs, -ă, -ŭm, *hard*
plānŭs, -ă, -ŭm, *level*
immortālĭs, -ĕ, *immortal*
simplex, -ĭcĭs, *simple*
paucī, -ae, -ă (pl.), *few*
ignōbĭlĭs, -ĕ, *ignoble*
ōtĭōsŭs, -ă, -ŭm, *unoccupied*
impār, -ărĭs, *odd*
expers, -tĭs, *without share*
fluxŭs, -ă, -ŭm, *frail*
invĭŭs, -ă, -ŭm, *unpassable*
văcŭŭs, -ă, -ŭm, *empty*
impŏtens, -tĭs, *unable, impotent*
praetĕrĭtŭs, -ă, -ŭm, *past*
grātŭĭtŭs, -ă, -ŭm, *free*
pūblĭcŭs, -ă, -ŭm, *public*
ăbălĭēnātŭs, -ă, -ŭm, *alienated*
longinquŭs, -ă, -ŭm, *far off*
vĕtŭs, -ĕrĭs, *old*

pŏpŭlārĭs, -ĕ, *popular*
prŏfānŭs, -ă, -ŭm, *profane*
perdĭtŭs, -ă, -ŭm, *ruined*
ēsŭrĭens, -tĭs, *hungry*
nūbĭlŭs, -ă,-ŭm, *cloudy*

sïmïlïs, -ĕ, *like*
supplex, -ĭcĭs, *suppliant*
ūsĭtātŭs, -ă, -ŭm, *customary*
vernācŭlŭs, -ă,-ŭm, *vernacular*
vĭrïlïs, -ĕ, *manly*

dissïmïlïs, -ĕ, *unlike*
mĭnax, -ācĭs, *threatening*
insŏlĭtŭs, -ă, -ŭm, *unusual*
pĕrĕgrĭnŭs, -ă, -ŭm, *foreign*
mŭlĭĕbrĭs, -ĕ, *womanly*

41. Adjectīvă mātĕrĭālĭă. *Material Adjectives.*

ăbĭegnŭs, -ă, -ŭm, *made of fir-
    wood*
aenĕŭs, -ă, -ŭm, *of bronze*
ărēnācĕŭs, -ă, -ŭm, *sandy*
argentĕŭs, -ă, -ŭm, *silver*
argillācĕŭs, -ă, -ŭm, *of clay*
aurĕŭs, -ă, -ŭm, *of gold, golden*
chălўbēĭŭs, -ă, -ŭm, *of steel*
cŏrĭārĭŭs, -ă, -ŭm, *of leather*
crystallĭnŭs, -ă, -ŭm, *of crystal*
cŭprĕŭs, -ă, -ŭm, *of copper*
ĕburnĕŭs, -ă, -ŭm, *of ivory*
farrĕŭs, -ă, -ŭm, *of corn*
ferrĕŭs, -ă, -ŭm, *of iron, iron*
fraxĭnĕŭs, -ă, -ŭm, *of ash-wood,
    ashen*
ĭlignĕŭs, -ă, -ŭm, *oaken*
lānĕŭs, -ă, -ŭm, *woollen*
lăpĭdĕŭs, -ă, -ŭm, *of stone*

lignĕŭs,-ă,-ŭm, *of wood,wooden*
lintĕŭs, -ă, -ŭm, *linen*
lūtĕŭs, -ă, -ŭm, *of mud, muddy*
marmŏrĕŭs, -ă, -ŭm, *of marble*
ŏlĕăgĭnĕŭs,-ă, -ŭm, *of the olive-
    tree*
păpўrācĕŭs, -ă, -ŭm, *of paper-
    reed*
pīnĕŭs, -ă, -ŭm, *of pine*
plumbĕŭs,-ă,-ŭm, *of lead,leaden*
plūmĕŭs, -ă, -ŭm, *downy*
sălīgnŭs, -ă, -ŭm, *of willow*
saxĕŭs, -ă, -ŭm, *of rock, rocky*
sērĭcŭs, -ă, -ŭm, *silken, silk*
stannĕŭs, -ă, -ŭm, *made of tin,
    tinnen*
terrēnŭs, -ă, -ŭm, *earthen*
testācĕŭs, -ă, -ŭm, *of bricks*
vĭtrĕŭs, -ă, -ŭm, *of glass*

42. Adjectīvă cŏlōrĕm nŏtantĭă. *Adjectives of Color.*

candĭdŭs, -ă, -ŭm ⎱ *white*
albŭs, -ă, -ŭm ⎰
ātĕr, -ră, -rŭm ⎱ *black*
nĭgĕr, -ră, -rŭm ⎰
cānŭs, -ă, -ŭm, *gray*
pullŭs, -ă, -ŭm, *dark-gray*
fulvŭs, -ă, -ŭm, *yellowish-
    brown, light-brown*
fuscŭs, -ă, -ŭm, *dark-brown*

rŭbĕr, -ră, -rŭm, *red*
rŏsĕŭs, -ă, -ŭm, *rose-colored*
flāvŭs, -ă, -ŭm, *yellow*
lūtĕŭs, -ă, -ŭm, *orange*
vĭrĭdĭs, -ĕ, *green*
caerŭlĕŭs, -ă, -ŭm, *dark-blue*
vĭŏlācĕŭs, -ă, -ŭm, *violet*
purpŭrĕŭs, -ă, -ŭm ⎱ *purple*
pūnĭcĕŭs, -ă, -ŭm ⎰

43. Verbă vōcāliă. *Verbs denoting sounds.*

vox sŏnăt	*the voice sounds*
hŏmŏ dīcĭt (lŏquĭtŭr)	*man speaks*
contĭŏ strĕpĭt	*the assembly makes a noise*
pŭĕr clămăt	*the boy cries*
pŭellă cantăt	*the girl sings*
infans vāgĭt	*the babe cries*
cĭcădă strīdĕt	*the tree-cricket shrills*
ŏvĭs bālăt	*the sheep bleats*
vaccă mūgĭt	*the cow lows*
porcŭs grŭnnĭt	*the hog grunts*
cănĭs lātrăt	*the dog barks*
lŭpŭs ŭlŭlăt	*the wolf howls*
lĕŏ rūgĭt	*the lion roars*
ĕquŭs hinnĭt	*the horse neighs*
asĭnŭs rŭdĭt	*the ass brays*
gallŭs cănĭt	*the cock crows*
ansĕr gingrĭt	*the goose gaggles*
ănăs tĕtrinnĭt	*the duck quacks*
pullŭs pīpăt	*the chicken peeps*
rănă cŏaxăt	*the frog croaks*
serpens sībĭlăt	*the snake hisses*
ăpĭs sŭsurrăt	*the bee hums*
tŭbă clangĭt	*the trumpet sounds*
caelŭm tŏnăt	*heaven thunders*
mărĕ murmŭrăt	*the sea roars*

ETYMOLOGICAL PART.

I. First Conjugation.

Regular Verbs.

Of all regular verbs the Infinitive ending alone is given.

aestĭmārĕ, *to estimate*

  aestĭmătĭŏ, –ŏnĭs (f.), *an esti-*
    mation
  existĭmārĕ, *to judge*
  existĭmătĭŏ, –ŏnĭs (f.), *an opin-*
    ion; reputation
  existĭmătŏr,–ŏrĭs(m.), *a judge,*
    critic

ămārĕ, *to love*

  ămŏr, –ŏrĭs (m.), *love*
  ămātŏr, –ŏrĭs (m.), *a lover,*
    friend
  ămābĭlĭs, –ĕ, *amiable*
  ădāmārĕ, *to become fond of*
  rĕdāmārĕ, *to love in return*
  ămīcŭs, –ī (m.), *a friend*
  ămīcĭtĭă, –ae (f.), *friendship*
  ĭnĭmīcŭs, –ī (m.), *an enemy*
  ĭnĭmīcĭtĭae, –ārŭm (f. pl.), *en-*
    mity

ărārĕ, *to plow*

  ărātŏr, –ŏrĭs (m.), *a plowman*
  ărātrŭm, –ī (n.), *a plow*
  arvŭm, –ī (n.), *an arable field*
  armentŭm, –ī (n.) *cattle for*
    plowing
  exărārĕ, *to plow up; to note*
    down

armārĕ, *to arm*

  armă, –ōrŭm (n. pl.), *arms*
  armĭgĕr,–ī (m.), *an armor-bear-*
  armātūră, –ae (f.), *armor* [*er*
  armāmentă, –ōrŭm (n. pl.),
    the tackle of a ship
  armāmentārĭŭm, –ī (n.), *an*
    armory
  ĭnermĭs, –ĕ, *unarmed*

caelārĕ, *to engrave*

  caelŭm, –ī (n.), *a chisel*
  caelātŏr, –ŏrĭs (m.), *a graver*

castīgārĕ, *to punish*

  castīgātĭŏ, –ŏnĭs (f.), *a punish-*
    [*ment*
cēlārĕ, *to conceal*

clāmārĕ, *to cry*

  clāmŏr, –ŏrĭs (m.), *a cry*
  classĭcŭm, –ī (n.), *a trumpet-*
  acclāmārĕ, *to cry at* [*signal*
  conclāmārĕ, *to call together*
  exclāmārĕ, *to exclaim*
  prōclāmārĕ, *to proclaim* [*ing*
  dĕclāmārĕ, *to practice speak-*
  dĕclāmātĭŏ, –ŏnĭs (f.), *a decla-*
    mation
  dĕclāmātŏr, –ŏrĭs (m.) *a de-*
    claimer
  rĕclāmārĕ, *to cry out against*

consīdĕrārĕ, to consider
consīdĕrātĭŏ, -ŏnĭs (f.) consideration
consīdĕrātŭs,-ă, -ŭm, consid-
erate
consīdĕrātĕ, considerately

cŏrōnārĕ, to crown
cŏrōnă, -ae (f.), a garland,
crown

crĕārĕ, to create
crĕātĭŏ, -ŏnĭs (f.),creation, ap-
pointment
crĕātŏr, -ŏrĭs (m.), a creator
prōcrĕārĕ, to bring forth
prōcrĕātŏr, -ŏrĭs (m.), a creator
rĕcrĕārĕ, to recreate

crĕmārĕ (trans.), to burn
concrĕmārĕ, to burn up

cūrārĕ, to care for
cūră, -ae (f.), care
cūrătŏr,-ŏrĭs (m.), a guardian
cūrĭōsŭs, -ă, -ŭm, careful
incūrĭă, -ae (f.), want of care
accūrārĕ, to do a thing with
care
accūrătŭs, -ă, -ŭm, exact,
careful
prōcūrārĕ, to attend to
prōcūrătŏr, -ŏrĭs (m.), a proc-
urator
sēcūrŭs, -ă, -ŭm, free from
care
sēcūrĭtās, -ătĭs (f.), freedom
from care

dēsīdĕrārĕ, to desire
dēsīdĕrĭŭm, -ī (n.), a desire

dissĭpārĕ, to disperse
dissĭpătĭŏ,-ŏnĭs (f.),a dispers-
ing

dōnārĕ, to give as a present
dōnŭm, -ī (n.), a gift
dōnătĭŏ, -ŏnĭs (f.), a donation
condōnārĕ, to pardon

errārĕ, to go astray; to err
errŏr, -ŏrĭs (m.), a mistake
ăberrārĕ, to go astray
ĭnerrans, -tĭs, fixed
errātŭm, -ī (n.), a mistake
errātĭcŭs, -ă,-ŭm, erratic

festīnārĕ, to hasten
festīnātĭŏ, -ŏnĭs (f.), haste
festīnantĕr, hastily
confestĭm, immediately

firmārĕ, to strengthen
firmŭs, -ă, -ŭm, strong
firmĭtās, -ătĭs (f.) } strength
firmĭtūdŏ, -ĭnĭs (f.) }
infirmŭs, -ă, -ŭm, weak
infirmĭtās, -ătĭs (f.), weakness
affirmārĕ, to affirm
affirmătĭŏ, -ŏnĭs (f.), an affir-
mation
confirmārĕ, to confirm
confirmătĭŏ, -ŏnĭs (f.), confir-
mation
infirmārĕ, to weaken   [ing
infirmătĭŏ, -ŏnĭs (f.),a weaken-

flāgĭtārĕ, to entreat
efflāgĭtārĕ, to entreat earnestly

flāgrārĕ (intrans.), to burn
conflāgrārĕ, to burn up

flammă, -ae (f.), *a flame*
inflammārĕ, *to inflame*
inflammătĭŏ, -ŏnĭs (f.), *an inflammation*

flārĕ, *to blow*
  afflārĕ, *to breathe on*
  conflārĕ, *to bring together*
  inflārĕ, *to blow into*
  inflātŭs, -ŭs (m.), *a blast*

formārĕ, *to shape, form*
  formă, -ae (f.), *figure, form*
  formōsŭs, -ă, -ŭm, *finely formed*
  dēformĭs, -ĕ, *deformed*
  dēformĭtās,-ātĭs (f.), *deformity*
  bĭformĭs, -ĕ, *two-formed*
  conformārĕ, *to shape, form*
  conformătĭŏ (f.), -ŏnĭs, *conformation*
  informārĕ, *to instruct*
  informătĭŏ, -ŏnĭs (f.), *an idea*

hŏnōrārĕ, *to honor*
  hŏnŏr, -ōrĭs (m.)) *honor; an*
  hŏnōs, -ōrĭs (m.)) *office*
  hŏnōrārĭŭs, -ă, -ŭm, *honorary*
  hŏnōrĭfĭcŭs, -ă, -ŭm, *honorable*
  hŏnestŭs, -ă, -ŭm, *honest*
  hŏnestās, -ātĭs (f.), *honesty, morality*
  hŏnestārĕ, *to honor*

jūdĭcārĕ, *to judge*
  dījūdĭcārĕ, *to decide*
  jūdex, -ĭcĭs (m.), *a judge*
  jūdĭcĭŭm,-ī (n.), *a judicial sentence; a court of justice*

lăbōrārĕ, *to work*
  lăbŏr, -ōrĭs (m.), *work*
  lăbōrĭōsŭs, -ă, -ŭm, *full of labor*
  ēlăbōrārĕ, *to elaborate, work out*

laudārĕ, *to praise*
  laus, -dĭs (f.), *praise*
  laudătĭŏ, -ŏnĭs (f.), *a eulogy*
  laudăbĭlĭs, -ĕ, *praiseworthy*
  laudātŏr, -ōrĭs (m.), *a praiser*

lēgārĕ, *to send with a commission, delegate*
  lēgătĭŏ, -ŏnĭs (f.), *an embassy*
  lēgătŭm, -ī (n.), *a legacy*
  lēgătŭs, -ī (m.), *a deputy, lieutenant-general, ambassador*
  allēgārĕ, *to deputy*
  allēgătĭŏ,-ŏnĭs (f.),*a delegation*
  dēlēgārĕ, *to assign*
  dēlēgătĭŏ, -ŏnĭs (f.), *an assignment*
  rēlēgārĕ, *to relegate* [ment
  rēlēgătĭŏ, -ŏnĭs (f.), *a banish-*
  lex, lēgĭs (f.), *a law* [ment
  lēgĭtĭmŭs,-ă,-ŭm,*lawful,legal*

lībĕrārĕ, *to free*
  lībĕrătĭŏ, -ŏnĭs (f.), *liberation*
  lībĕrătŏr, -ōrĭs (m.), *a deliverer*
  lībĕr, -ă, -ŭm, *free*
  lībĕrī, -ōrŭm (m. pl.), *children*
  lībĕrtās, -ātĭs (f.), *liberty*
  lībĕrtŭs, -ī (m.), *a freedman*
  lībĕrālĭs, -ĕ, *liberal, noble*
  lībĕrālĭtās, -ātĭs (f.),*liberality, generosity*

lĭbrārĕ, *to weigh (in a balance)*

lībră, -ae (f.), *a pair of scales; a pound*

lĭbrāmentŭm, -Ĭ (n.), *weight*

dēlĭbĕrārĕ, *to weigh well, deliberate*

dēlĭbĕrātĭŏ, -ŏnĭs (f.), *deliberation*

lĭgārĕ, *to tie, bind*

allĭgārĕ, *to bind up*

collĭgārĕ, *to bind together*

dēlĭgārĕ, *to bind fast*

oblĭgārĕ, *to bind up, oblige*

rĕlĭgārĕ, *to bind fast*

lŏcārĕ, *to place*

lŏcātĭŏ, -ŏnĭs (f.), *a letting for hire*

lŏcŭs, -Ĭ (m.), *a place*

Ĭlĭcō, *on the spot*

lŏcŭlĬ, -ŏrŭm (m. pl.), *a box*

collŏcārĕ, *to place*

collŏcātĭŏ, -ŏnĭs (f.), *collocation*

mānārĕ, *to flow*

ēmānārĕ, *to spring out*

permānārĕ, *to flow through*

mandārĕ, *to commit, enjoin*

mandātŭm, -Ĭ (n.), *a charge, order*

commendārĕ, *to recommend*

commendātĭŏ, -ŏnĭs (f.), *a recommendation*

mĭgrārĕ, *to wander*

mĭgrātĭŏ, -ŏnĭs (f.), *a change of residence*

commĭgrārĕ ⎱ *to remove into a*
immĭgrārĕ ⎰ *country*

dēmĭgrārĕ ⎱ *to remove from a*
ēmĭgrārĕ ⎰ *place*

rĕmĭgrārĕ, *to remove back*

mŭltārĕ, *to punish with fine*

multă, -ae (f.), *a fine*

mūtārĕ, *to change*

mūtātĭŏ, -ŏnĭs (f.) ⎱ *a change*
immūtātĭŏ, -ŏnĭs (f.) ⎰

mūtăbĭlĭs, -ĕ, *changeable*

commūtārĕ ⎱ *to change, exchange*
permūtārĕ ⎰ *change*

immūtārĕ, *to change*

immūtătŭs, -ă, -ŭm, *unchanged*

nătārĕ ⎱ *to swim, float*
nārĕ ⎰

ēnătārĕ, *to swim away*

nāvĭgārĕ, *to sail*

nāvĭs, - (f.), *a ship*

naută, -ae (m.) *a seaman*

nāvĭgĭŭm, -Ĭ (n.), *a vessel*

nāvĭgātĭŏ, -ŏnĭs (f.), *a sailing*

optārĕ, *to choose, wish*

optĭŏ, -ŏnĭs (f.) ⎱ *choice*
optātĭŏ, -ŏnĭs (f.) ⎰

optăbĭlĭs, -ĕ, *desirable*

ădoptārĕ, *to choose, adopt*

exoptātŭs, -ă, -ŭm, *longed for*

ŏrārĕ, *to speak, pray*

ŏrātĭŏ, -ŏnĭs (f.), *a speech, oration*

ŏrātŏr, -ŏrĭs (m.), *a speaker, orator*

ŏrācŭlŭm, -Ĭ (n.), *an oracle (answer of a god)*

exōrārĕ, *to move by entreaty*
ĭnexōrăbĭlĭs,–ĕ, *not to be moved by entreaty*
ădōrārĕ, *to worship*
ădōrătĭŏ, –ōnĭs (f.), *worship*

ornārĕ, *to fit out*

ornātŭs,–ūs(m.),*a preparation*
ornāmentŭm, –ī (n.), *an orna-*
ornātĕ, *elegantly* [*ment*
ădornārĕ) *to adorn, embellish*
exornārĕ)

părārĕ, *to prepare*

părăbĭlĭs, –ĕ, *easy to be had*
părātŭs, –ă, –ŭm, *ready*
impărātŭs, –ă, –ŭm, *not ready*
appărārĕ, *to make ready*
appărātŭs,–ūs (m.),*equipment*
compărārĕ, *to bring together;*
to compare
compărătĭŏ, –ōnĭs (f.), *a com-*
parison
praepărārĕ, *to prepare*
praepărătĭŏ, –ōnĭs (f.), *a prep-*
aration
sēpărārĕ, *to separate*
sēpărātĭm, *asunder, separately*
impĕrārĕ, *to command*
impĕrātōr, –ōrĭs (m.), *a com-*
mander-in-chief,an emperor
impĕrĭŭm, –ī (n.), *dominion,*
empire

pătrārĕ, *to bring to pass*

impĕtrārĕ, *to obtain (by en-*
treaty)

(–pellārĕ)

appellārĕ, *to address, call*
appellātĭŏ, –ōnĭs (f.), *a name,*
an appellation

compellārĕ, *to accost*
compellātĭŏ, –ōnĭs (f.), *a re-*
buking
interpellārĕ, *to interrupt by*
speaking
interpellātĭŏ, –ōnĭs (f.), *an in-*
terruption
interpellātŏr, –ōrĭs (m.), *a*
disturber

plōrārĕ, *to cry, weep aloud*

plōrātŭs, –ūs (m.), *a weeping*
complōrārĕ) *to deplore*
dēplōrārĕ)
implōrārĕ, *to implore*
implōrătĭŏ,–ōnĭs(f.),*an earnest*
supplication
explōrārĕ, *to search out*
explōrātŏr, –ōrĭs (m.), *a spy*

portārĕ, *to carry*

apportārĕ, *to carry to*
asportārĕ, *to carry away*
comportārĕ, *to bring together*
transportārĕ, *to transport*
dēportārĕ) *to carry off*
rĕportārĕ)
exportārĕ, *to export*
exportātĭŏ, –ōnĭs (f.), *export*
importārĕ, *to import*
supportārĕ, *to carry to*

prīvārĕ, *to deprive*

prīvătĭŏ,–ōnĭs (f.), *a privation*
prīvātŭs, –ă, –ŭm, *private*
prīvātĭm, *in private*
prīvīlēgĭŭm,–ī (n.), *a privilege*

prŏbārĕ, *to try, test*

apprŏbārĕ) *to approve*
comprŏbārĕ)

prŏbătĭŏ, -ŏnĭs (f.), *a trial*
apprŏbătĭŏ, -ŏnĭs (f.), *approval*
prŏbăbĭlĭs, -ĕ, *acceptable*
prŏbăbĭlĭtĕr, *probably*
prŏbăbĭlĭtās, -ātĭs (f.), *proba-*
bility
imprŏbārĕ, *to disapprove*
imprŏbătĭŏ, -ŏnĭs (f.), *disap-*
probation
prŏbŭs, -ă, -ŭm, *upright*
prŏbĭtās,-ātĭs (f.), *uprightness*
imprŏbŭs, -ă, -ŭm, *wicked*
imprŏbĭtās, -ātĭs (f.), *wicked-*
ness

pugnārĕ, *to fight*

pugnă, -ae (f.), *a fight*
pugnax, -ācĭs, *fond of fighting*
pugnŭs, -ĭ (m.), *a fist*
expugnārĕ, *to capture*
expugnătĭŏ,-ŏnĭs(f.), *a capture*
ĭnexpugnăbĭlĭs,-ĕ, *that can not*
be taken by assault, impreg-
nable
impugnārĕ, *to attack*
oppugnārĕ, *to assault* [*sault*
oppugnătĭŏ, -ŏnĭs (f.), *an as-*
prŏpugnārĕ, *to defend*
prŏpugnătĭŏ, -ŏnĭs (f.), *a de-*
fense
prŏpugnătŏr, -ŏrĭs (m.), *a de-*
fender
prŏpugnăcŭlŭm, -ĭ (n.), *a bul-*
wark
rĕpugnārĕ, *to resist, oppose*
rĕpugnantĭă, -ae (f.), *a contra-*
diction

purgārĕ, *to clean*

purgătĭŏ, -ŏnĭs (f.), *an apology*
pūrŭs, -ă, -ŭm, *clean*
impūrŭs, -ă, -ŭm, *unclean*

pŭtārĕ, *to think*
compŭtārĕ, *to compute*
dispŭtārĕ, *to discuss* [*sion*
dispŭtătĭŏ, -ŏnĭs (f.), *a discus-*
rĕpŭtārĕ, *to reflect upon*

rŏgārĕ, *to ask*

rŏgătĭŏ, -ŏnĭs (f.), *a bill, a pro-*
jected law
abrŏgārĕ, *to repeal*
arrŏgārĕ,*to claim as one's own*
arrŏgantĭă, -ae (f.), *arrogance*
dĕrŏgārĕ, *to repeal*
ĕrŏgārĕ, *to expend*
ĕrŏgătĭŏ,-ŏnĭs(f.),*a paying out*
interrŏgārĕ, *to ask*
interrŏgătĭŏ, -ŏnĭs (f.), *a ques-*
irrŏgārĕ, *to impose* [*tion*
prŏrŏgārĕ, *to prolong*
prŏrŏgătĭŏ,-ŏnĭs (f.), *a prolon-*
gation

săcrārĕ, *to hallow*

consĕcrārĕ, *to consecrate*
obsĕcrārĕ, *to conjure*
obsĕcrătĭŏ, -ŏnĭs (f.), *an en-*
treaty
săcĕr, -ră, -rŭm, *sacred*
săcrŭm, -ĭ (n.), *a sacred thing*
săcellŭm, -ĭ (n.), *a chapel*
săcrārĭŭm, -ĭ (n.), *a shrine*
săcerdōs, -ōtĭs (m.), *a priest*
săcerdōtĭŭm, -ĭ (n.), *the priest-*
hood
săcrămentŭm, -ĭ (n.), *the mili-*
tary oath
săcrĭfĭcĭŭm, -ĭ (n.), *a sacrifice*
săcrĭlĕgŭs, -ă, -ŭm, *sacrile-*
gious
săcrĭlĕgĭŭm,-ĭ (n.), *a sacrilege*
săcrōsanctŭs, -ă, -ŭm, *invio-*
lable, sacrosanct

sānārĕ, *to cure*

sānăbĭlĭs, -ĕ, *curable*
sānătĭŏ, -ōnĭs (f.), *a healing*
sānŭs, -ă, -ŭm, *sound*
sānĭtās, -ātĭs (f.), *health*
sānĕ, *well, indeed*
insānŭs, -ă, -ŭm, *mad*
insānĭă, -ae (f.), *madness*
insānīrĕ, *to be mad*
vēsānŭs, -ă, -ŭm, *mad*

servārĕ, *to keep*

servătŏr, -ōrĭs (m.), *a savior*
asservārĕ, *to preserve*
conservārĕ, *to keep, preserve*
conservătĭŏ,-ōnĭs(f.), *a keeping*
conservătŏr,-ōrĭs(m.), *a keeper*
observārĕ, *to observe*
observătĭŏ, -ōnĭs (f.), *an obser-*
vation
observantĭă,-ae(f.),*regard, ob-*
servance
rĕservārĕ, *to save up*

signārĕ, *to mark*

signŭm, -ī (n.), *a sign*
signĭfĭcārĕ, *to show*
signĭfĭcătĭŏ, -ōnĭs (f.), *a signi-*
fication
signĭfĕr, -ī (m.), *a standard-*
bearer
assignārĕ, *to assign*
obsignārĕ, *to seal up*
dēsignārĕ, *to designate*
rĕsignārĕ, *to unseal*
insignĭs, -ĕ, *distinguished*
insignĕ, -ĭs (n.), *a decoration*

sĭmŭlārĕ, *to feign*

sĭmŭlătĭŏ, -ōnĭs (f.), *pretense*
dissĭmŭlārĕ, *to dissemble*

dissĭmŭlătĭŏ, -ōnĭs (f.), *a dis-*
sembling
insĭmŭlārĕ, *to charge*
sĭmĭlĭs, -ĕ, *like*
dissĭmĭlĭs, -ĕ, *unlike*
sĭmĭlĭtūdŏ, -ĭnĭs (f.), *resem-*
blance
dissĭmĭlĭtūdŏ, -ĭnĭs (f.), *differ-*
ence
sĭmŭlăcrŭm, -ī (n.), *a likeness*

somnĭārĕ, *to dream*

somnŭs, -ī (m.), *sleep*
somnĭŭm, -ī (n.), *a dream*
somnĭcŭlōsŭs, -ă, -ŭm, *sleepy*
insomnĭă, -ae (f.), *sleeplessness*
sēmĭsomnŭs, -ă, -ŭm, *drowsy*

spērārĕ, *to hope*

spēs, -ĕī (f.), *hope*
dēspērārĕ, *to despair*
dēspērătĭŏ, -ōnĭs (f.), *despair*
inspērātŭs, -ă, -ŭm, *unhoped*
for
dēspērātŭs,-ă,-ŭm, *despaired*
of

spīrārĕ, *to breathe*

spīrĭtŭs,-ūs(m.),*a breath; high*
spirit
aspīrārĕ, *to aspire*
aspīrătĭŏ, -ōnĭs (f.), *a breath-*
ing
conspīrārĕ, *to agree together*
conspīrătĭŏ,-ōnĭs(f.),*an agree-*
ment
respīrārĕ, *to respire*
respīrătĭŏ, -ōnĭs (f.), *respira-*
tion
suspīrārĕ, *to sigh*
suspīrĭŭm, -ī (n.), *a sigh*

spŏllãrĕ, *to rob of clothing*

spŏllãtlŏ,–ŏnĭs (f.), *plundering*

spŏllã, –ŏrŭm (n. pl.), *spoils*

sũdãrĕ, *to sweat*

sũdŏr, –ŏrĭs (m.), *sweat*

sũdãrĭŭm, –ĭ (n.), *a napkin (to wipe off perspiration)*

dēsũdãrĕ, *to fatigue one's self*

tempĕrãrĕ, *to temper*

tempĕrantlã, –ae (f.), *temperance*

intempĕrantlã, –ae (f.), *intemperance*

tempĕrãtlŏ, –ŏnĭs (f.), *a temobtempĕrãrĕ, to obey [pering*

tŏlĕrãrĕ, *to suffer*

tŏlĕrantlã, –ae (f.), *endurance*

intŏlĕrantlã, –ae (f.), *intolerance*

tŏlĕrãbĭlĭs, –ĕ, *tolerable*

tŏlĕrantĕr, *tolerably*

intŏlĕrãbĭlĭs, –ĕ ⎫ *intoler-*
intŏlĕrandŭs,–ã,–ŭm ⎭ *able*

intŏlĕrantĕr, *intolerably*

trĕpĭdãrĕ, *to hurry with alarm*

trĕpĭdũs, –ã, –ŭm, *alarmed*

trĕpĭdãtlŏ, –ŏnĭs (f.), *trepidation, fear*

turbãrĕ, *to trouble*

turbã, –ae (f.), *turmoil, crowd*

turbĭdũs, –ã, –ŭm, *troubled*

turbũlentũs, –ã, –ŭm, *stormy*

conturbãrĕ, *to confound*

conturbãtlŏ, –ŏnĭs (f.), *confusion*

dēturbãrĕ, *to throw down*

disturbãrĕ, *to drive asunder, disturb*

exturbãrĕ, *to drive away*

perturbãrĕ, *to confuse*

perturbãtlŏ, –ŏnĭs (f.), *confusion*

vãcãrĕ, *to be free from*

vãcãtlŏ, –ŏnĭs (f.), *freedom (from a duty)*

vãcũũs, –ã, –ŭm, *empty*

vãcũĭtãs,–ãtĭs (f.), *a being free from any thing [less*

sũpervãcãnĕũs, –ã, –ŭm, *need-*

vastãrĕ, *to lay waste*

vastũs, –ã, –ŭm, *waste*

vastĭtãs, –ãtĭs (f.), *a waste*

verbĕrãrĕ, *to beat*

verbĕrã, –ŭm (n. pl.), *blows*

vestĭgãrĕ, *to track*

investĭgãrĕ, *to track, investigate*

pervestĭgãrĕ, *to trace out*

investĭgãtlŏ,–ŏnĭs (f.) ⎫ *an investi-*
pervestĭgãtlŏ,–ŏnĭs (f.) ⎬ *gation*
investĭgãtŏr, –ŏrĭs (m.), *an investigator*

vestĭgĭŭm,–ĭ (n.), *a trace, track*

vexãrĕ, *to trouble*

vexãtlŏ, –ŏnĭs (f.), *trouble*

vexãtŏr, –ŏrĭs (m.), *a troubler*

vĭŏlãrĕ, *to injure*

vĭŏlentũs, –ã, –ŭm, *violent*

vĭŏlentlã, –ae (f.), *violence*

vītārĕ, *to shun*

dēvītārĕ }
ēvītārĕ } *to avoid*

vĭtŭpĕrārĕ, *to blame*

vĭtŭpĕrātĭŏ, –ōnĭs (f.), *blame, censure*

vĭtŭpĕrātŏr, –ōrĭs (m.) *a censurer*

vĭtĭŭm, –ī (n.), *vice*

vĭtĭōsŭs, –ă, –ŭm, *vicious*

vĭtĭārĕ, *to injure*

vŏcārĕ, *to call*

vŏcĭtārĕ, *to name*

vox, vōcĭs (f.), *a voice*

vŏcăbŭlŭm, –ī (n.), *a word, vocable*

vŏcālĭs, – (f.), *a vowel*

vŏcātĭŏ, –ōnĭs (f.) }
vŏcātŭs, –ūs (m.) } *an invitation*

āvŏcārĕ, *to call away*

advŏcārĕ, *to summon*

convŏcārĕ, *to call together*

dēvŏcārĕ, *to call off*

ēvŏcārĕ, *to call out*

invŏcārĕ, *to invoke*

prōvŏcārĕ, *to challenge*

prōvŏcātĭŏ, –ōnĭs(f.), *an appeal*

rĕvŏcārĕ, *to recall*

sēvŏcārĕ, *to call aside*

vŏlārĕ, *to fly*

vŏlĭtārĕ, *to fly about*

vŏlātŭs, –ūs (m.), *a flight*

vŏlŭcĕr, –rĭs, –rĕ }
vŏlātĭlĭs, –ĕ } *winged*

āvŏlārĕ, *to fly away*

advŏlārĕ, *to fly to*

convŏlārĕ, *to run together*

ēvŏlārĕ, *to fly out*

invŏlārĕ, *to fly at*

pervŏlārĕ, *to fly through*

praetervŏlārĕ, *to fly over*

praevŏlārĕ, *to fly before*

prōvŏlārĕ, *to rush out*

rĕvŏlārĕ, *to fly back*

subvŏlārĕ, *to fly upward*

vŏrārĕ, *to swallow up*

dēvŏrārĕ, *to devour*

vŏrax, –ācĭs, *voracious*

vŏrāgŏ, –ĭnĭs (f.), *an abyss*

vulgārĕ, *to make common*

vulgŭs, –ī (n.), *the rabble*

vulgārĭs, –ĕ, *vulgar*

vulgō, *before every body*

dīvulgārĕ }
pervulgārĕ } *to publish*

vulnĕrārĕ, *to wound*

vulnĕrātĭŏ, –ōnĭs (f.), *a wounding*

vulnŭs, –ĕrĭs (n.), *a wound*

invulnĕrātŭs, –ă, –ŭm, *unwounded*

Irregular Verbs.

The Principal Parts are given in full:

1. of all Irregular Simple Verbs,
2. of such of their Compounds as deviate in any important particular from the simple verbs.

The Infinitive ending alone is given:

1. of all verbs (simple and compound) of regular formation,
2. of such Irregular Compounds as do not deviate in Perfect and Supine from their simple verbs.

Obsolete forms are inclosed within brackets, and such as are but little used, within parentheses.

crĕpŏ, crĕpŭī, crĕpĭtŭm, crĕpārĕ, *to creak*

crĕpĭtŭs, -ūs (m.), *a creaking*
discrĕpārĕ, *to sound discordantly*
discrĕpantĭă, -ae (f.), *discrep-*
incrĕpārĕ, *to scold* [*ancy*

cūbŏ, cūbŭī, cūbĭtŭm, cūbārĕ, *to lie down*

cūbĭtŭs, -ī (m.), *the elbow*
cūbĭlĕ, -ĭs (n.), *a bed*
cūbĭcŭlŭm, -ī (n.), *a bedroom*
accūbārĕ, *to recline at table*
incūbārĕ, *to lie upon*
rĕcūbārĕ, *to lie back*

dŏmŏ, dŏmŭī, dŏmĭtŭm, dŏmārĕ, *to tame*

ĕdŏmārĕ } *to overcome*
perdŏmārĕ }
dŏmĭtŏr, -ōrĭs (m.), *a tamer*
dŏmĭtŭs, -ūs (m.), *a taming*
indŏmĭtŭs, -ă, -ŭm, *untamed*

sŏnŏ, sŏnŭī, sŏnĭtŭm, sŏnārĕ, *to sound* Part. Fut. sŏnātūrŭs

consŏnārĕ, *to resound*
consŏnŭs, -ă, -ŭm, *harmonious*

dissŏnārĕ, *to disagree*
persŏnārĕ, *to sound through*
rĕsŏnārĕ, *to resound*
persŏnă, -ae (f.), *a mask*
sŏnŭs, -ī (m.) } *a sound,*
sŏnĭtŭs, -ūs (m.) } *noise*
absŏnŭs, -ă, -ŭm } *dissonant*
dissŏnŭs, -ă, -ŭm }

tŏnŏ, tŏnŭī, (tŏnĭtŭm), tŏnārĕ, *to thunder*

attŏnārĕ, *to thunder at*
attŏnĭtŭs, -ă, -ŭm, *thunderstruck*
circumtŏnārĕ, *to thunder a-*
intŏnārĕ, *to thunder* [*round*
tŏnĭtrŭs, -ūs (m.) } *thunder*
tŏnĭtrŭŭm, -ī (n.) }

vĕtŏ, vĕtŭī, vĕtĭtŭm, vĕtārĕ, *to forbid*

vĕtĭtŭm, -ī (n.), *a prohibition*

mīcŏ, mīcŭī, (without Sup.) mīcārĕ, *to shine*

ēmīcŏ, ēmīcŭī, ēmīcātŭm, ēmīcārĕ, *to shine forth*
dīmīcŏ, -āvī, -ātŭm, -ārĕ, *to fight*

frĭcŏ, frĭcŭĭ, frĭcātŭm or frĭc-
tŭm, frĭcārĕ, to rub
dēfrĭcārĕ, to rub off
infrĭcārĕ, to rub in
perfrĭcārĕ, to rub all over
rĕfrĭcārĕ, to renew

sĕcŏ,sĕcŭĭ, sectŭm, sĕcārĕ, to cut
Part. Fut. sĕcātŭrŭs
sĭcă, -ae (f.), a poniard
serră, -ae (f.), a saw
sĕcūrĭs, – (f.), a hatchet
dēsĕcārĕ, to cut down
dissĕcārĕ, to cut asunder

jŭvŏ, jŭvī, jūtŭm, jŭvārĕ, to assist
Part. Fut. jŭvātŭrŭs
jūcundŭs, -ă, -ŭm, pleasant
adjŭvārĕ, to help
Part. Fut. { adjūtŭrŭs
{ adjŭvātŭrŭs
adjūmentŭm, -ī (n.), assistance
adjūtŏr, -ōrĭs (m.), an assistant

lăvŏ, lăvī, lăvātŭm, lautŭm or
lōtŭm, lăvārĕ, to wash
lautŭs, -ă, -ŭm, elegant
lautĭtĭă, -ae (f.), elegance (in
one's style of living)
ablŭŏ, ablŭī, ablūtŭm, ablŭĕrĕ,
to wash off
allŭĕrĕ, to flow along, wash
ēlŭĕrĕ, to wash out
prōlŭĕrĕ, to wash off
allŭvĭēs, -ēī (f.), an inundation
illŭvĭēs, -ēī (f.), dirt

nĕcŏ, -āvī, -ātŭm -ārĕ, to kill
ēnĕcŏ { -āvī, -ātŭm, -ārĕ) to
{ -ŭī, -tŭm, -ārĕ } kill

nex, nĕcĭs (f.), a violent death
pernĭcĭēs, -ēī (f.), destruction
pernĭcĭōsŭs, -ă, -ŭm, destructive
internĭcĭŏ, -ōnĭs (f.), extermi-
nation

[-plĭcŏ, fold]
applĭcŏ, -āvī, -ātŭm (applĭ-
cŭī, applĭcĭtŭm), applĭcārĕ,
to attach; to apply
complĭcŏ, -āvī, -ātŭm (com-
plĭcŭī, complĭcĭtŭm), com-
plĭcārĕ, to fold together
explĭcŏ, -āvī, -ātŭm (explĭ-
cŭī, explĭcĭtŭm), explĭcārĕ,
to unfold, explain
implĭcŏ, -āvī, -ātŭm (implĭ-
cŭī, implĭcĭtŭm), implĭcārĕ,
to entangle

Regular:
dŭplĭcŏ, -āvī, -ātŭm, -ārĕ, to
double
multĭplĭcŏ, -āvī, -ātŭm, -ārĕ,
to multiply
supplĭcŏ, -āvī, -ātŭm, -ārĕ, to
beseech
supplex, -ĭcĭs, kneeling down,
humbly begging
supplĭcātĭŏ, -ōnĭs (f.), a public
prayer
supplĭcĭŭm, -ī (n.), a kneeling
down to receive capital punishment
dŭplex, -ĭcĭs, double
multĭplex, -ĭcĭs, manifold

pōtŏ, -āvī, -ātŭm, usually pō-
tŭm, pōtārĕ, to drink
pōtŭs, -ă, -ŭm, that has drunk,
that has been drunk
appōtŭs, -ă, -ŭm, tipsy

ĕpōtŭs, -ă, -ŭm, *drunk up*
pōcŭlŭm, -ī (n.), *a goblet*

dō, dĕdī, dătŭm, dărĕ, *to give*

circumdărĕ, *to surround*
pessundărĕ, *to destroy*
sătisdărĕ, *to give back*
vēnundărĕ, *to sell*
dŏs, dōtĭs (f.), *a dowry*
dōnŭm, -ī (n.), *a gift*
dōnărĕ, *to give as a present*
dōnătĭŏ, -ōnĭs (f.), *a donation*

stō, stĕtī, stătŭm, stărĕ, *to stand*

Without Supine:
antestō, -ĕtī, -ărĕ, *to excel*
circumstō, -ĕtī, -ărĕ, *to sur-*
round
interstō, -ĕtī, -ărĕ, *to stand*
between
sŭperstō, -ĕtī, -ărĕ, *to stand*
over
adstō, -ĭtī, -ărĕ, *to stand at*
constō, -ĭtī, -ărĕ, *to exist*
instō, -ĭtī, -ărĕ, *to insist*
obstō, -ĭtī, -ărĕ, *to stand in*
the way

perstō, -ĭtī, -ărĕ, *to persevere*
praestō, -ĭtī, -ărĕ, *to surpass*
restō, -ĭtī, -ărĕ, *to remain*
Without Perfect and Supine:
distărĕ, *to be distant*
exstărĕ, *to be conspicuous*
constantĭă, -ae (f.), *constancy*
distantĭă, -ae (f.), *diversity*
praestantĭă,-ae(f.),*superiority*

coenō, -āvī,-ātŭm,-ărĕ, *to dine*
coenătŭs, -ă, -ŭm, *having*
dined
coenă, -ae (f.), *dinner*
coenăcŭlŭm, -ī (n.), *a dining-*
room

jūrō, -āvī,-ātŭm,-ărĕ, *to swear*
jūrătŭs, -ă, -ŭm, *having sworn*
conjūrătŭs,-ī(m.),*a conspirator*
conjūrătĭŏ, -ōnĭs(f.), *a conspir-*
acy
perjūrărĕ } *to forswear*
pējĕrărĕ }
perjūrŭs, -ă, -ŭm, *perjured*
jūsjūrandŭm, jūrisjūrandī (n.),
an oath

II. SECOND CONJUGATION.
Regular Verbs.

cālērĕ, *to be warm*
cālŏr, -ōrĭs (m.), *warmth*
cālĭdŭs, -ă, -ŭm, *warm*

cărērĕ, *to want*

dŏlērĕ, *to feel pain*
dŏlŏr, -ōrĭs (m.), *pain*
dŏlentĕr, *with pain* [*ity*
indŏlentĭă, -ae (f.), *insensibil-*

hăbērĕ, *to have*
hăbĭtŭs, -ŭs (m.), *appearance*
hăbĭlĭs, -ĕ, *able*
hăbēnă, -ae (f.),*a rein*
hăbĭtărĕ, *to live, dwell*
hăbĭtătĭŏ, -ōnĭs (f.), *a dwelling*
ădhĭbērĕ, *to employ*
cōhĭbērĕ, *to hold together*
exhĭbērĕ, *to show, confer*

pĕrhĭbērĕ, *to assert*
posthäbērĕ, *to neglect*
prŏhĭbērĕ, *to hinder*
praebērĕ, *to offer*
rĕdhĭbērĕ, *to receive back ; to give back*
dēbērĕ (dĕhĭbērĕ), *to owe*
dēbĭtŏr, -ōrĭs (m.), *a debtor*
dēbĭtŭm, -ī (n.), *a debt*

jăcērĕ, *to lie*
adjăcērĕ, *to lie near*

lĭcērĕ, *to be for sale*
lĭcĕt, *it is permitted*
lĭcentĭă, -ae (f.), *license*
illĭcĭtŭs, -ă, -ŭm, *not allowed*
lĭcentĕr, *without restraint*

mĕrērĕ, *to deserve, merit*
mĕrĭtŭm, -ī (n.), *merit*
mĕrĭtō, *justly*
immĕrĭtō, *unjustly*
mercēs, -ēdĭs (f.), *wages*
mercēnārĭŭs, -ī (m.), *a hireling*

mŏnērĕ, *to warn, advise*
mŏnĭtŏr, -ōrĭs (m.), *an adviser*
mŏnŭmentŭm, -ī (n.), *a monument*
admŏnērĕ, *to admonish*
commŏnērĕ, *to put in mind*

nŏcērĕ, *to do harm*
innŏcens, -tĭs, *guiltless*
innŏcentĭă, -ae (f.), *innocence*
noxă, -ae (f.), *harm*
noxĭă, -ae (f.), *a trespass*

noxĭŭs, -ă, -ŭm, *hurtful*
innoxĭŭs, -ă, -ŭm, *harmless*
obnoxĭŭs, -ă, -ŭm, *subject*

pārērĕ, *to obey; to appear*
appārērĕ, *to appear*
appārĭtŏr,-ōrĭs (m.), *an officer of a magistrate*

plăcērĕ, *to please*
plăcĭtŭm, -ī (n), *an opinion*
displĭcērĕ, *to displease*
plăcĭdŭs, -ă, -ŭm, *gentle*
plăcārĕ, *to appease*
plăcābĭlĭs, -ĕ, *easily appeased*
implăcābĭlĭs, -ĕ, *implacable*

tăcērĕ, *to be silent*
tăcĭtŭs, -ă, -ŭm, *silent*
tăcĭturnĭtās, -ātĭs (f.), *reserve in speaking*
rĕtĭcērĕ, *to keep silence*
rĕtĭcentĭă, -ae (f.), *reticence*

terrērĕ, *to frighten*
terrŏr, -ōrĭs (m.), *great fear*
terrĭbĭlĭs, -ĕ, *frightful*
exterrērĕ ⎱ *to strike with*
perterrērĕ ⎰ *terror*
absterrērĕ ⎱ *to deter*
dēterrērĕ ⎰

vălērĕ, *to be strong, healthy*
vălĭdŭs, -ă, -ŭm, *strong*
invălĭdŭs, -ă, -ŭm, *infirm*
vălētūdŏ, -ĭnĭs (f.), *state of health*
valdĕ, *very*
praevălērĕ, *to prevail*

The following have no Supine:

arcērĕ, *to keep off*

  arx, –cĭs (f.), *a citadel*

  artŭs, –ă, –ŭm, *narrow*

  cŏartārĕ, *to press together*

  cŏercērĕ, *to restrain*

  exercērĕ, *to exercise*

  exercĭtŭs, –ă, –ŭm, *vexed*

  exercĭtātŭs, –ă, –ŭm, *trained*

  exercĭtātĭŏ, –ŏnĭs (f.), *exercise*

  exercĭtŭs, –ŭs (m.), *an army*

callērĕ, *to be versed*

  callĭdŭs, –ă, –ŭm, *shrewd*

  callĭdĭtăs, –ātĭs (f.), *shrewd-ness*

candērĕ, *to glitter*

  candŏr, –ŏrĭs (m.), *brightness*

  candĭdŭs, –ă, –ŭm, *white*

ĕgērĕ ⎫
indĭgērĕ ⎰ *to be in want*

  ĕgestăs, –ātĭs (f.) ⎱ *need, want*
  indĭgentĭă, –ae (f.) ⎰

flōrērĕ, *to blossom*

  flōs, flōrĭs (m.), *a flower, blossom*

  floscŭlŭs, –ĭ (m.), *a floweret*

frondērĕ, *to put forth leaves*

  frons, –dĭs (f.), *foliage*

horrērĕ, *to bristle, to shiver*

  horrĭdŭs, –ă, –ŭm, *bristly; dreadful*

  horrŏr, –ŏrĭs (m.), *a shudder*

  horrĭbĭlĭs, –ĕ, *horrible*

  ăbhorrērĕ, *to shrink back*

  pĕrhorrescērĕ, *to have a great horror*

languērĕ, *to be weary*

  languĭdŭs, –ă, –ŭm, *weary*

  languŏr, –ŏrĭs (m.), *weariness*

lătērĕ, *to be hidden*

  lătentĕr, *secretly*

  lătĕbră, –ae (f.) ⎱ *a hiding-*
  lătĭbŭlŭm, –ĭ (n.) ⎰ *place*

mădērĕ, *to be wet*

  mădĭdŭs, –ă, –ŭm, *wet*

nĭtērĕ, *to glitter*

  nĭtŏr, –ŏrĭs (m.), *splendor*

  nĭtĭdŭs, –ă, –ŭm, *glittering*

  ēnĭtērĕ, *to shine forth*

ŏlērĕ, *to smell*

  ŏlĭdŭs, –ă, –ŭm, *stinking*

  rĕdŏlērĕ, *to smell like*

  sŭbŏlērĕ, *to emit some smell*

  ŏdŏr, –ŏrĭs (m.), *smell*

  ŏdŏrŭs, –ă, –ŭm, *fragrant*

pallērĕ, *to look pale*

  pallĭdŭs, –ă, –ŭm, *pale*

  pallŏr, –ŏrĭs (m.), *paleness*

pătērĕ, *to stand open*

  pătŭlŭs, –ă, –ŭm, *open*

rĭgērĕ, *to be stiff*

  rĭgĭdŭs, –ă, –ŭm, *stiff, hard*

  rĭgŏr, –ŏrĭs (m.), *hardness*

rŭbērĕ, *to be red*

  rŭbĕr, –ră, –rŭm ⎱ *red*
  rŭbĭdŭs, –ă, –ŭm ⎰

  rŭbŏr, –ŏrĭs (m.), *redness*

sĭlērĕ, *to be silent*

  sĭlentĭŭm, –ĭ (n.), *silence*

sorbĕrĕ, *to sip*

absorbĕrĕ }
exsorbĕrĕ } *to swallow down*

sordĕrĕ, *to be dirty*

sordĭdŭs, -ă, -ŭm, *dirty*
sordēs, -ĭŭm (f. pl.), *dirt*

splendĕrĕ, *to gleam*

splendĭdŭs, -ă, -ŭm, *glittering*
splendŏr, -ōrĭs (m.), *splendor*

stŭdĕrĕ, *to busy one's self*

stŭdĭŭm, -ī (n.), *zeal*
stŭdĭōsŭs, -ă, -ŭm, *zealous*

stŭpĕrĕ, *to be amazed*

stŭpĭdŭs, -ă, -ŭm, *dull*
stŭpŏr, -ōrĭs (m.), *dullness*

tĭmĕrĕ, *to fear*

tĭmĭdŭs, -ă, -ŭm, *timid*
tĭmŏr, -ōrĭs (m.), *fear*
tĭmĭdĭtās, -ātĭs (f.), *fearfulness*

torpĕrĕ, *to be stiff, numb*

torpĭdŭs, -ă, -ŭm, *stiff*
torpŏr, -ōrĭs (m.), *numbness*

tŭmĕrĕ, *to swell*

tŭmĭdŭs, -ă, -ŭm, *elated*
tŭmŏr, -ōrĭs (m.), *a swelling*
tŭmŭlŭs, -ī (m.), *a sepulchral mound*
tŭmultŭs, -ŭs (m.), *an uproar*
tŭmultŭārī, *to raise a tumult*
tŭmultŭōsŭs, -ă, -ŭm, *full of tumult*

vĭgĕrĕ, *to be lively*

vĕgĕtŭs, -ă, -ŭm, *lively*
vĭgŏr, -ōrĭs (m.), *liveliness*
vĭgĭlārĕ, *to watch*
pervĭgĭlārĕ, *to watch all night*
vĭgĭl, -ĭs, *watchful*
vĭgĭlēs, -ŭm (m. pl.), *watchmen*
vĭgĭlĭae, -ārŭm (f. pl.), *the watch (sentinels)*
vĭgĭlantĭă, -ae (f.), *watchful-*
vĭgĭlantĕr, *watchfully* [*ness*

vĭrĕrĕ, *to be green, flourish*

vĭrĭdĭs, -ĕ, *green*
vĭrĭdĭtās, -ātĭs (f.), *freshness*
vĭrĭdārĭŭm, -ī (n.), *a pleasure garden*

The following have neither Perfect nor Supine:

ăvērĕ, *to long for*

ăvĭdŭs, -ă, -ŭm, *greedy*
ăvĭdĭtās, -ātĭs (f.), *greediness*
ăvārŭs, -ă, -ŭm, *avaricious*
ăvārĭtĭă, -ae (f.), *avarice*

calvērĕ, *to be bald*

calvŭs, -ă, -ŭm, *bald*
calvĭtĭŭm, -ī (n.), *baldness*

cānērĕ, *to be gray*

cānŭs, -ă, -ŭm, *gray*

flāvērĕ, *to be golden-yellow*

flāvŭs, -ă, -ŭm, *golden-yellow*

foetērĕ, *to stink*

foetĭdŭs, -ă, -ŭm, *stinking*
foetŏr, -ōrĭs (m.), *stench*

hĕbērĕ, to be blunt
hĕbĕs, -ĕtĭs, blunt

hūmērĕ, to be moist
hūmĭdŭs, -ă, -ŭm, moist
hūmŏr, -ōrĭs (m.), moisture

līvērĕ, to be pale
līvĭdŭs, -ă, -ŭm, envious
līvŏr, -ōrĭs (m.), leaden color

[mĭnērĕ, to jut]
immĭnērĕ, to lean towards
ēmĭnērĕ, to stand out
prōmĭnērĕ, to project
ēmĭnentĭă, -ae (f.), a prominence

maerērĕ, to grieve
maerŏr, -ōrĭs (m.), grief
maestŭs, -ă, -ŭm, sorrowful
maestĭtĭă, -ae (f.), grief

pollērĕ, to be powerful
pollex, -ĭcĭs (m.), the thumb

rĕnĭdērĕ, to shine, to smile

scătērĕ, to gush

squālērĕ, to be filthy
sqălĭdŭs, -ă, -ŭm, filthy
squālŏr, -ōrĭs (m.), filthiness;
filthy garments (as a sign of
mourning)

Irregular Verbs.

1. Perfect ēvī, Supine ētŭm (ĭtŭm, tŭm).

dēlĕō, dēlēvī, dēlētŭm, dēlērĕ, to destroy

flĕō, flēvī, flētŭm, flērĕ, to weep
flētŭs, -ūs (m.), weeping
flēbĭlĭs, -ĕ, lamentable

nĕō, nēvī, nētŭm, nērĕ, to spin

[-plĕō, fill]
plēnŭs, -ă, -ŭm, full
complĕō, complēvī, complētŭm, complērĕ, to fill up
complēmentŭm, -ī (n.), a complement
explĕō, explēvī, explētŭm, explērĕ, to fill up
implĕō, implēvī, implētŭm, implērĕ, to fill up

rĕplĕō, rĕplēvī, rĕplētŭm, rĕplērĕ, to supply
supplĕō, supplēvī, supplētŭm, supplērĕ, to supply
supplēmentŭm, -ī (n.), a supply

[-ŏlĕō, grow]
ăbŏlĕō, ăbŏlēvī, ăbŏlĭtŭm, ăbŏlērĕ, to abolish
ădŏlĕō, ădŏlēvī, ădultŭm, ădŏlērĕ, to grow up
exŏlĕō, exŏlēvī, exŏlētŭm, exŏlērĕ, to grow obsolete
obsŏlĕō, obsŏlēvī, obsŏlētŭm, obsŏlērĕ, to grow obsolete
ădŭlescens, -tĭs (m.), a youth
ădŭlescentĭă, -ae (f.), youth
ădultŭs, -ă, -ŭm, grown up
obsŏlētŭs, -ă, -ŭm, obsolete
prōlēs, -ĭs }
sŭbŏlēs, -ĭs } (f.), offspring

— 48 —

2. Perfect ī, Supine tŭm.

căvĕŏ, căvī, cautŭm, căvērĕ, to
  be on one's guard
cautŭs, -ă, -ŭm, careful
incautŭs, -ă, -ŭm, careless
cautĭŏ, -ōnĭs (f.), caution
praecăvērĕ, to prevent

făvĕŏ, făvī, fautŭm, făvērĕ, to
  favor
făvŏr, -ōrĭs (m.), a favor
fantŏr, -ōrĭs (m.), a favorer
faustŭs, -ă, -ŭm, favorable

fŏvĕŏ, fŏvī, fōtŭm, fŏvērĕ, to
  cherish
fōmentŭm, -ī (n.), a lenitive

mŏvĕŏ, mōvī, mōtŭm, mŏvērĕ,
  to move
mōtŭs, -ūs (m.), motion
mōmentŭm, -ī (n.), a circum-
  stance
mōbĭlĭs, -ĕ, movable   [ness
mōbĭlĭtās, -ātĭs (f.), movable-
commŏvērĕ } to move deeply;
permŏvērĕ } to excite

ămŏvērĕ ⎫
dēmŏvērĕ ⎪
dīmŏvērĕ ⎬ to remove
rĕmŏvērĕ ⎪
submŏvērĕ ⎭
admŏvērĕ, to draw near to
prōmŏvērĕ, to promote

vŏvĕŏ, vŏvī, vōtŭm, vŏvērĕ, to
  vow
vōtŭm, -ī (n.), a vow
vōtīvŭs,-ă,-ŭm, given by vow
dēvŏvērĕ, to devote
dēvōtĭŏ, -ōnĭs (f.), a devoting

păvĕŏ, păvī,(without Sup.) păvērĕ,
  to fear
păvŏr, -ōrĭs (m.), fear
păvĭdŭs, -ă, -ŭm, trembling

fervĕŏ, fervī, ferbŭī,(without Sup.)
  fervērĕ, to glow
fervŏr, -ōrĭs (m.), heat
fervĭdŭs, -ă, -ŭm, glowing

cōnīvĕŏ, cōnīvī, cōnixī, (without
  Sup.) cōnīvērĕ, to shut the eyes

3. Dropping the I of the Supine.

dŏcĕŏ, dŏcŭī, doctŭm, dŏcērĕ,
  to teach
doctŏr, -ōrĭs (m.), a teacher
doctrīnă, -ae (f.), teaching
dŏcĭlĭs, -ĕ, easily taught
dŏcĭlĭtās, -ātĭs (f.), docility
dŏcŭmentŭm, -ī (n.), a lesson,
  proof
ēdŏcērĕ } to teach thoroughly
perdŏcērĕ }
dēdŏcērĕ, to unteach

tĕnĕŏ, tĕnŭī (tentŭm), tĕnērĕ,
  to hold
tĕnŏr, -ōrĭs (m.), a holding on
tĕnax, -ācĭs, holding fast
tĕnācĭtās, -ātĭs (f.), tenacity
pertĭnax, -ācĭs, obstinate
pertĭnācĭă, -ae (f.), obstinacy
abstĭnērĕ, to abstain
abstĭnentĭă, -ae (f.), abstinence
attĭnērĕ, to belong somewhere
contĭnērĕ, to hold together

contĭnentĭă, -ae (f.), *a restraining of one's self*
contĭnens, -tĭs (f.), *a continent*
contĭnŭŭs, -ă, -ŭm, *continu-*
contĭnŭō, *forthwith* [*ous*
contĭnŭārĕ, *to connect*
contĭnŭātĭŏ, -ŏnĭs (f.), *a continuation*
contentŭs, -ă, -ŭm, *contented*
dĕtĭnērĕ, *to hold off*
rĕtĭnērĕ, *to keep back*
distĭnērĕ, *to keep asunder*
pertĭnērĕ, *to reach, extend*
sustĭnērĕ, *to hold up*
sustentārĕ, *to support*
sustentātĭŏ, -ŏnĭs (f.), *support*

miscĕō, miscŭī, mixtŭm (mistŭm), miscērĕ, *to mix*

mixtūră, -ae (f.), *a mixture*
admiscērĕ, *to mix up*

commiscērĕ }
permiscērĕ } *to mix together*
immiscērĕ, *to mix in*
prōmiscŭŭs, -ă, -ŭm, *mixed*

torrĕō, torrŭī, tostŭm, torrērĕ, *to dry, roast*

torrĭdŭs, -ă, -ŭm, *dried up*
torrens, -tĭs (m.), *a torrent*

censĕō, censŭī, censŭm, censērĕ, *to value, think*

censŏr, -ŏrĭs (m.), *a censurer*
censūră, -ae (f.), *a judgment*
censŭs, -ūs (m.), *a valuation, census*
succensērĕ, *to be angry*
percensērĕ, (without Sup.), *to reckon up*
rĕcensērĕ, *to review*

4. Perfect sī (xī), Supine tŭm (ctŭm).

indulgĕō, indulsī, indultŭm, indulgērĕ, *to be kind to one*
indulgentĭă, -ae (f.), *indulgence*

torquĕō, torsī, tortŭm, torquērĕ, *to twist*

tortŏr, -ŏrĭs (m.), *a torturer*
tormentŭm, -ī (n.), *a rack; a shot*
torquĭs, - (f.) }
torquēs,-ĭs (f.) } *a neck chain*
tortŭōsŭs, -ă, -ŭm, *full of crooks*
tornārĕ, *to round off*
contorquērĕ, *to turn*
distorquērĕ, *to twist*
extorquērĕ, *to extort*
rĕtorquērĕ, *to turn back*

augĕō, auxī, auctŭm, augērĕ, *to augment*

ădaugērĕ, *to augment*
auctŭs, -ūs (m.), *increase*
auctĭŏ, -ŏnĭs (f.), *an auction*
auctŏr, -ŏrĭs (m.), *an author*
auctōrĭtās, -ātĭs (f.), *authority*
auctumnŭs, -ī (m.), *autumn*
auxĭlĭŭm, -ī (n.), *help*
auxĭlĭārēs, -ĭŭm (m. pl.), *auxiliary troops*

frīgĕō, frixī, (without Sup.), frīgērĕ, *to be cold*

frīgŭs, -ŏrĭs (n.), *cold*
frīgĭdŭs, -ă, -ŭm, *cold*
rĕfrīgĕrārĕ, *to make cold*
rĕfrīgescĕrĕ, *to grow cold*

lūcĕō, luxī, (without Sup.), lūcērĕ, to shine

lux, lūcis (f.), daylight
lūcŭs, -ī (m.), a grove [star
Lūcīfĕr, -ī (m.), the morning-
lūcĭdŭs, -ă, -ŭm, shining
lūcŭlentŭs, -ă, -ŭm, bright
lūcĭfūgŭs, -ă,-ŭm, light-shun-
ning
dīlūcĭdŭs, -ă, -ŭm, clear
lūcernă, -ae (f.), a lamp
lūcŭbrārĕ, to work by lamp-
light
lūmĕn, -ĭnĭs (n.), light
illūmĭnārĕ, to illume

ēlūcērĕ, to shine forth
illustrĭs, -ĕ, lighted up, distinguished
illustrārĕ, to illuminate
pellūcērĕ, to shine through, be
transparent
pellūcĭdŭs, -ă,-ŭm, transparent

lūgĕō, luxī, (without Sup.), lūgērĕ, to mourn

luctŭs, -ūs (m.), mourning
luctŭōsŭs, -ă, -ŭm, full of sorrow
lūgŭbrĭs, -ĕ, mournful

5. Perfect sī, Supine sŭm.

ardĕō, arsī, arsŭm, ardērĕ, to burn

ardentĕr, eagerly
ardŏr,-ōrĭs (m.), burning heat

haerĕō, haesī, haesŭm, haerērĕ, to hang, stick

haesĭtārĕ, to stick fast
haesĭtātĭŏ, -ōnĭs (f.), hesitating
ădhaerērĕ)
cŏhaerērĕ } to stick
ĭnhaerērĕ)

jŭbĕō, jussī, jussŭm, jŭbērĕ, to order

jussă, -ōrŭm (n. pl.), orders
jussū, by order
injussū, without command

mănĕō, mansī, mansŭm, mă-
nērĕ, to stay

mansĭŏ, -ōnĭs (f.), a stay
permănērĕ, to hold out

permansĭŏ, -ōnĭs (f.), a remaining
rĕmănērĕ, to stay behind

mulcĕō, mulsī, mulsŭm, mul-
cērĕ, to stroke

dēmulcērĕ)
permulcērĕ } to rub gently
mulcārĕ, to beat

mulgĕō, mulsī, mulsŭm, mul-
gērĕ, to milk

rīdĕō, rīsī, rīsŭm, rīdērĕ, to laugh

rīsŭs, -ūs (m.), laughing
rīdĭcŭlŭs, -ă, -ŭm, laughable
arrīdērĕ, to laugh at
dērīdērĕ)
irrīdērĕ } to scoff at
irrīsĭŏ, -ōnĭs (f.), mockery
irrīsŏr, -ōrĭs (m.), a scoffer
subrīdērĕ, to smile

suádĕō, suásī, suásŭm, suádĕrĕ, to advise

suásŏr, -ōrĭs (m.), an adviser
dissuádĕrĕ, to advise against
persuádĕrĕ, to prevail upon
persuásĭŏ, -ōnĭs (f.), conviction

tergĕō (tergō), tersī, tersŭm, tergĕrĕ (tergĕrĕ), to wipe

tersŭs, -ă, -ŭm, neat
abstergĕrĕ) to wipe away,
dĕtergĕrĕ) remove

algĕō, alsī, (without Sup.), algĕrĕ, to be cold, to starve

fulgĕō, fulsī, (without Sup.), fulgĕrĕ, to shine

fulgŏr, -ōrĭs (m.), brightness
fulgŭr, -ĭs (n.), lightning
fulgŭrārĕ, to lighten
fulmĕn, -ĭnĭs (n.), a thunderbolt
effulgĕrĕ, to shine forth

turgĕō, tursī, (without Sup.), turgĕrĕ, to swell
turgĭdŭs, -ă, -ŭm, swollen

urgĕō, ursī, (without Sup.), urgĕrĕ, to urge

6. Perfect I, Supine sŭm.

prandĕō, prandī, pransŭm, prandĕrĕ, to breakfast, lunch

pransŭs, -ă, -ŭm, that has breakfasted, lunched
prandĭŭm, -ī (n.), a breakfast, lunch

sĕdĕō, sĕdī, sessŭm, sĕdĕrĕ, to sit
assĭdĕō, assĕdī, assessŭm, assĭdĕrĕ, to sit by
assĭdŭŭs, -ă, -ŭm, unremitting
assĭdŭĭtās, -ātĭs (f.), closeness of application
circumsĕdĕrĕ, to sit around
dĕsĭdĭă, -ae (f.), a sitting idle
dĕsĭdĭōsŭs, -ă, -ŭm, idle
dissĭdĕō, dissĕdī, (without Sup.), dissĭdĕrĕ, to sit apart
insĭdĕō, insĕdī, insessŭm, insĭdĕrĕ, to sit upon
insĭdĭae, -ārŭm (f. pl.), an ambush
insĭdĭōsŭs, -ă, -ŭm, deceitful

obsĭdĕō, obsĕdī, obsessŭm, obsĭdĕrĕ, to besiege
obsĭdĭŏ, -ōnĭs (f.)) a siege
obsessĭŏ, -ōnĭs (f.))
possĭdĕō, possĕdī, possessŭm, possĭdĕrĕ, to have and hold, possess
possessĭŏ, -ōnĭs (f.), possession
possessŏr, -ōrĭs (m.), a possessor
praesĭdĕō, praesĕdī, (without Sup.), praesĭdĕrĕ, to preside
praesĭdĭŭm, -ī (n.), a garrison
praesĕs, -ĭdĭs (m.), a president
subsĭdĭŭm, -ī (n.), support
rĕsĭdĕō, rĕsĕdī, (without Sup.), rĕsĭdĕrĕ, to remain behind
rĕsĭdŭŭs, -ă, -ŭm, remaining
supersĕdĕrĕ, to forbear, omit
sĕdārĕ, to calm
sĕdātŭs, -ă, -ŭm, calm
sĕdātĭŏ, -ōnĭs (f.), the act of calming

strīdĕō (strīdō), strīdī, (without Sup.), strīdĕrĕ (strīdĕrĕ), to creak

strīdŏr, -ōrĭs (m.), a creaking sound

vīdĕō, vīdī, vīsŭm, vīdĕrĕ, to see

vīsĭŏ, -ōnĭs (f.), a vision
vīsŭs, -ūs (m.), sight
ĕvīdens, -tĭs, evident
ĕvīdentĭă, -ae (f.); distinctness
invīdĕrĕ, to envy
invīdĭă, -ae (f.), envy
invīdŭs, -ă, -ŭm, envious
invīdĭōsŭs, -ă, -ŭm } hated
invīsŭs, -ă, -ŭm
praevīdĕrĕ } to foresee
prōvīdĕrĕ
prōvīdŭs, -ă, -ŭm, foreseeing
prōvīdentĭă, -ae (f.), foresight
prūdens, -tĭs, sensible
imprūdens, -tĭs, imprudent
prūdentĭă, -ae (f.), prudence
imprōvīsŭs, -ă, -ŭm, unforeseen

Reduplicated in the Perfect.

mordĕō, mŏmordī, morsŭm, mordĕrĕ, to bite

morsŭs, -ūs (m.), a bite

mordax, -ācĭs, biting
mordĭcŭs, with the teeth

pendĕō, pĕpendī, pensŭm, pendĕrĕ, to hang

impendĕrĕ, (without Perf. & Sup.), to hang over

dependĕrĕ } (without Perf. & Sup.)
prōpendĕrĕ } to hang down
prōpensŭs, -ă, -ŭm, inclined

spondĕō, spŏpondī, sponsŭm, spondĕrĕ, to pledge

sponsĭŏ, -ōnĭs (f.), a pledge
sponsŏr, -ōrĭs (m.), a bondsman
sponsŭs, -ī (m.), a bridegroom
sponsă, -ae (f.), a bride
despondĕō, despondī, desponsŭm, despondĕrĕ, to promise
respondĕō, respondī, responsŭm, respondĕrĕ, to answer
responsĭŏ, -ōnĭs (f.) } an answer
responsŭm, -ī (n.)

tondĕō, tŏtŏndī, tonsŭm, tondĕrĕ, to shear

tonsŏr, -ōrĭs (m.), a barber
tonstrīnă, -ae (f.), a barber's shop

7. Semi-Deponent Verbs.

audĕō, ausŭs sŭm, audĕrĕ, to dare

audax, -ācĭs, daring
audactĕr, daringly
audācĭă, -ae (f.), daring

gaudĕō, gāvīsŭs sŭm, gaudĕrĕ, to rejoice

gaudĭŭm, -ī (n.), joy

sŏlĕō, sŏlĭtŭs sŭm, sŏlĕrĕ, to be wont, use

assŏlet, it is customary
insŏlens, -tĭs, unusual; insolent
insŏlentĕr, unusually
insŏlentĭă, -ae (f.), unusualness; insolence
insŏlĭtŭs, -ă, -ŭm, unusual

Mark the solitary verb:

cĭĕō, cīvī, cītŭm, ciērĕ } *to*
cĭō, cīvī, cītŭm, cīrĕ } *arouse*
cītŭs, -ă, -ŭm, *quick*
cītō, *quickly*
accīrĕ, *to summon*
concīrĕ, *to call together*
concĭlĭŭm, -ī (n.), *a meeting*
concĭlĭārĕ, *to unite*

rĕconcĭlĭārĕ, *to reconcile*
excīrĕ, *to call out*
concĭtārĕ, *to move violently*
excītārĕ, *to call out*
incītārĕ, *to rouse*
rĕcĭtārĕ, *to say by heart*
suscĭtārĕ, *to stir up*
exsuscĭtārĕ, *to awaken*

III. THIRD CONJUGATION.

1. Verbs in ŭō and vō.

ăcŭō, ăcŭī, ăcūtŭm, ăcŭĕrĕ, *to whet, sharpen*

ăcūtŭs, -ă, -ŭm, *sharp, keen*
ăcūmĕn, -ĭnĭs (n.), *acuteness*
ăcĭēs, -ēī (f.), *an edge; battle-array*
exăcŭĕrĕ } *to make very*
pĕrăcŭĕrĕ } *sharp*
praeăcŭĕrĕ, *to sharpen at one end*

argŭō, argŭī, (argūtŭm), argŭĕrĕ, *to accuse, convict; Perf. Part.* convictŭs, -ă, -ŭm, *convicted*

argūtŭs, -ă, -ŭm, *sagacious*
argūmentŭm, -ī (n.), *a proof*
cōargŭĕrĕ, *to convict*
rĕdargŭĕrĕ, *to disprove*

imbŭō, imbŭī, imbūtŭm, imbŭĕrĕ, *to dip, imbue*

indŭō, indŭī, indūtŭm, indŭĕrĕ, *to put on*

exŭō, exŭī, exūtŭm, exŭĕrĕ, *to put off*
exŭvĭae, -ārŭm (f. pl.), *spoils*

lŭō, lŭī, (lŭĭtŭm), lŭĕrĕ, *to pay, atone*

lŭō, lŭī, lūtŭm, lŭĕrĕ, *to wash*
ablŭĕrĕ, *to wash off*
dīlŭĕrĕ, *to wash away*
dīlŭvĭŭm, -ī (n.), *a flood*
dīlūtŭs, -ă, -ŭm, *thin*
ēlŭĕrĕ, *to wash out*
pollŭĕrĕ, *to defile*

mĭnŭō, mĭnŭī, mĭnūtŭm, mĭnŭĕrĕ, *to lessen*
dēmĭnŭĕrĕ, *to lessen*
dēmĭnūtĭō, -ōnĭs (f.), *decrease*
commĭnŭĕrĕ } *to break into*
dīmĭnŭĕrĕ } *pieces*
immĭnŭĕrĕ, *to lessen*

[nŭō, nod]

nūtŭs, -ūs (m.) a nod

nūtārĕ, to nod

nūmĕn, -ĭnĭs (n.), Godhead

Without Supine:

abnŭō, abnŭī, abnŭĕrĕ, to deny

annŭō, annŭī, annŭĕrĕ, to give assent

innŭō, innŭī, innŭĕrĕ, to nod to

rĕnŭō, rĕnŭī, rĕnŭĕrĕ, to disapprove

rŭō, rŭī,(rŭĭtŭm), rŭĕrĕ, to rush down

rŭīnă, -ae (f.), a fall, ruin

rŭīnōsŭs, -ă, -ŭm, tumbling down

dīrŭō, dīrŭī, dīrŭtŭm, dīrŭĕrĕ, to destroy, demolish

ērŭō, ērŭī, ērŭtŭm, ērŭĕrĕ, to cast forth

ŏbrŭō, ŏbrŭī, ŏbrŭtŭm, ŏbrŭĕrĕ, to overwhelm

prōrŭō, prōrŭī, prōrŭtŭm, prōrŭĕrĕ, to rush forth

corrŭō, corrŭī, (without Sup.), corrŭĕrĕ, to tumble down

irrŭō, irrŭī, (without Sup.), irrŭĕrĕ, to rush into

spŭō, spŭī, spŭtŭm, spŭĕrĕ, to spit

spūmă, -ae (f.), foam

spūmārĕ, to foam

conspŭĕrĕ, to spit upon

despŭĕrĕ, to abhor

respŭĕrĕ, to reject

stătŭō, stătŭī, stătŭtŭm, stătŭĕrĕ, to set, place

stătŭă, -ae (f.), a statue

constĭtŭĕrĕ, to establish

constĭtūtĭō, -ōnĭs (f.), a regulation

destĭtŭĕrĕ, to foresake

instĭtŭĕrĕ, to institute, found

instĭtūtĭō, -ōnĭs (f.), instruction

instĭtūtŭm,- ī (n.), an institution

restĭtŭĕrĕ, to restore [tion

restĭtūtĭō,-ōnĭs (f.), a restoration

restĭtūtŏr, -ōrĭs (m.), a restorer

substĭtŭĕrĕ, to put in the place of another

sternŭō, sternŭī, (without Sup.), sternŭĕrĕ, to sneeze

steŕnūtārĕ, to sneeze

sŭō, sŭī, sūtŭm, sŭĕrĕ, to sew

sūtŏr, -ōrĭs (m.), a shoemaker

sūtūră, -ae (f.), a seam

consŭĕrĕ, to sew together

dissŭĕrĕ } to rip open
rĕsŭĕrĕ {

trĭbŭō, trĭbŭī, trĭbūtŭm, trĭbŭĕrĕ, to allot

trĭbūtŭm, -ī (n.), a contribution

trĭbūtārĭŭs,-ă, -ŭm, tributary

attrĭbŭĕrĕ, to assign

distrĭbŭĕrĕ, to distribute

distrĭbūtĭō, -ōnĭs (f.), a distribution

contrĭbŭĕrĕ, to contribute

solvō, solvī, solūtŭm, solvĕrĕ, to loose

absolvĕrĕ, to acquit [quittal

absŏlūtĭō, -ōnĭs (f.), an acquittal

absŏlūtŭs, -ă, -ŭm, complete

dissolvĕrĕ, *to dissolve*

dissŏlūtŭs, -ă, -ŭm, *loose*

dissŏlūtĭŏ, -ōnĭs (f.), *a breaking up, dissolution*

exsolvĕrĕ } *to pay*
persolvĕrĕ }

volvō, volvī, vŏlūtŭm, volvĕrĕ, *to roll*

vŏlūtārĕ, *to roll about*

vŏlūbĭlĭs, -ĕ, *rolling*

vŏlūbĭlĭtās, -ātĭs (f.), *aptness to roll*

vŏlūmĕn, -ĭnĭs (n.), *a roll of writing*

ēvolvĕrĕ, *to unroll*

involvĕrĕ, *to wrap up*

invŏlūcrŭm, -ī (n.), *a wrapper*

congrūō, congrūī, (**without Sup.**), congrŭĕrĕ, *to coincide, agree*

ingrŭō, ingrūī, (**without Sup.**), ingrŭĕrĕ, *to rush into*

mĕtŭō, mĕtŭī, (**without Sup.**), mĕtŭĕrĕ, *to fear*

mĕtŭs, -ūs (m.), *fear*

plŭō, plŭī (plūvī), (**without Sup.**), plŭĕrĕ, *to rain*

plŭĭt, *it rains*

implŭĭt, *it rains upon*

perplŭĭt, *it rains in, through*

plŭvĭă, -ae (f.), *rain*

implŭvĭŭm, -ī (n.), *a court-yard*

plŭvĭŭs, -ă, -ŭm, *rainy*

flŭō, fluxī, fluxŭm, flŭĕrĕ, *to flow*

fluxŭs, -ă, -ŭm, *fleeting*

flŭĭtārĕ, *to flow about*

fluxĭŏ, -ōnĭs (f.) } *a flowing*
fluxŭs, -ūs (m.) }

flŭĭdŭs, -ă, -ŭm, *flowing*

flŭvĭŭs, -ī (m.) } *a river*
flūmĕn, -ĭnĭs (n.) }

flŭvĭātĭlĭs, -ĕ, *belonging to a river*

fluctŭs, -ūs (m.), *a flood*

fluctŭārĕ, *to wave*

afflŭĕrĕ, *to flow to*

conflŭĕrĕ, *to run together*

dēflŭĕrĕ, *to flow down*

difflŭĕrĕ, *to flow every way*

efflŭĕrĕ, *to flow out*

inflŭĕrĕ, *to flow into*

interflŭĕrĕ, *to flow between*

praeterflŭĕrĕ, *to flow past*

prōflŭĕrĕ, *to flow forth*

rēflŭĕrĕ, *to flow back*

strŭō, struxī, structŭm, strŭĕrĕ, *to join together, build*

structūră, -ae (f.), *a building*

structōrēs,-ŭm (m. pl.), *builders*

strŭēs, -ĭs (f.), *a heap*

constrŭĕrĕ, *to construct*

constructĭŏ, -ōnĭs (f.), *a construction*

dēstrŭĕrĕ, *to pull down, destroy*

exstrŭĕrĕ, *to build up*

exstructĭŏ, -ōnĭs (f.), *a building up*

instrŭĕrĕ, *to set in order*

instructĭŏ, -ōnĭs (f.), *a setting in array*

instrūmentŭm, -ī (n.), *a tool*

obstrŭĕrĕ, *to stop up, obstruct*

obstructĭŏ, -ōnĭs (f.), *an obstruction*

vīvō, vīxī, victŭm, vīvĕrĕ, *to live*
vīvŭs, -ă, -ŭm, *living*
vīvĭdŭs, -ă, -ŭm, *full of life*
vīvax, -ācĭs, *having vital force*
vīvācĭtās, -ātĭs (f.), *vital force*
vīvărĭŭm, -ī (n.), *an enclosure for keeping living animals*

vītă, -ae (f.), *life*
vītālĭs, -ĕ, *vital*
victŭs, -ūs (m.), *victuals*
convictŭs, -ūs (m.), *social intercourse*
convīvĭŭm, -ī (n.), *a banquet*
convīvă, -ae (m. & f.), *a guest*

2. Verbs in ĬŌ.

căpĭō, cēpī, captŭm, căpĕrĕ, *to take, seize, catch*

căpax, -ācĭs, *ample, capacious*
căpācĭtās, -ātĭs (f.), *capaciousness*
căpŭlŭs, -ī (m.), *the hilt*
captŭs, -ūs (m.), *capacity*
captārĕ, *to catch*
captātĭō, -ōnĭs (f.), *the practice of catching favor*
captĭōnēs, -ŭm (f. pl.), *subtleties*
captĭōsŭs, -ă, -ŭm, *subtle*
captīvŭs, -ă, -ŭm, *a captive in war*
accĭpĭō, accēpī, acceptŭm, accĭpĕrĕ, *to accept*
acceptŭs, -ă, -ŭm, *agreeable*
concĭpĭō, concēpī, conceptŭm, concĭpĕrĕ, *to take in*
dēcĭpĭō, dēcēpī, dĕceptŭm, dēcĭpĕrĕ, *to deceive*
excĭpĭō, excēpī, exceptŭm, excĭpĕrĕ, *to except*
exceptĭō, -ōnĭs (f.), *an exception*
incĭpĭō, incēpī, inceptŭm, incĭpĕrĕ, *to begin*
intercĭpĭō, intercēpī, interceptŭm, intercĭpĕrĕ, *to intercept*

interceptĭō, -ōnĭs (f.), *the act of intercepting*
percĭpĭō, percēpī, perceptŭm, percĭpĕrĕ, *to perceive*
praecĭpĭō, praecēpī, praeceptŭm, praecĭpĕrĕ, *to prescribe*
praeceptŭm, -ī (n.), *a precept*
praeceptŏr, -ōrĭs (m.), *a teacher*
praecĭpŭŭs, -ă, -ŭm, *extraordinary*
rĕcĭpĭō, rĕcēpī, rĕceptŭm, rĕcĭpĕrĕ, *to take back*
rĕcŭpĕrārĕ, *to regain, recover*
rĕceptŭs, -ūs (m.), *a retreat*
rĕceptăcŭlŭm, -ī (n.), *a place of refuge*
rĕcĭprŏcārĕ, *to give backward and forward*
suscĭpĭō, suscēpī, susceptŭm, suscĭpĕrĕ, *to undertake*
susceptĭō, -ōnĭs (f.), *an undertaking*
antĭcĭpārĕ, *to take up beforehand*
occŭpārĕ, *to take possession of*
occŭpātĭō, -ōnĭs (f.), *an employment*

făcĭō, fēcī, factŭm, făcĕrĕ, *to do*
factĭtārĕ, *to be wont to do*
ărᵉfăcĕrĕ, *to dry up*

assuēfăcĕrĕ } *to accustom to*
consuēfăcĕrĕ } *something*
călĕfăcĕrĕ } *to make warm,*
tĕpĕfăcĕrĕ } *heat*
frĭgĕfăcĕrĕ, *to make cool*
lăbĕfăcĕrĕ, *to shake*
pătĕfăcĕrĕ, *to open*
sătisfăcĕrĕ, *to satisfy*
Compounds of făcĭō which retain ă, have fĭō in the Passive. Other compounds change ă to ĭ; they form their Passive in ĭcĭŏr and their Supine in ectŭm.

factŭm, -ī (n.) } *a deed*
făcĭnŭs, -ŏrĭs (n.) } *a deed*
făcĭnŏrōsŭs, -ă, -ŭm, *wicked*
factĭō, -ōnĭs (f.), *a party*
făcĭlĭs, -ĕ, *easy*
făcĭlĭtās, -ātĭs (f.), *easiness*
făcultās,-ātĭs (f.), *skill, ability*
diffĭcĭlĭs, -ĕ, *difficult*
diffĭcultās, -ātĭs (f.), *difficulty*
afﬁcĭō, affĕcī, affectŭm, affĭcĕrĕ, *to affect*
affectārĕ, *to strive after*
affectātĭō,-ōnĭs (f.), *a striving after*
affectĭō,-ōnĭs (f.), *an affection*
affectŭs, -ŭs (m.), *an affect*
confĭcĭō, confēcī, confectŭm, confĭcĕrĕ, *to make ready*
dēfĭcĭō, dēfēcī, dēfectŭm, dēfĭcĕrĕ, *to desert, fail*
dēfectĭō, -ōnĭs (f.), *a defection*
dēfectŭs, -ŭs (m.), *a failure*
effĭcĭō, effēcī, effectŭm, effĭcĕrĕ, *to bring to pass*
effĭcax, -ācĭs, *powerful*
effĭcĭentĕr, *efficiently*
effĭcăcĭtās, -ātĭs (f.) } *efficacy*
effĭcĭentĭă, -ae (f.) } *efficacy*

inﬁcĭō, infēcī, infectŭm, infĭcĕrĕ, *to infect, dye*
infectŭs, -ă, -ŭm, *unfinished*
interﬁcĭō, interfēcī, interfectŭm, interfĭcĕrĕ, *to kill, murder* [*derer*
interfectŏr, -ōrĭs (m.), *a murofﬁcĭō,* offēcī, offectŭm, offĭcĕrĕ, *to come in the way*
ofﬁcĭŭm, -ī (n.), *duty*
officĭōsŭs, -ă, -ŭm, *obliging, ready to serve*
perﬁcĭō, perfēcī, perfectŭm, perfĭcĕrĕ, *to achieve*
perfectĭō, -ōnĭs (f.), *perfection*
praeﬁcĭō, praefēcī, praefectŭm, praefĭcĕrĕ, *to set over*
praefectŭs, -ī (m.), *a prefect, commander*
prōﬁcĭō, prōfēcī, prōfectŭm, prōﬁcĕrĕ, *to make progress*
prōfectŭs, -ŭs (m.), *progress*
rēﬁcĭō, rēfēcī, rēfectŭm, rēfĭcĕrĕ, *to repair*
sufﬁcĭō, suffēcī, suffectŭm, sufﬁcĕrĕ,*to substitute, to suffice*
amplĭfĭcārĕ, *to enlarge*
amplĭfĭcātĭō, -ōnĭs (f.), *enlargement*
săcrĭfĭcārĕ, *to sacrifice*
săcrĭfĭcĭŭm, -ī (n.), *a sacrifice*
săcrĭfĭcătĭō,-ōnĭs (f.), *a sacrificing*

ĭcō (ĭcĭō), ĭcī, ĭctŭm, ĭcĕrĕ, *to strike*
ĭctŭs, -ă, -ŭm, *struck*
ĭctŭs, -ŭs (m.), *a stroke*

jăcĭō, jēcī, jactŭm, jăcĕrĕ, *to throw, cast*
jactŭs, -ŭs (m.), *a throw*

jăcŭlŭm, -ĭ (n.), *a javelin*
jactārĕ, *to throw about, to boast*
jactătĭō, -ōnĭs (f.), *vanity*
jactūră, -ae (f.), *loss*
abjĭcĭō, abjēcĭ, abjectŭm, abjĭcĕrĕ, *to cast away*
adjĭcĭō, adjēcĭ, adjectŭm, adjĭcĕrĕ, *to add*
conjĭcĭō, conjēcĭ, conjectŭm, conjĭcĕrĕ, *to throw together, infer*
conjectūră,-ae (f.),*a conjecture*
dējĭcĭō, dējēcĭ, dējectŭm, dējĭcĕrĕ, *to throw down*
disjĭcĭō, disjēcĭ, disjectŭm, disjĭcĕrĕ, *to throw asunder*
ējĭcĭō, ējēcĭ, ējectŭm, ējĭcĕrĕ, *to drive out*
înjĭcĭō, injēcĭ, injectŭm, injĭcĕrĕ, *to throw in*
interjĭcĭō, interjēcĭ, interjectŭm, interjĭcĕrĕ, *to throw between*
objĭcĭō, objēcĭ, objectŭm, objĭcĕrĕ, *to cast in the way*
ōbex, -ĭcĭs (m. & f.), *a bolt*
prōjĭcĭō, prōjēcĭ, prōjectŭm, prōjĭcĕrĕ, *to throw forth*
rējĭcĭō, rējēcĭ, rējectŭm, rējĭcĕrĕ, *to throw back*
subjĭcĭō, subjēcĭ, subjectŭm, subjĭcĕrĕ, *to place under*
transjĭcĭō, transjēcĭ, transjectŭm, transjĭcĕrĕ, *or* trājĭcĭō, trājēcĭ, trājectŭm, trājĭcĕrĕ, *to convey across*
trājectŭs, -ūs (m.), *a crossing*

[lăcĭō, *entice*]

allĭcĭō, allexĭ, allectŭm, allĭcĕrĕ, *to allure*

illĭcĭō, illexĭ, illectŭm, illĭcĕrĕ, *to allure*
illĕcĕbră, -ae (f.), *an enticement*
pellĭcĭō, pellexĭ, pellectŭm, pellĭcĕrĕ, *to decoy*
ēlĭcĭō, ēlĭcŭĭ, ēlĭcĭtŭm, ēlĭcĕrĕ, *to entice out*
dēlectārĕ } *to delight*
ŏblectārĕ }
dēlĭcĭae, -ārŭm (f. pl.), *delight*
dēlectătĭō, -ōnĭs (f.) } *amusement*
ŏblectătĭō, -ōnĭs (f.) }
dēlectāmentŭm, -ĭ (n.) } *pastime*
ŏblectāmentŭm, -ĭ (n.) }

[spĕcĭō, *see*]

spectārĕ, *to look on*
spĕcĭēs, -ēĭ (f.), *the outward appearance*
spĕcĭōsŭs, -ă, -ŭm, *good-looking*
spĕcĭmĕn, -ĭnĭs (n.), *a sample*
spĕcŭlŭm, -ĭ (n.), *a mirror*
spĕcŭlă, -ae (f.), *a watch-tower*
spectātŏr,-ōrĭs (m.), *a looker-on*
spectācŭlŭm, -ĭ (n.), *a show*
exspectārĕ, *to look out for*
exspectătĭō, -ōnĭs (f.), *an awaiting*
adspĭcĭō, adspexĭ, adspectŭm, adspĭcĕrĕ, *to look at*
adspectŭs, -ūs (m.), *a look*
circumspĭcĭō, circumspexĭ, circumspectŭm,circumspĭcĕrĕ, *to look about*
conspĭcĭō, conspexĭ, conspectŭm, conspĭcĕrĕ, *to look at*
conspectŭs, -ūs (m.), *a view*
despĭcĭō, despexĭ, despectŭm, despĭcĕrĕ, *to despise*

dēspĭcĭentĭă, -ae (f.), *contempt*
dispĭcĭō, dispexī, dispectŭm, dispĭcĕrĕ, *to look up*
inspĭcĭō, inspexī, inspectŭm, inspĭcĕrĕ, *to look into*
introspĭcĭō, introspexī, introspectŭm, introspĭcĕrĕ, *to look closely into*
perspĭcĭō, perspexī, perspectŭm, perspĭcĕrĕ, *to perceive*
perspĭcax, -ācĭs, *sharp-sighted*
perspĭcŭŭs, -ă, -ŭm, *clear*
perspĭcŭĭtās, -ātĭs (f.), *clearness*
prospĭcĭō, prospexī, prospectŭm, prospĭcĕrĕ, *to look forward*
prospectŭs, -ūs (m.), *a lookout*
respĭcĭō, respexī, respectŭm, respĭcĕrĕ, *to look back; to regard*
respectŭs, -ūs (m.), *respect*
suspĭcĭō, suspexī, suspectŭm, suspĭcĕrĕ, *to look up*
suspectŭs, -ă, -ŭm, *suspected*
suspīcĭō, -ōnĭs (f.), *suspicion*
suspĭcax, -ācĭs, *distrustful*
suspĭcĭōsŭs, -ă, -ŭm, *suspicious*

fŏdĭō, fōdī, fossŭm, fŏdĕrĕ, *to dig*
fossă, -ae (f.), *a ditch*
fŏvĕă, -ae (f.), *a pit*
effŏdĕrĕ, *to dig up*
confŏdĕrĕ, *to stab*
perfŏdĕrĕ, *to dig through*

fŭgĭō, fūgī, (fŭgĭtŭm), fŭgĕrĕ, *to flee*
fŭgă, -ae (f.), *flight*
fŭgārĕ, *to put to flight*
fŭgax, -ācĭs, *fleeting*
fŭgĭtīvŭs, -ī (m.), *a fugitive*
aufŭgĕrĕ, *to run off*
effŭgĕrĕ, *to escape*
confŭgĕrĕ, **perfŭgĕrĕ**, **transfŭgĕrĕ** } *to flee to*
perfŭgă, -ae (m.), **transfŭgă**, -ae (m.) } *a transfuge*
rĕfŭgĕrĕ, *to flee back*
rĕfŭgĭŭm, -ī (n.), **perfŭgĭŭm**, -ī (n.) } *a refuge*
subterfŭgĕrĕ, *to escape*

cŭpĭō, cŭpīvī, cŭpītŭm, cŭpĕrĕ, *to wish*
cŭpĭdŭs, -ă, -ŭm, *desirous*
cŭpīdō, -ĭnĭs (f.), *a desire*
cŭpĭdĭtās, -ātĭs (f.), *a passion*

răpĭō, răpŭī, raptŭm, răpĕrĕ, *to rob*
raptŭs, -ūs (m.), *rapine*
răpīnă, -ae (f.), *robbery*
raptĭm, *hastily*
răpĭdŭs, -ă, -ŭm, *swift*
răpĭdē, *swiftly*
răpax, -ācĭs, *rapacious*
răpācĭtās, -ātĭs (f.), *rapacity*
arrĭpĭō, arrĭpŭī, arreptŭm, arrĭpĕrĕ, *to seize*
abrĭpĭō, abrĭpŭī, abreptŭm, abrĭpĕrĕ; **ērĭpĭō**, ērĭpŭī, ēreptŭm, ērĭpĕrĕ } *to tear away*
corrĭpĭō, corrĭpŭī, correptŭm, corrĭpĕrĕ, *to take hold of*
dīrĭpĭō, dīrĭpŭī, dīreptŭm, dīrĭpĕrĕ, *to plunder*
surrĭpĭō, surrĭpŭī, surreptŭm, surrĭpĕrĕ, *to steal*

părĭō, pĕpĕrĭ, partŭm, părĕrĕ, to bring forth
Part. Fut. părĭtūrŭs
partŭs, -ūs (m.), a birth
părens, -tĭs (m. or f.), father or mother
părentēs, -ŭm (m. pl.), the parents
părentārĕ, to offer a sacrifice in honor of deceased parents

quătĭō, (without Perf.), quassŭm, quătĕrĕ, to shake
concŭtĭō, concussĭ, concussŭm, concŭtĕrĕ, to shake
discŭtĭō, discussĭ, discussŭm, discŭtĕrĕ, to break up
excŭtĭō, excussĭ, excussŭm, excŭtĕrĕ, to shake off
incŭtĭō, incussĭ, incussŭm, incŭtĕrĕ, to strike into

percŭtĭō, percussĭ, percussŭm, percŭtĕrĕ, to pierce through
percussĭō, -ōnĭs (f.), a beating time
percussŏr, -ōrĭs (m.), a murderer
rĕpercŭtĭō, rĕpercussĭ, rĕpercussŭm, rĕpercŭtĕrĕ, to push back

săpĭō, săpĭvĭ & săpŭĭ, (without Sup.), săpĕrĕ, to savor, be wise
săpŏr, -ōrĭs (m.), taste
săpĭens, -tĭs, wise
săpĭentĭă, -ae (f.), wisdom
insĭpĭens, -tĭs, foolish
dēsĭpĭō, dēsĭpŭĭ, (without Sup.), dēsĭpĕrĕ, to be foolish
insĭpĭentĭă, -ae (f.), folly

3. Verbs in dō, tō.

claudō, clausĭ, clausŭm, claudĕrĕ, to shut, close
clāvĭs, - (f.), a key
claustră, -ōrŭm (n. pl.), a lock
clausŭlă, -ae (f.), a close
conclūdō, conclūsĭ, conclūsŭm, conclūdĕrĕ, to close up
inclūdō, inclūsĭ, inclūsŭm, inclūdĕrĕ, to enclose
exclūdō, exclūsĭ, exclūsŭm, exclūdĕrĕ, to shut out
sēclūdō, sēclūsĭ, sēclūsŭm, sēclūdĕrĕ, to shut off [sion
conclūsĭō, -ōnĭs (f.), a conclu-

dīvĭdō, dīvīsĭ, dīvīsŭm, dīvĭdĕrĕ, to divide
dīvĭsĭō, -ōnĭs (f.), a division

dīvĭdŭŭs, -ă, -ŭm, divisible
indīvĭdŭŭs,-ă,-ŭm, indivisible
indīvĭdŭŭm, -ī (n.), an atom

laedō, laesĭ, laesŭm, laedĕrĕ, to hurt
allīdō, allīsĭ, allīsŭm, allīdĕrĕ, to dash against
illīdō, illīsĭ, illīsŭm, illīdĕrĕ, to dash upon
collīdō, collīsĭ, collīsŭm, collīdĕrĕ, to dash together
ēlīdō, ēlīsĭ, ēlīsŭm, ēlīdĕrĕ, to strike out

lūdō, lūsĭ, lūsŭm, lūdĕrĕ, to play
lūsĭō, -ōnĭs (f.), a playing
lūdŭs, -ī (m.), a play; a school

lŭdĭbrĭŭm, -ī (n.), *mockery*
lŭdĭcĕr, -ră, -rŭm, *sportive*
lŭdĭbundŭs, -ă, -ŭm, *playful*
allŭdĕrĕ, *to play with*
collŭdĕrĕ, *to play together*
ēlŭdĕrĕ, *to make sport of*
illŭdĕrĕ, *to mock*

plaudō, plausī, plausŭm, plau-
dĕrĕ, *to clap the hands*
plausŭs, -ūs (m.), *applause*
applaudĕrĕ, *to applaud*
explōdō, explōsī, explōsŭm,
explōdĕrĕ, *to hiss off*
complōdō, complōsī, complō-
sŭm, complōdĕrĕ, *to clap
the hands together*

rādō, rāsī, rāsŭm, rādĕrĕ, *to
scrape*
abrādĕrĕ) *to rub off*
ērādĕrĕ)
corrādĕrĕ, *to rake together*
rastrŭm, -ī (n.), *a prong hoe*

rōdō, rōsī, rōsŭm, rōdĕrĕ, *to
gnaw*
rostrŭm, -ī (n.), *a beak*
arrōdĕrĕ, *to gnaw at*
dērōdĕrĕ, *to gnaw away*
perrōdĕrĕ, *to gnaw through*

trŭdō, trŭsī, trŭsŭm, trŭdĕrĕ,
to thrust
dētrŭdĕrĕ, *to thrust down*
extrŭdĕrĕ, *to thrust out*
prōtrŭdĕrĕ, *to thrust forward*
abstrŭdĕrĕ, *to conceal*

vādō, (without Perf. & Sup.), vādĕrĕ,
to go
vădŭm, -ī (n.), *a ford*
vădōsŭs, -ă, -ŭm, *shallow*
ēvādō, ēvāsī, ēvāsŭm, ēvā-
dĕrĕ, *to go, turn out*
invādō, invāsī, invāsŭm, invā-
dĕrĕ, *to fall upon*
pervādō, pervāsī, pervāsŭm,
pervādĕrĕ, *to pass through*

With Reduplication.

cădō, cĕcĭdī, cāsŭm, cădĕrĕ, *to
fall*
cāsŭs, -ūs (m.), *an accident*
cădŭcŭs, -ă, -ŭm, *frail*
cădāvĕr, -ĭs (n.), *a corpse*
incĭdō, incĭdī, incāsŭm, incĭ-
dĕrĕ, *to fall into or upon*
occĭdō, occĭdī, occāsŭm, occĭ-
dĕrĕ, *to set*
rĕcĭdō, rĕcĭdī, rĕcāsŭm, rĕcĭ-
dĕrĕ, *to fall back*
Without Supine:
concĭdō, concĭdī, concĭdĕrĕ, *to
tumble down*

dēcĭdō, dēcĭdī, dēcĭdĕrĕ, *to
fall down*
excĭdō, excĭdī, excĭdĕrĕ, *to
fall out*
accĭdō, accĭdī, accĭdĕrĕ, *to fall
upon;* accĭdĭt, *it happens*

caedō, cĕcĭdī, caesŭm, caedĕrĕ,
to cut, fell
caedēs, -ĭs (f.), *a murder*
caementŭm, -ī (n.), *a quarry
stone*
concĭdō, concĭdī, concīsŭm,
concĭdĕrĕ, *to strike down*

abscīdō, abscīdī, abscīsŭm, abscīdĕrĕ, *to cut off*
circumcīdō, circumcīdī, circumcīsŭm, circumcīdĕrĕ, *to cut around*
excīdō, excīdī, excīsŭm, excīdĕrĕ, *to hew out*
excīdĭŭm, -ī (n.), *destruction*
incīdō, incīdī, incīsŭm, incīdĕrĕ, *to cut into*
praecīdō, praecīdī,praecīsŭm, praecīdĕrĕ, *to cut off*
praecīsē, *in short*
dēcīdō, dēcīdī, decīsŭm, dēcīdĕrĕ, *to decide, compound with one*
dēcīsĭō, -ōnĭs (f.), *agreement*
occīdō, occīdī, occīsŭm, occīdĕrĕ, *to kill*
occīdĭō, -ōnĭs (f.), *destruction*

pendō, pĕpendī, pensŭm, pendĕrĕ, *to weigh*
pensŭm, -ī (n.), *a task*
pensĭō, -ōnĭs (f.), *payment*
pondŭs, -ĕrĭs (n.), *weight*
pondō (indecl.), *a pound in weight*
pondĕrārĕ, *to weigh*
pensārĕ }
pensĭtārĕ } *to pay*
compensārĕ }
compensĭtārĕ } *to make good*
compensātĭō, -ōnĭs (f.), *a compensation*
compendĭŭm, -ī (n.), *a profit*
dispendĭŭm, -ī (n.), *expense*
dispensārĕ, *to manage*
dispensātŏr,-ōrĭs (m.), *a manager*
dispensātĭō,-ōnĭs (f.), *management*

appendō, appendī, appensŭm, appendĕrĕ, *to weigh out*
dēpendō, dēpendī, dēpensŭm, dēpendĕrĕ, *to pay*
expendō, expendī, expensŭm, expendĕrĕ, *to pay out*
expensŭm, -ī (n.), *a payment*
impendĭŭm, -ī (n.) }
impensă, -ae (f.) } *expense*
perpendō, perpendī, perpensŭm, perpendĕrĕ, *to consider*
suspendō, suspendī, suspensŭm,suspendĕrĕ, *to hang up*

tendō, tĕtendī, tensŭm & tentŭm, tendĕrĕ, *to stretch*
tentŏrĭŭm, -ī (n.), *a tent*
tentārĕ, *to try*
attendō, attendī, attentŭm, attendĕrĕ, *to attend to*
attentĭō, -ōnĭs (f.), *attention*
attentŭs, -ă, -ŭm, *attentive*
attentē, *attentively*
attentārĕ, *to attempt*
contendō, contendī, contentŭm, contendĕrĕ, *to exert*
contentĭō, -ōnĭs (f.), *strife; quarrel*
distendō, distendī, distentŭm, distendĕrĕ, *to stretch out*
extendō, extendī, extensŭm & extentŭm, extendĕrĕ, *to stretch out*
intendō, intendī, intentŭm, intendĕrĕ, *to strain*
intentĭō, -ōnĭs (f.), *an exertion*
intentārĕ, *to threaten*
obtendō, obtendī, obtentŭm, obtendĕrĕ, *to cover*
ostendō, ostendī, ostensŭm, ostendĕrĕ, *to show*

ostentŭm, -ĭ (n.), *a prodigy*
ostentārĕ, *to present to view*
ostentātĭŏ, -ŏnĭs (f.), *ostenta-
tion*
praetendŏ, praetendĭ, praeten-
tŭm, praetendĕrĕ, *to pre-
tend*
prōtendŏ, prōtendĭ, prōten-
sŭm, prōtendĕrĕ, *to stretch
forth*
portendŏ, portendĭ, portentŭm, portendĕrĕ, *to fore-
show*
portentŭm, -ĭ (n.), *an omen*

tundŏ, tŭtŭdĭ, tunsŭm & tŭ-
sŭm, tundĕrĕ, *to beat, pound*
contundŏ, contŭdĭ, cǫntŭsŭm,
contundĕrĕ, *to break to
pieces*
rĕtundŏ, rĕtŭdĭ, rĕtŭsŭm, rĕ-
tundĕrĕ, *to blunt*
obtundŏ, obtŭdĭ, obtŭsŭm, ob-
tundĕrĕ, *to stun*
obtŭsŭs, -ă, -ŭm, *blunt*

crēdŏ, crēdĭdĭ, crēdĭtŭm, crē-
dĕrĕ, *to believe*
crēdĭtŏr,-ōrĭs (m.), *a creditor*
crēdĭbĭlĭs, -ĕ, *credible*
ĭncrēdĭbĭlĭs, -ĕ, *incredible*
crēdĭbĭlĭtās,-ātĭs (f.), *credible-
ness*
crēdŭlŭs, -ă, -ŭm, *credulous*
ĭncrēdŭlŭs, -ă, -ŭm, *incredul-
ous*
accrēdĕrĕ, *to trust*

**Compounds of
dărĕ**, *to give* (see p. 43).

condŏ, condĭdĭ, condĭtŭm,
condĕrĕ, *to build, found*

condĭtŏr, -ōrĭs (m.), *a foun-
der*
abdŏ, abdĭdĭ, abdĭtŭm, ab-
dĕrĕ, *to hide*
abscondŏ, abscondĭdĭ, abscon-
dĭtŭm, abscondĕrĕ, *to hide
carefully*
rĕcondŏ, rĕcondĭdĭ, rĕcon-
dĭtŭm, rĕcondĕrĕ, *to lay
up*
addŏ, addĭdĭ, addĭtŭm, ad-
dĕrĕ, *to add*
addĭtāmentŭm, -ĭ (n.), *an addition*
dēdŏ, dēdĭdĭ, dēdĭtŭm, dē-
dĕrĕ, *to give up*
dēdĭtĭŏ, -ŏnĭs (f.), *a surrender*
ēdŏ, ēdĭdĭ, ēdĭtŭm, ēdĕrĕ, *to
give out*
ēdĭtĭŏ,-ŏnĭs (f.), *a declaration;
an edition*
perdŏ, perdĭdĭ, perdĭtŭm,
perdĕrĕ, *to ruin*
praedĭtŭs, -ă, -ŭm, *endowed*
prōdŏ, prōdĭdĭ, prōdĭtŭm,
prōdĕrĕ, *to bring forth, be-
tray*
prōdĭtĭŏ, -ŏnĭs (f.), *treason*
prōdĭtŏr, -ōrĭs (m.), *a traitor*
reddŏ, reddĭdĭ, reddĭtŭm,
reddĕrĕ, *to give back*
subdŏ, subdĭdĭ, subdĭtŭm, sub-
dĕrĕ, *to put under*
trādŏ, trādĭdĭ, trādĭtŭm, trā-
dĕrĕ, *to deliver*
trādĭtĭŏ, - ŏnĭs (f.), *a giving
up*
vendŏ, vendĭdĭ, vendĭtŭm,
vendĕrĕ, *to sell*
vendĭtĭŏ, -ŏnĭs (f.), *a sale*
vendĭtŏr, -ōrĭs (m.), *a seller*

Perfect ī, Supine sŭm.

accendō, accendī, accensŭm, accendĕrĕ, *to kindle*

incendĕrĕ \
succendĕrĕ } *to set fire to*

incendĭŭm, -ī (n.), *a fire*

cūdō, cūdī, cūsŭm, cūdĕrĕ, *to forge*

incūs, -ūdĭs (f.), *an anvil*
excūdĕrĕ, *to beat out*

[fendō, *thrust*]

dēfendō, dēfendī, dēfensŭm, dēfendĕrĕ, *to defend*
dēfensĭō, -ōnĭs (f.), *a defense*
dēfensŏr,-ōrĭs (m.), *a defender*
offendō, offendī, offensŭm, offendĕrĕ, *to offend*

offensă, -ae (f.) \
offensŭm, -ī (n.) } *an offense* \
offensĭō, -ōnĭs (f.)

ĕdō, ĕdī, ĕsŭm, ĕdĕrĕ, *to eat*

ĕdax, -ācĭs, *voracious*
ĕdācĭtās, -ātĭs (f.), *voracity*
ĕdūlĭs, -ĕ, *eatable*
ĕdūlĭă, -ĭŭm (n. pl.), *eatables*
escă, -ae (f.), *a bait*
ĕsŭrīrĕ, *to be hungry*

exĕdĕrĕ, \
cŏmĕdĕrĕ } *to eat up*

pĕrĕdĕrĕ, *to devour*
cŏmĕdō, -ōnĭs (m.), *a glutton*

mandō, (mandī), mansŭm, mandĕrĕ, *to chew, masticate*

mălă, -ae (f.), *a jaw, cheek*

prĕhendō, prĕhendī, prĕhensŭm, prĕhendĕrĕ, *to seize*
prensārĕ, *to grasp, seize*

apprĕhendĕrĕ \
comprĕhendĕrĕ } *to seize*

dēprĕhendĕrĕ, *to detect*
rĕprĕhendĕrĕ, *to censure*
rĕprĕhensĭō, -ōnĭs (f.), *a censure*

scandō, scandī, scansŭm, scandĕrĕ, *to climb*

scālae, -ārŭm (f. pl.), *a staircase*
scamnŭm, -ī (n.), *a bench*
scăbellŭm, -ī (n.), *a footstool*

ascendō, ascendī, ascen- \
sŭm, ascendĕrĕ \ *to* \
escendō, escendī, escen- } *climb* \
sŭm, escendĕrĕ / *up*

ascensĭō, -ōnĭs (f.) \
ascensŭs, -ūs (m.) } *an ascent*

conscendō, conscendī, conscensŭm, conscendĕrĕ, *to embark*
descendō, descendī, descensŭm, descendĕrĕ, *to go down*
descensĭō, -ōnĭs (f.), *a going down*

fundō, fūdī, fūsŭm, fundĕrĕ, *to pour*

fūsē, *at length*
affundĕrĕ, *to pour upon*
effundĕrĕ, *to pour out*
infundĕrĕ, *to pour in*
confundĕrĕ, *to confound*
confūsĭō,-ōnĭs (f.), *a confusion*
diffundĕrĕ, *to diffuse*
offundĕrĕ, *to spread over*
prŏfundĕrĕ, *to pour out; to lavish*

Various Irregularities.

cēdō, cessī, cessŭm, cēdĕrĕ, to
go, yield

cessārĕ, to leave off

cessātĭŏ, –ōnĭs (f.), inactivity

cessātŏr, –ōrĭs (m.), a loiterer

accēdĕrĕ, to come near to

accessĭŏ,–ōnĭs (f.), an increase

abscēdĕrĕ, to go off

antĕcēdĕrĕ, to go before

antĕcessĭŏ, –ōnĭs (f.), a going
before

rĕcēdĕrĕ, to go back

rĕcessŭs, –ŭs (m.), a retreat

dēcēdĕrĕ, to depart

dēcessĭŏ, –ōnĭs (f.), a decrease

concēdĕrĕ, to yield, concede

incessŭs, –ŭs (m.), the gait

intercēdĕrĕ, to interfere

intercessĭŏ,–ōnĭs (f.), an inter-
vention

prōcēdĕrĕ, to go forth or before

prōcessĭŏ, –ōnĭs (f.) } an ad-
prōcessŭs, –ŭs (m.) } vance

sēcēdĕrĕ, to go aside

sēcessĭŏ, –ōnĭs (f.), a going
aside

succēdĕrĕ, to come into the
place of

successĭŏ,–ōnĭs (f.), succession

successŏr, –ōrĭs (m.), a suc-
cessor

findō, fĭdī, fissŭm, findĕrĕ, to
split, cleave

diffindĕrĕ, to cleave asunder

scindō, scĭdī, scissŭm, scindĕrĕ,
to cut

conscindĕrĕ, to rend to pieces

discindĕrĕ, to tear asunder

discĭdĭŭm, –ī (n.), a separation

rescindĕrĕ, to annul

abscindō, abscĭdī, abscĭsŭm,
abscindĕrĕ, to tear off

exscindō, excĭdī, excĭsŭm,
exscindĕrĕ, to destroy

frendō (frendĕō), (without Perf.),
fressŭm & frēsŭm, fren-
dĕrĕ, to gnash (the teeth)

mĕtō,(messŭī),messŭm,mĕtĕrĕ,
to cut off, gather

messŏr, –ōrĭs (m.), a reaper

messĭs, – (f.), harvest

dēmĕtĕrĕ, to cut off

mittō, mīsī, missŭm, mittĕrĕ, to
send

missĭŏ, –ōnĭs (f.), a sending
away, discharge

missĭlĭs, –ĕ, capable of being
thrown

āmittĕrĕ, to lose

admittĕrĕ, to admit

committĕrĕ, to bring together

dēmittĕrĕ, to drop

dīmittĕrĕ, to discharge

dīmissĭŏ, –ōnĭs (f.), a dischar-
ging

ēmittĕrĕ, to send out

ēmissārĭŭs, –ī (m.), a spy

immittĕrĕ, to discharge at

intermittĕrĕ, to leave off

intrōmittĕre, to let in

ōmittĕrĕ } to omit
praetermittĕrĕ }

permissŭs, –ŭs (m.), leave

permittĕrĕ, to permit

praemittĕrĕ, to send forward

prōmittĕrĕ, *to promise*
prōmissĭŏ,–ōnĭs (f.), *a promise*
rĕmittĕrĕ, *to send back*
submittĕrĕ, *to lower, sink*
transmittĕrĕ, *to convey across*

pandō, pandĭ, passŭm (pansŭm),
pandĕrĕ, *to spread out*
passŭs, –ūs (m.), *a step*
passĭm, *hither and thither*

pĕtō, pĕtīvī (pĕtĭī), pĕtītŭm,
pĕtĕrĕ, *to beg, seek*
pĕtītĭŏ, –ōnĭs (f.), *an attack; a request*
pĕtītŏr, –ōrĭs (m.), *a plaintiff*
compĕtītŏr, –ōrĭs (m.), *a rival*
pĕtŭlans, –tĭs, *wanton*
pĕtŭlantĭă,–ae (f.), *wantonness*
appĕtĕrĕ, *to strive after*
appĕtītŭs, –ūs (m.), *a desire*
expĕtĕrĕ, *to long for*
oppĕtĕrĕ, *to go to meet*
rĕpĕtĕrĕ, *to demand back*
rĕpĕtītĭŏ;–ōnĭs (f.), *a repetition*
suppĕtĕrĕ, *to suffice*
impĕtŭs, –ūs (m.), *an attack*
perpĕtŭŭs, –ă, –ŭm, *perpetual*
perpĕtŭĭtăs, –ātĭs (f.), *continual duration*

sīdō, sēdī (sīdī), sessŭm, sīdĕrĕ,
to sit down
assīdĕrĕ, *to sit down*
consīdĕrĕ, *to sit down*
dēsīdĕrĕ, *to sink*
possīdĕrĕ, *to take possession of*
rĕsīdĕrĕ, *to settle*
subsīdĕrĕ, *to settle down*

sistō, stĭtĭ, stătŭm, sistĕrĕ, *to cause to stand, to place*
stătĭm, *at once*
stătŭs, –ă, –ŭm, *fixed*
stătŭs, –ūs (m.), *a standing*
stătĭŏ, –ōnĭs (f.), *a station*
obsistō, obstĭtĭ, obstĭtŭm, ob-
sistĕrĕ, *to oppose*
Without Supine:
absistĕrĕ, *to cease*
adsistĕrĕ, *to stand by*
consistĕrĕ, *to stand*
dēsistĕrĕ, *to leave off*
exsistĕrĕ, *to come forth*
insistĕrĕ, *to tread upon*
persistĕrĕ, *to persist*
rĕsistĕrĕ, *to withstand*
subsistĕrĕ, *to stand still*

stertō, stertŭĭ, (without Sup.), ster-
tĕrĕ, *to snore*

vertō, vertī, versŭm, vertĕrĕ,
to turn
versūtŭs, –ă, –ŭm, *adroit*
vertex, –ĭcĭs (m.), *an eddy*
vertĭgŏ, –ĭnĭs (f.), *giddiness*
versŭs, –ūs (m.) { *a verse,*
versĭcŭlŭs, –ī (m.) { *line*
versārĕ, *to turn about*
versūră, –ae (f.), *a loan*
āvertĕrĕ, *to turn off*
advertĕrĕ, *to turn to*
adversŭs, *opposite to*
adversārĭŭs, –ī (m.), *an antag-
onist*
ănĭmadvertĕrĕ, *to perceive*
ănĭmadversĭŏ, –ōnĭs (f.), *per-
ception*
antĕvertĕrĕ, *to prevent*
convertĕrĕ, *to turn about*

conversĭŏ, -ōnĭs (f.), a change
dĕvertĕrĕ, to put up
dĕvertĭcŭlŭm, -ī (n.), a by-way
dĕversōrĭŭm, -ī (n.), an inn
ĕvertĕrĕ, to destroy
ĕversĭŏ, -ōnĭs (f.), destruction
ĕversŏr,-ōrĭs (m.),a destructor
invertĕrĕ, to upset
intervertĕrĕ, to embezzle
pervertĕrĕ, to overturn
perversŭs, -ă, -ŭm, wrong
perversĭtās, -ātĭs (f.), perversity
contrŏversĭă,-ae (f.), a controversy
dīversŭs, -ă, -ŭm, contrary
rĕtrorsŭm (rĕtrōversŭm), backward
prorsŭs, -ă, -ŭm (prōversŭs), straight, prosaic
prōsă, -ae (f.), prose

prorsŭs, forwards
rūrsŭs (rĕvorsŭm),again
sūrsŭm (subvorsŭm), on high
transversŭs, -ă, -ŭm, cross-
praevertĕrĕ, to outrun [wise
rĕvertĕrĕ, to come back

fīdŏ, fīsŭs sŭm, fīdĕrĕ, to trust
fīdŭs, -ă, -ŭm, trusty
infīdŭs, -ă, -ŭm, faithless
fīdūcĭă, -ae (f.), confidence
fīdēs, -ĕī (f.), faith
fīdēlĭs, -ĕ, faithful
fīdēlĭtās,-ātĭs (f.),faithfulness
infīdēlĭs, -ĕ, faithless
perfīdŭs, -ă,-ŭm, treacherous
perfīdĭă, -ae (f.), treachery
confīdĕrĕ, to rely upon
confīdentĭă, -ae (f.), confidence
diffīdĕrĕ, to distrust

4. Verbs in bō, pō.

glūbō, glupsī, gluptŭm, glūbĕrĕ, to peel
dēglūbĕrĕ, to skin

nūbō, nupsī, nuptŭm, nūbĕrĕ, to marry (of the woman)
nuptă, -ae (f.), a wife
nuptĭae,-ārŭm (f. pl.), a marriage
connūbĭŭm,-ī (n.), marriage
nuptĭālĭs, -ĕ, nuptial

scrībō, scripsī, scriptŭm, scrībĕrĕ, to write
scrība, -ae (m.), a clerk
scriptĭŏ, -ōnĭs (f.) } the art of
scriptūră, -ae (f.) } writing
scriptŭm, -ī (n.), a writing

scriptŏr, -ōrĭs (m.), an author
scriptĭtārĕ, to use to write
adscrībĕrĕ, to add to a writing
circumscrībĕrĕ, to determine the limits
cònscrībĕrĕ, to draw up in writing
descrībĕrĕ, to sketch off
descriptĭŏ, -ōnĭs (f.), a description
inscrībĕrĕ, to write upon
inscriptĭŏ, -ōnĭs (f.), a title
perscrībĕrĕ, to write down
praescrībĕrĕ, to prescribe
praescriptĭŏ,-ōnĭs (f.) } a precept,
praescriptŭm, -ī (n.) } order
proscrībĕrĕ, to outlaw
proscriptĭŏ,-ōnĭs (f.), outlawry

rescrībĕrĕ, *to write back*
subscrībĕrĕ, *to sign*
transcrībĕrĕ, *to copy*

carpō, carpsī, carptŭm, carpĕrĕ,
to pluck, crop

concerpō, concerpsī, concerp-
tŭm, concerpĕrĕ, *to tear in
pieces*
discerpō, discerpsī, discerptŭm,
discerpĕrĕ, *to tear in pieces*
excerpō, excerpsī, excerptŭm,
excerpĕrĕ, *to pick out*

rēpō, repsī, reptŭm, rēpĕrĕ, *to
creep, crawl*

arrēpĕrĕ, *to creep along*
subrēpĕrĕ, *to creep under*

irrēpĕrĕ, *to creep in*
prōrēpĕrĕ, *to creep forth*
obrēpĕrĕ, *to creep up*

scalpō, scalpsī, scalptŭm, scal-
pĕrĕ, *to carve*
scalpellŭm, -ī (n.), *a lancet*

sculpō, sculpsī, sculptŭm, scul-
pĕrĕ, *to chisel*
exsculpĕrĕ, *to carve*
insculpĕrĕ, *to engrave*
sculptŏr, -ōrĭs (m.), *a sculptor*
sculptūră, -ae (f.), *sculpture*

serpō, serpsī, (serptŭm), serpĕrĕ,
to creep (of animals only)
serpens, -tĭs (f.), *a serpent*

The following are irregular:

accumbō, accŭbŭī, accŭbĭtŭm,
accumbĕrĕ, *to recline at table*
incumbĕrĕ, *to apply one's self to*
prōcumbĕrĕ, *to sink down*
occumbĕrĕ, *to die*
succumbĕrĕ, *to succumb*
(Compounds of cŭbārĕ, *to lie*, p. 41.)

bībō, bībī, (bībĭtŭm), bībĕrĕ, *to
drink*
ēbībĕrĕ, *to drink up*
imbībĕrĕ, *to drink in*

rumpō, rūpī, ruptŭm, rumpĕrĕ,
to break
rūpēs, -ĭs (f.), *a rock*
abrumpĕrĕ, *to tear off*
abruptŭs, -ă, -ŭm, *steep*
corrumpĕrĕ, *to corrupt, spoil*
corruptĭŏ, -ōnĭs (f.), *corruption*
corruptŏr, -ōrĭs (m.), *a cor-
ruptor*

ērumpĕrĕ, *to break out*
ēruptĭŏ, -ōnĭs (f.), *a sally*
interrumpĕrĕ, *to interrupt*
irrumpĕrĕ, *to break in*
irruptĭŏ, -ōnĭs (f.), *an invasion*
perrumpĕrĕ, *to break through*
prōrumpĕrĕ, *to break forth*
praerumpĕrĕ, *to break off*
praeruptŭs, -ă, -ŭm, *steep*

strĕpō, strĕpŭī, strĕpĭtŭm, strĕ-
pĕrĕ, *to make a noise*
strĕpĭtŭs, -ūs (m.), *a noise*
obstrĕpĕrĕ, *to annoy*

lambō, lambī, (lambĭtŭm), lam-
bĕrĕ, *to lick*
lăbră, -ōrŭm (n. pl.), *the lips*

scăbō, scăbī, (without Sup.), scă-
bĕrĕ, *to scratch*
scăbĭēs, -ēī (f.), *the mange*
scăbĕr, -ră, -rŭm, *mangy*

5. Verbs in cō, gō (guō), hō, ctō, quō.

cingō, cinxī, cinctům, cingěrě, *to gird*

cingŭlŭs, -ī (m.), *a girdle*
discinctŭs, -ă, -ŭm, *ungirt*
accingěrě, *to gird on*
succingěrě, *to gird*

[flīgō, *strike*]
afflīgō, afflixī, afflictům, afflī-gěrě, *to strike down*
afflictārě, *to trouble*
afflictătĭŏ, -ōnĭs (f.), *trouble*
conflīgō, conflixī, conflictům, conflīgěrě, *to fight*
inflīgō, inflixī, inflictům, inflī-gěrě, *to strike upon*
prōflīgārě, *to strike to the ground*
flăgellŭm, -ī (n.), *a scourge*

frīgō, frixī, frictům (frixům), frīgěrě, *to roast*

jungō, junxī, junctům, jungěrě, *to join*

jŭgŭm, -ī (n.), *a yoke*
jūmentům, -ī (n.), *draught cattle*
jŭgŭlŭm,-ī (n.), *the collar-bone*
jŭgŭlārě, *to cut the throat*
adjungěrě, *to join to*
conjungěrě, *to join together*
conjunctĭŏ, -ōnĭs (f.), *a connecting*
conjux, -ŭgĭs (m.), *a husband*
conjŭgĭŭm, -ī (n.), *a marriage*
disjungěrě) *to separate* [tion
sējungěrě } *to separate* [tion
disjunctĭŏ, -ōnĭs (f.), *a separa-*

injungěrě, *to attach to*
subjungěrě, *to subdue*
lingō, linxī, linctům, lingěrě, *to lick*

līgŭrīrě, *to lick*
līgŭrītĭŏ, -ōnĭs (f.), *daintiness*
linguă, -ae (f.), *the tongue*

[mungō, *blow the nose*]
ēmungō, ēmunxī, ēmunctům, ēmungěrě, *to blow the nose*

plangō, planxī, planctům, plan-gěrě, *to bewail*

rěgō, rexī, rectům, rěgěrě, *to rule, govern*

rectŭs, -ă, -ŭm, *right*
rectē, *rightly*
rectĭŏ, -ōnĭs (f.)) *a leading*
rěgĭmĕn,-ĭnĭs (n.) } *a leading*
rectŏr, -ōrĭs (m.), *a ruler*
rex, rēgĭs (m.), *a king*
rēgīnă, -ae (f.), *a queen*
regnům, -ī (n.), *a kingdom*
regnārě, *to reign*
rēgĭŭs, -ă, -ŭm) *kingly*
rēgălĭs, -ě } *kingly*
rēgĭă, -ae (f.), *a royal palace*
rēgĭŏ, -ōnĭs (f.), *a direction*
rēgŭlă, -ae (f.), *a rule*
corrīgō, correxī, correctům, corrīgěrě, *to correct*
correctĭŏ, -ōnĭs (f.), *a correction*
correctŏr, -ōrĭs (m.), *a corrector*
dīrĭgō, dīrexī, dīrectům, dīrĭ-gěrě, *to direct to*

dīrectŭs, -ă, -ŭm, *straight*
ērīgō, ērexī, ērectŭm, ērī-
gĕrĕ, *to raise*
porrīgō, porrexī, porrectŭm,
porrīgĕrĕ, *to stretch out*
pergō (per-rĕgō), perrexī, per-
rectŭm, pergĕrĕ, *to go on*
surgō (sub-rĕgō), surrexī, sur-
rectŭm, surgĕrĕ, *to rise*
assurgĕrĕ ⎫
consurgĕrĕ ⎬ *to rise up*
exsurgĕrĕ ⎭

sūgō, suxī, suctŭm, sūgĕrĕ, *to
suck*

exsūgĕrĕ, *to suck out*
sūcŭs, -ī (m.), *sap*

tĕgō, texī, tectŭm, tĕgĕrĕ, *to
cover*

tĕgĕs, -ĕtĭs (f.) ⎫ a
tĕgĭmĕn, -ĭnĭs (n.) ⎬ *covering,*
tĕgĭmentŭm, -ī (n.) ⎭ *cover*
tĕgŭlă, -ae (f.), *a tile*
tectŭm, -ī (n.), *a roof*
contĕgĕrĕ ⎫ *to cover*
obtĕgĕrĕ ⎭
dĕtĕgĕrĕ, *to uncover*
prōtĕgĕrĕ, *to protect*
rĕtĕgĕrĕ, *to uncover*

tingō (tinguō), tinxī, tinctŭm,
tingĕrĕ, *to dip*

tinctŭs, -ūs (m.), *a dipping
into*
tinctūră, -ae (f.), *a dyeing*
tinctŏr, -ōrĭs (m.), *a dyer*

[stinguō, *put out*]
distinguĕrĕ, *to distinguish*

distinctŭs, -ă, -ŭm, *distinct*
distinctē, *distinctly*
distinctĭŏ, -ōnĭs (f.), *a distinction*
exstinguō, exstinxī, exstinc-
tŭm, exstinguĕrĕ, *to ex-
tinguish*
restinguĕrĕ, *to put out*

trăhō, traxī, tractŭm, trăhĕrĕ,
to draw

attrăhĕrĕ, *to attract*
contrăhĕrĕ, *to draw together*
dĕtrăhĕrĕ, *to draw off*
extrăhĕrĕ, *to draw out*
prōtrahĕrĕ, *to draw forth*
rĕtrahĕrĕ, *to withdraw*
subtrăhĕrĕ, *to carry off*
tractŭs, -ūs (m.), *a tract of
land*
tractārĕ, *to treat*
tractātĭŏ, -ōnĭs (f.) ⎫ *treatment*
tractŭs, -ūs (m.) ⎭
tractăbĭlĭs, -ĕ, *manageable*
attrectārĕ ⎫ *to handle*
contrectārĕ ⎭
dĕtrectārĕ, *to refuse*
obtrectārĕ, *to decry*
obtrectātĭŏ, -ōnĭs (f.), *dispar-
agement*
obtrectātŏr, -ōrĭs (m.), *a tra-
ducer*
pertractārĕ, *to investigate*
rĕtractārĕ, *to handle again,
to refuse*
rĕtractātĭŏ, -ōnĭs (f.), *a refusal*

unguō (ungō), unxī, unctŭm,
unguĕrĕ, *to anoint*
unctĭŏ, -ōnĭs (f.), *an anoint-
ing*

unguentŭm, -ī (n.), *an oint-
ment*
unguentărĭŭs, -ī (m.), *a per-
fumer*

vĕhō, vexī, vectŭm, vĕhĕrĕ,
to carry
vĕhĭcŭlŭm, -ī (n.), *a vehicle*
vectŏr, -ōrĭs (m.), *a passenger*
vectīgăl, -ālĭs (n.), *a toll*
ăvĕhĕrĕ, *to carry away*
advĕhĕrĕ, *to carry to a place*
convĕhĕrĕ, *to gather in*
dēvĕhĕrĕ, *to carry down*
ēvĕhĕrĕ, *to carry forth*
invĕhĕrĕ, *to carry to a place*
transvĕhĕrĕ, *to carry over*
pervĕhĕrĕ, *to carry through*
prōvĕhĕrĕ, *to carry forwards*
subvĕhĕrĕ, *to carry up stream*

dīcō, dixī, dictŭm, dīcĕrĕ,
to say
dīcax, -ācĭs, *witty*
dīcăcĭtās, -ātĭs (f.), *wit*
dictārĕ, *to dictate*
dictītārĕ, *to declare*
addīcĕrĕ, *to award*
condīcĕrĕ, *to agree upon*
condīcĭō, -ōnĭs (f.), *a condi-
tion*
ēdīcĕrĕ, *to make known*
ēdictŭm, -ī (n.), *an ordi-
nance*
indīcĕrĕ, *to proclaim*
interdīcĕrĕ, *to forbid*
praedīcĕrĕ, *to foretell*
mălēdīcĕrĕ, *to revile*
mălēdīcŭs, -ă, -ŭm, *abusive*
dīcārĕ } *to dedicate*
dēdīcārĕ }

abdīcārĕ, *to renounce*
indīcārĕ, *to show*
index, -ĭcĭs (m.), *a pointer*
indĭcĭŭm, -ī (n.), *a notice*
praedīcārĕ, *to proclaim; to
praise*
praedīcătĭō, -ōnĭs (f.), *praise*
praedīcătŏr, -ōrĭs (m.), *a
crier*

dūcō, duxī, ductŭm, dūcĕrĕ, *to
lead, guide*
ductŭs, -ūs (m.), *command*
dux, dŭcĭs (m.), *a leader*
ductŏr, -ōrĭs (m.), *a chief*
abdūcĕrĕ, *to lead away*
circumdūcĕrĕ, *to lead around*
condūcĕrĕ, *to hire*
dēdūcĕrĕ, *to lead to a place*
dīdūcĕrĕ, *to divide*
ēdūcĕrĕ, *to lead forth*
indūcĕrĕ, *to lead into*
intrōdūcĕrĕ, *to bring in*
perdūcĕrĕ, *to lead through*
praedūcĕrĕ, *to put before*
prōdūcĕrĕ, *to bring forth*
rēdūcĕrĕ, *to bring back*
rēdux, -ŭcĭs, *returned*
sēdūcĕrĕ, *to lead aside*
subdūcĕrĕ, *to lead away*
trādūcĕrĕ, *to convey across*
trādux, -ŭcĭs (m.), *a vine-
layer*

cŏquō, coxī, coctŭm, cŏquĕrĕ,
to cook
cŏquŭs, -ī (m.), *a cook*
concŏquĕrĕ, *to digest*
dēcŏquĕrĕ, *to boil down*
dēcoctŭm, -ī (n.), *a decoction*
praecox, -ŏcĭs, *early ripe*

The Supine is irregular.

fingō, finxī, fictŭm, fingĕrĕ, to
  fashion, feign
affingĕrĕ, to add by fashioning
confingĕrĕ, to devise
effingĕrĕ, to fashion
effĭgĭēs, -ēī (f.), a likeness
fĭgŭlŭs, -ī (m.), a potter
fictĭŏ, -ōnĭs (f.), a fashioning
fictĭlĭs, -ĕ, earthen

pingō, pinxī, pictŭm, pingĕrĕ,
  to paint
pictŏr, -ōrĭs (m.), a painter
pictūră, -ae (f.), a picture
pigmentŭm, -ī (n.), a paint
appingĕrĕ, to add by painting
dēpingĕrĕ } to depict
expingĕrĕ }

stringō, strinxī, strictŭm, strin-
  gĕrĕ, to bind tight
strictĭm, briefly
adstringĕrĕ, to draw close
constringĕrĕ, to bind together
destringĕrĕ, to strip off
distringĕrĕ, to molest
obstringĕrĕ, to oblige
perstringĕrĕ, to touch
praestringĕrĕ, to blind
restrictŭs,-ă,-ŭm, close

fīgō,fixī, fixŭm, fīgĕrĕ, to fasten
affīgĕrĕ, to fix upon
confīgĕrĕ } to pierce through
transfīgĕrĕ }
dēfīgĕrĕ } to thrust in
infīgĕrĕ }
praefīgĕrĕ, to fix before
rĕfīgĕrĕ, to unfasten

flectō, flexī, flexŭm, flectĕrĕ,
  to bend

flexĭŏ, -ōnĭs (f.) } a bending
flexŭs, -ūs (m.) }
dēflectĕrĕ, to bend aside
inflectĕrĕ, to bend
rĕflectĕrĕ, to bend back

nectō, nexŭī & nexī, nexŭm,
  nectĕrĕ, to bind
nexŭs, -ī (m.), a person en-
  slaved for debt
nexŭs, -ūs (m.) } a tying
cōnexŭs, -ūs (m.) } together
nexŭm, -ī (n.), slavery for debt
annectō, annexŭī, annexŭm,
  annectĕrĕ, to bind to
cōnectō, cōnexŭī, cōnexŭm,
  cōnectĕrĕ, to bind together

pectō, pexī, pexŭm, pectĕrĕ,
  to comb
pectĕn, -ĭnĭs (m.), a comb

angō, anxī, (without Sup.), angĕrĕ,
  to torment
angŏr, -ōrĭs (m.), anguish
anxĭŭs, -ă, -ŭm, anxious
anxĭĕtās, -ātĭs (f.), anxiety
angustŭs, -ă, -ŭm, narrow
angustĭae, -ārŭm (f. pl.), a
  narrow place

ningō, ninxī, (without Sup.), nin-
  gĕrĕ, to snow
nix, nĭvĭs (f.), snow
(nĭvĭt, it snows)
nĭvĕŭs, -ă, -ŭm } snowy
nĭvālĭs, -ĕ }
nĭvōsŭs, -ă, -ŭm, full of snow

clangō, (without Perf. & Sup.), clan-
  gĕrĕ, to clang
clangŏr, -ōrĭs (m.), a noise

The Perfect is irregular.

A. Reduplication.

parcō, pĕpercī, parsŭm, par-
cĕrĕ, *to spare*

parcŭs, -ă, -ŭm, *thrifty*

parsĭmōnĭă, -ae (f.), *frugality*

comparcō, comparsī (comper-
sī), comparsŭm, comparcĕ-
rĕ, *to save*

pungō, pŭpŭgī, punctŭm, pun-
gĕrĕ, *to pierce*

punctŭm, -ī (n.), *a point*

pŭgĭŏ, -ōnĭs (m.), *a dagger*

compungō, compunxī, com-
punctŭm, compungĕrĕ, *to
prick severely*

interpungō, interpunxī, inter-
punctŭm, interpungĕrĕ, *to
punctuate*

interpunctĭŏ, -ōnĭs (f.), *punc-
tuation*

tangō, tĕtĭgī, tactŭm, tangĕrĕ,
to touch

tactŭs, -ūs (m.), *touch*

attingō, attĭgī, attactŭm, at-
tingĕrĕ, *to touch*

contingō, contĭgī, contactŭm,
contingĕrĕ, *to touch*

contingĭt ⎱ *it happens*
obtingĭt ⎰

contāgĭŏ, -ōnĭs (f.), *a contact,
infection*

contāmĭnārĕ, *to stain*

intactŭs, -ă, -ŭm, *untouched*

intĕgĕr,-ră,-rŭm, *untouched,
entire*

intĕgrĭtās, -ātĭs (f.), *integrity*

intĕgrārĕ ⎱ *to renew*
rĕdintĕgrārĕ ⎰

pangō, panxī, panctŭm, pan-
gĕrĕ, *to drive in*

pangō, pĕpĭgī, pactŭm, pan-
gĕrĕ, *to bargain*

pactĭŏ, -ōnĭs (f.) ⎱ *an agree-
pactŭm, -ī (n.) ⎰ ment*

pax, pācĭs (f.), *peace*

pācārĕ, *to pacify*

pāgŭs, -ī (m.), *a district, country*

pāgānŭs, -ī (m.), *a countryman*

pāgĭnă, -ae (f.), *a page*, or *leaf*

compingō, compēgī, compac-
tŭm, compingĕrĕ, *to join together*

compāgēs, -ĭs (f.), *a joint*

impingō, impēgī, impactŭm,
impingĕrĕ, *to push at*

B. The Stem-Vowel is lengthened.

ăgō, ēgī, actŭm, ăgĕrĕ, *to drive,
do*

actĭŏ, -ōnĭs (f.), *a doing*

actŭs, -ūs (m.), *an act*

actŏr, -ōrĭs (m.), *a doer*

actă, -ōrŭm (n. pl.), *records*

ăgĭlĭs, -ĕ, *nimble*

ăgĭlĭtās, -ātĭs (f.), *nimbleness*

ăgĭtārĕ, *to drive at*

exăgĭtārĕ, *to stir up*

agmĕn, -ĭnĭs (n.), *a train,
an army*

ăbĭgō, ăbēgī, ăbactŭm, ăbĭ-
gĕrĕ, *to drive away*

ăbĭgĕātŭs,–ūs (m.), *cattle stealing*
ădĭgō, ădēgī, ădactŭm, ădīgĕrĕ, *to drive to*
cĭrcŭmägĕrĕ, *to turn around*
ambĭgō, (without Perf. & Sup.), ambĭgĕrĕ, *to contend*
ambĭgŭŭs, –ă, –ŭm, *moving to both sides*
ambĭgŭītăs, –ātĭs (f.), *double sense*
ambăgēs, –ŭm (f. pl.), *a round about way*
cōgō, cŏēgī, cŏactŭm, cōgĕrĕ, *to drive together; to compel*
cŏactŏr, –ōrĭs (m.), *a collector*
cōgĭtārĕ, *to think*
cōgĭtātĭŏ, –ōnĭs (f.), *a thought*
excōgĭtārĕ, *to think out*
dēgō (dē–ăgō), dēgī, (without Sup.), dēgĕrĕ, *to spend, pass*
exĭgō, exēgī, exactŭm, exĭgĕrĕ, *to drive off, demand*
exactŭs, –ă, –ŭm, *precise*
exactĭŏ, –ōnĭs (f.), *a driving out, exacting*
exactŏr, –ōrĭs (m.), *a collector*
exāmĕn, –ĭnĭs (n.), *a swarm; the tongue of a balance*
exāmĭnārĕ, *to weigh*
pĕrăgĕrĕ, *to finish*
rĕdĭgō, rĕdēgī, rĕdactŭm, rĕdĭgĕrĕ, *to bring back*
prōdĭgŭs, –ă, –ŭm, *wasteful*
sŭbĭgō, sŭbēgī, sŭbactŭm, sŭbĭgĕrĕ, *to subdue*
transĭgō, transēgī, transactŭm, transĭgĕrĕ, *to accomplish*

frangō, frēgī, fractŭm, frangĕrĕ, *to break*
frăgĭlĭs, –ĕ, *easily broken*

frăgĭlĭtăs, –ātĭs (f.), *fragility*
frăgŏr, –ōrĭs (m.), *a breaking*
fragmentŭm, –ī (n.), *a piece*
anfractŭs, –ūs (m.), *a turning*
confringō, confrēgī, confractŭm, confringĕrĕ, *to break in two*
dēfringō, dēfrēgī, dēfractŭm, dēfringĕrĕ, *to break off*
perfringō, perfrēgī, perfractŭm, perfringĕrĕ, *to shiver*
praefringō, praefrēgī, praefractŭm, praefringĕrĕ, *to break to pieces*
effringō, effrēgī, effractŭm, effringĕrĕ, *to break open*
rĕfringō, rĕfrēgī, rĕfractŭm, rĕfringĕrĕ, *to break up*

lĕgō, lēgī, lectŭm, lĕgĕrĕ, *to read*
lectĭŏ, –ōnĭs (f.), *reading*
lectŏr, –ōrĭs (m.), *a reader*
lectĭtārĕ, *to read often*
perlĕgĕrĕ, *to read through, to read aloud*
praelĕgĕrĕ, *to read to others*
rĕlĕgĕrĕ, *to go over again*
collĭgō, collēgī, collectŭm, collĭgĕrĕ, *to collect*
dēlĭgō, dēlēgī, dēlectŭm, dēlĭgĕrĕ, *to choose*   [levy
dēlectŭs, –ūs (m.), *a choice, a*
ēlĭgō, ēlēgī, ēlectŭm, ēlĭgĕrĕ, *to elect*
ēlĕgans, –tĭs, *choice*
ēlĕgantĕr, *elegantly*
ēlĕgantĭă, –ae (f.), *elegance*
sēlĭgō, sēlēgī, sēlectŭm, sēlĭgĕrĕ, *to select*
dīlĭgō, dīlexī, dīlectŭm, dīlĭgĕrĕ, *to love*
dīlĭgens, –tĭs, *careful*

dĭlĭgentĕr, *carefully*
dĭlĭgentĭă, -ae (f.), *care*
nĕglĕgō, nĕglexĭ, nĕglectŭm, nĕglĕgĕrĕ, *not to care for, to neglect*
nĕglĕgentĭă, -ae (f.), *carelessness*
intellĕgō, intellexĭ, intellectŭm, intellĕgĕrĕ, *to perceive*
intellĕgentĭă,-ae (f.)) *under-*
intellectŭs,-ūs (m.),) *standing*

vincō, vīcĭ, victŭm, vincĕrĕ, *to conquer*
victŏr, -ōrĭs (m.), *a conqueror*
victŏr, -ōrĭs (adj.), *victorious*
victrix, -īcĭs (f.), *a conqueress*
victōrĭă, -ae (f.), *a victory*
dēvincĕrĕ, *to conquer completely*

convincĕrĕ) *to convict*
ēvincĕrĕ)
pervincĕrĕ, *to carry a point*
pervĭcax, -ācĭs, *obstinate*
pervĭcācĭă, -ae (f.), *obstinacy*
rĕvincĕrĕ, *to refute*
invictŭs,-ă,-ŭm, *unconquered*

linquō, līquĭ, (**without Sup.**), linquĕrĕ, *to leave*
dēlinquō, dēlīquĭ, dēlictŭm, dēlinquĕrĕ, *to commit a fault*
dēlictŭm, -ī (n.), *an offense*
rĕlinquō, rĕlīquĭ, rĕlictŭm, rĕlinquĕrĕ, *to leave behind*
dērēlinquō, dērēlīquĭ, dērēlictŭm, dērēlinquĕrĕ, *to abandon*
rĕlīquŭs, -ă, -ŭm, *remaining*
rĕlīquĭae, -ārŭm (f. pl.), *relics*

Perfect sī, Supine sŭm.

mergō, mersĭ, mersŭm, mergĕrĕ, *to dip in*
ēmergĕrĕ, *to rise up*
dēmergĕrĕ)
immergĕrĕ) *to dip under*
submergĕrĕ)

spargō, sparsĭ, sparsŭm, spargĕrĕ, *to strew*
aspergō, aspersĭ, aspersŭm, aspergĕrĕ, *to scatter*

conspergō, conspersĭ, conspersŭm, conspergĕrĕ, *to sprinkle*
inspergō, inspersĭ, inspersŭm, inspergĕrĕ, *to scatter upon*
respergō, respersĭ,respersŭm, respergĕrĕ, *to besprinkle*
dispergō, dispersĭ, dispersŭm, dispergĕrĕ, *to scatter about*

vergō, (**without Perf. & Sup.**), vergĕrĕ, *to incline towards*

6. Verbs in lō, mō, nō, rō.

cōmō, compsĭ, comptŭm, cōmĕrĕ, *to adorn*
dēmō, dempsĭ, demptŭm, dēmĕrĕ, *to take away*

prōmō, prompsĭ, promptŭm, prōmĕrĕ, *to bring out*
dēprōmĕrĕ) *to draw out*
exprōmĕrĕ)

promptŭs, -ă, -ŭm, *brave*
promptē, *readily*

sūmŏ, sumpsī, sumptŭm, sū-
mĕrĕ, *to take*

sumptŭs, -ûs (m.), *expense*
sumptŭŏsŭs, -ă, -ŭm, *costly*
absûmĕrĕ)
consûmĕrĕ } *to consume*
insûmĕrĕ)
assûmĕrĕ, *to take in addition*

temnō, (**without Perf. & Sup.**), tem-
nĕrĕ, *to slight* (**poet.**)

contemnō, contempsī, contemp-
tŭm, contemnĕrĕ, *to de-
spise*

contemptĭŏ, -ōnīs (f.) } *con-
contemptŭs, -ûs (m.) } tempt*

contemptŏr, -ōrīs (m.), *a de-
spiser*

contemptĭm, *with contempt*

Aooording to the analogy of the Second Conjugation.

ălŏ, ălûī, (ălĭtŭm) altŭm, ălĕrĕ,
to nourish

ălumnŭs, -ī (m.), *a pupil*
ălĭmentŭm, -ī (n.), *nourishment*
almŭs, -ă, -ŭm, *bountiful*
altŏr, -ōrīs (m.), *a nourisher*
altŭs, -ă, -ŭm, *high*
altĭtudŏ, -ĭnīs (f.), *height*
altŭm, -ī (n.), *a height*

cŏlŏ, cŏlûī, cultŭm, cŏlĕrĕ, *to
till, care for*

cŏlŏnŭs,-ī (m.), *a husbandman*
cŏlŏnĭă, -ae (f.), *a settlement*
cultŏr, -ōrīs (m.), *a planter*
cultŭs, -ûs (m.) }
cultûră, -ae (f.) } *culture*
cultĕr, -rī (m.), *a plowshare,
knife*
ăgrĭcŏlă, -ae (m.), *a farmer*
ăgrĭcultûră,-ae(f.),*agriculture*
accŏlĕrĕ, *to dwell by*
accŏlă, -ae (m.), *a neighbor*
excŏlĕrĕ, *to improve*
incŏlĕrĕ, *to inhabit*
incŏlă, -ae (m.), *an inhabitant*
incultŭs, -ă, -ŭm, *untilled*
incultē, *roughly*

consŭlŏ, consŭlûī, consultŭm,
consŭlĕrĕ, *to ask advice*

consultŏ, *deliberately*
consultârĕ, *to consult*
consultâtĭŏ, -ōnīs (f.), *a con-
sultation*
consŭl, -īs (m.), *a consul*
consĭlĭŭm, -ī (n.), *counsel*

mŏlŏ, mŏlûī, mŏlĭtŭm, mŏlĕrĕ,
to grind

mŏlă, -ae (f.), *a mill*
mŏlârīs, -- (m.), *a millstone; a
grinder*

occŭlŏ, occŭlûī, occultŭm, occŭ-
lĕrĕ, *to hide*

occultă, -ōrŭm (n. pl.), *secrets*
occultē, *secretly*
occultârĕ, *to hide*
occultâtĭŏ, -ōnīs (f.), *a hiding*
occultâtŏr, -ōrīs (m.), *a con-
cealer*

frĕmŏ, frĕmûī, frĕmĭtŭm, frĕ-
mĕrĕ, *to growl, murmur*

frĕmĭtŭs, -ûs (m.), *a murmur-
ing*

gĕmō, gĕmŭī, (gĕmĭtŭm), gĕ-
mĕrĕ, to sigh

gĕmĭtŭs, -ŭs (m.), a sigh
congĕmĕrĕ, (without Sup.), to
bewail
ingĕmĕrĕ, (without Sup.), to wail

trĕmō, trĕmŭī, (without Sup.),
trĕmĕrĕ, to tremble

trĕmŏr, -ŏrĭs (m.), a trembling
contrĕmĕrĕ, to tremble all over
trĕmendŭs, -ă, -ŭm, frightful
trĕmĕbundŭs, -ă, -ŭm, trembling

vŏmō, vŏmŭī, vŏmĭtŭm, vŏmĕrĕ,
to throw up, vomit
vŏmĭtĭŏ, -ōnĭs (f.)) vomiting
vŏmĭtŭs, -ŭs (m.))
ĕvŏmĕrĕ, to spew out
ignĭvŏmŭs, -ă, -ŭm, vomiting
fire

gignō, gĕnŭī, gĕnĭtŭm, gignĕrĕ,
to beget, bring forth

gĕnĭtŏr, -ŏrĭs (m.), a parent
gĕnŭs, -ĕrĭs (n.), a kind, race
gĕnĕrārĕ, to produce
gĕnĕrātĭm, by kinds
gĕnĕrōsŭs, -ă, -ŭm, of noble
birth
dēgĕnĕr, -ĭs, degenerate
gens, -tĭs (f.), a tribe, clan
gentīlĭs, - (m. & f.), a person
belonging to the same clan
ingignĕrĕ, to implant
gĕnĭŭs, -ī (m.), a genius
ingĕnĭŭm, -ī (n.), natural
capacity
ingĕnĭōsŭs, -ă, -ŭm, gifted
with genius

ingĕnŭŭs, -ă, -ŭm, free-born
ingĕnŭĕ, frankly
ingĕnŭĭtās, -ātĭs (f.), noble-
mindedness
prōgignĕrĕ, to bring forth
prōgĕnĭēs, -ēī (f.), offspring

pōnō, pŏsŭī, pŏsĭtŭm, pōnĕrĕ,
to put
antĕpōnĕrĕ, to prefer
appōnĕrĕ, to put near
compōnĕrĕ, to join together
compŏsĭtĭŏ, -ōnĭs (f.), a draw-
ing up, composition
compŏsĭtē, in good order
dēpōnĕrĕ, to lay down
dispōnĕrĕ, to set in order
dispŏsĭtĭŏ, -ōnĭs (f.), disposi-
expōnĕrĕ, to expose [tion
expŏsĭtĭŏ, -ōnĭs (f.), exposition
oppōnĕrĕ, to oppose
oppŏsĭtĭŏ, -ōnĭs (f.), opposition
postpōnĕrĕ, to postpone [fer
praepōnĕrĕ, to set before, pre-
praepŏsĭtĭŏ, -ōnĭs (f.), a prep-
osition
prōpōnĕrĕ, to lay before
prōpŏsĭtŭm, -ī (n.), a purpose
prōpŏsĭtĭŏ, -ōnĭs (f.), a sentence
rĕpōnĕrĕ, to replace
sēpōnĕrĕ, to lay apart
suppōnĕrĕ, to put in the place
of another

[cellō, impel]
celsŭs, -ă, -ŭm) high
excelsŭs, -ă, -ŭm)
excellentĭă, -ae (f.), superiority
antĕcellĕrĕ) without Perf. & Sup.,
excellĕrĕ) to excel
praecellĕrĕ)
percellō, percŭlī, perculsŭm,
percellĕrĕ, to beat down

With Reduplication.

cănō, cĕcĭnī, cantŭm, cănĕrĕ, to sing, sound

cantārĕ } to sing
cantĭtārĕ }

cănōrŭs, -ă, -ŭm, melodious

cantŭs, -ūs (m.), singing

cantĭcŭm, -ī (n.), a song

cantŏr, -ōrĭs (m.), a singer

cantĭlēnă, -ae (f.), a sing-song

carmĕn, -ĭnĭs (n.), a song

concĭnō, concĭnŭī, concentŭm, concĭnĕrĕ, to sound together

concentŭs, -ūs (m.), harmony

tūbĭcĕn, -ĭnĭs (m.), a trumpeter

tĭbĭcĕn, -ĭnĭs (m.), a fluteplayer

currō, cŭcurrī, cursŭm, currĕrĕ, to run

cursŭs, -ūs (m.), a running

currŭs, -ūs (m.), a chariot

currĭcŭlŭm, -ī (n.), a course, career

cursŏr, -ōrĭs (m.), a runner

cursārĕ, to run hither and thither

Without reduplication:

accurrĕrĕ, to run to

dēcurrĕrĕ, to run down

concurrĕrĕ, to run together

discurrĕrĕ, to run to and fro

excurrĕrĕ, to run out

incurrĕrĕ, to run upon

occurrĕrĕ, to meet

percurrĕrĕ, to run over

prōcurrĕrĕ, to run forth

rĕcurrĕrĕ, to run back

transcurrĕrĕ, to run past

succurrĕrĕ, to succor

concursŭs, -ūs (m.), a running together

dēcursĭō, -ōnĭs (f.) } a maneuvre
dēcursŭs, -ūs (m.) }

excursĭō, -ōnĭs (f.) } a sally
excursŭs, -ūs (m.) }

incursĭō, -ōnĭs (f.), an assault

fallō, fĕfellī, falsŭm, fallĕrĕ, to deceive

falsŭs, -ă, -ŭm, false

falsŭm, -ī (n.), falsehood

falsō, untruly

fallax, -ācĭs, deceitful

fallācĭtĕr, deceitfully

fallācĭă, -ae (f.), deceit

rĕfellō, rĕfellī, (without Sup.), rĕfellĕrĕ, to refute

pellō, pĕpŭlī, pulsŭm, pellĕrĕ, to drive away

pulsŭs, -ūs (m.), a push

pulsārĕ, to push

prōpulsārĕ, to ward off

Without reduplication :

appellĕrĕ, to land

compellĕrĕ, to compel

dēpellĕrĕ, to drive away

expellĕrĕ, to drive out

impellĕrĕ, to impel

perpellĕrĕ, to drive

prōpellĕrĕ, to drive forward

rĕpellĕrĕ, to drive back

impulsĭō, -ōnĭs (f.), influence

rĕpulsă, -ae (f.), a rejection

cernō, (crēvī, crētŭm), cernĕrĕ,
to sift; to see

Only the following compounds are
used in the Perfect & Supine:
dēcernĕrĕ, to determine
discernĕrĕ, to distinguish
sēcernĕrĕ, to put apart

certŭs, -ă, -ŭm, certain
incertŭs, -ă, -ŭm, uncertain
certārĕ, to fight
certātĭm, eagerly
certāmĕn, -ĭnĭs (n.), a contest
concertārĕ, to debate
dēcertārĕ, to fight it out
dēcrētŭm, -ī (n.), a decree
discrīmĕn, -ĭnĭs (n.), a differ-
sēcrētō, secretly   [ence

līnō, lēvī, lĭtŭm, lĭnĕrĕ, to smear
lĭtūră, -ae (f.), an erasure
allĭnĕrĕ, to besmear
illĭnĕrĕ, to bedaub
perlĭnĕrĕ, to smear all over
ŏblĭnĕrĕ, to smear over

sĭnō, sīvī, sĭtŭm, sĭnĕrĕ, to let,
suffer
dēsĭnō, dēsĭvī & dēsĭī, dēsĭ-
tŭm, dēsĭnĕrĕ, to leave off

spernō, sprēvī, sprētŭm, sper-
nĕrĕ, to despise

sternō, strāvī, strātŭm, ster-
nĕrĕ, to spread out
strātŭm, -ī (n.), a bed
strāmentŭm, -ī (n.), straw
strāgēs, -ĭs (f.), a massacre
strāgŭlŭm, -ī (n.), a carpet

consternĕrĕ, to bestrew
consternārĕ, to alarm
consternātŭs, -ă, -ŭm, alarmed
prosternĕrĕ, to throw to the
ground
substernĕrĕ, to spread under-
neath

sĕrō, sēvī, sătŭm, sĕrĕrĕ, to sow
sēmĕn, -ĭnĭs (n.), seed
sēmentĭs, - (f.), a seeding
sĕgĕs, -ĕtĭs (f.), a crop
consĕrō, consēvī, consĭtŭm,
consĕrĕrĕ, to plant
insĕrō, insēvī, insĭtŭm, insĕ-
rĕrĕ, to plant in
dissēmĭnārĕ, to spread abroad
sătŭs, -ūs (m.) } a sowing
sătĭŏ, -ōnĭs (f.) }
sătŏr, -ōrĭs (m.), a sower

sĕrō, sĕrŭī, sertŭm, sĕrĕrĕ, to
join, connect
sertă, -ōrŭm (n. pl.),garlands
sĕrĭēs, -ēī (f.), a row
sermō, -ōnĭs (m.), speech
consĕrō, consĕrŭī, consertŭm,
consĕrĕrĕ, to connect
dēsĕrō, dēsĕrŭī, dēsertŭm, dē-
sĕrĕrĕ, to forsake
dēsertŏr, -ōrĭs (m.), a deserter
dēsertŭm, -ī (n.), a desert
dissĕrō, dissĕrŭī, dissertŭm,
dissĕrĕrĕ, to speak of
dīsertŭs, -ă, -ŭm, skillful in
speaking
dissertātĭŏ, -ōnĭs (f.), a dis-
course
insĕrō, insĕrŭī, insertŭm, in-
sĕrĕrĕ, to insert
praesertĭm, especially

tĕrō, trīvī, trītŭm, tĕrĕrĕ, to rub

tĕrĕs, –ĕtĭs, smooth

contĕrĕrĕ, to rub off

dĕtĕrĕrĕ, to wear away, weaken

dĕtĕrĭŏr, –ŭs, worse

dētrĭmentŭm, –ī (n.), damage

obtĕrĕrĕ, to break to pieces

trībŭlŭm, –ī (n.), a threshing-sled

tĕrĕbrā, –ae (f.), a borer

trītŭs, –ă, –ŭm, common-place

Various Irregularities.

vellō, vellī (vulsī), vulsŭm, vel-lĕrĕ, to pluck, pull

vellĭcārĕ, to twitch

āvellĕrĕ, to tear off

convellĕrĕ, to pull up

ēvellĕrĕ, to pull out

dēvellĕrĕ, to tear in pieces

psallō, psallī, (withoṳt Sṳp.), psal-lĕrĕ, to play on a stringed instrument

psaltrĭā, –ae (f.), a lutist

ĕmō, ĕmī, emptŭm, ĕmĕrĕ, to buy

emptĭō, –ōnĭs (f.), a purchase

emptŏr, –ōrĭs (m.), a buyer

cŏĕmĕrĕ, to buy together

rĕdĭmĕrĕ, to buy back

rĕdemptŏr, –ōrĭs (m.), a con-tractor

ădīmō, ădēmī, ădemptŭm, ădī-mĕrĕ, to take away

dīrĭmō, dīrēmī, dīremptŭm, dīrĭmĕrĕ, to separate

exīmō, exēmī, exemptŭm, ex-īmĕrĕ, to take out

exĭmĭŭs, –ă, –ŭm, choice

exemplŭm –ī (n.), an example

exemplăr, –ārĭs (n.), a pattern

ĭntĕrĭmō, ĭntĕrēmī, ĭntĕremp-tŭm, ĭntĕrĭmĕrĕ, to slay, kill

pĕrĭmō, pĕrēmī, pĕremptŭm, pĕrĭmĕrĕ, to slay, kill

prĕmō, pressī, pressŭm, prĕ-mĕrĕ, to press

pressē, with pressure, violently

comprĭmō, compressī, com-pressŭm, comprĭmĕrĕ, to press together

dēprĭmō, dēpressī, dēpressŭm, dēprĭmĕrĕ, to press down

exprĭmō, expressī, expres-sŭm, exprĭmĕrĕ, to press out

expressŭs, –ă, –ŭm, clear

opprĭmō, oppressī, oppres-sŭm, opprĭmĕrĕ, to put down

oppressŏr, –ōrĭs (m.), a de-stroyer

oppressĭō, –ōnĭs (f.), an over-throw

supprĭmō, suppressī, suppres-sŭm, supprĭmĕrĕ, to keep back

suppressĭō, –ōnĭs (f.), embezzle-ment

gĕrō, gessī, gestŭm, gĕrĕrĕ, to carry, manage

gestārĕ, to bear

gestŭs, –ŭs (m.), carriage

gestīrĕ, to exult

gestĭō, –ōnĭs (f.), a performing

rēs gestă, rĕī –ae (f.), a deed

gĕrundĭŭm, –ī (n.), a gerund

aggĕrĕrĕ, *to carry to*
aggĕr, -ĭs (m.), *a dike*
congĕrĕrĕ, *to bring together*
congestŭs, -ŭs (m.), *a bring-*
ing together
dīgĕrĕrĕ, *to arrange*
ēgĕrĕrĕ, *to carry out*
ingĕrĕrĕ, *to carry into*
suggĕrĕrĕ, *to afford, suggest*
suggestŭm, -ī (n.) } *a plat-*
suggestŭs, -ŭs (m.) } *form*

ūrō, ussī, ustŭm, ūrĕrĕ, *to burn*
ădūrĕrĕ, *to burn*
combūrĕrĕ, *to consume by fire*
exūrĕrĕ, *to burn out*
inūrĕrĕ, *to burn in*
ambustŭs, -ă, -ŭm, *singed*
sēmĭustŭs, -ă, -ŭm, *half-burnt*

verrō, verrī, versŭm, verrĕrĕ,
to sweep out

quaerō, quaesīvī, quaesītŭm,
quaerĕrĕ, *to seek*
quaestĭŏ,-ōnĭs (f.), *an inquiry*
quaestŭs, -ŭs (m.), *gain*
quaestŭōsŭs, -ă, -ŭm, *gainful*
acquīrō, acquīsīvī, acquīsītŭm,
acquīrĕrĕ, *to acquire*
anquīrō, anquīsīvī, anquīsītŭm,
anquīrĕrĕ, *to search after*
conquīrō, conquīsīvī, conquīsī-
tŭm, conquīrĕrĕ, *to seek for*
exquīrō, exquīsīvī, exquīsī-
tŭm, exquīrĕrĕ, *to inquire*
conquīsītĭŏ, -ōnĭs (f.), *a levy*
conquīsītŏr, -ōrĭs (m.), *a re-*
cruiting officer
inquīrō, inquīsīvī, inquīsītŭm,
inquīrĕrĕ, *to inquire*

inquīsītĭŏ, -ōnĭs (f.), *a search-*
ing into
inquīsītŏr, -ōrĭs (m.), *a detect-*
ive
perquīrō, perquīsīvī, perquīsī-
tŭm, perquīrĕrĕ, *to search*
thoroughly
rĕquīrō, rĕquīsīvī, rĕquīsītŭm,
rĕquīrĕrĕ, *to miss*
rĕquīsītŭm, -ī (n.), *a want*
rĕquīsītĭŏ,-ōnĭs (f.), *an exami-*
nation

fūrō, (without Perf. & Sup.), fūrĕrĕ,
to rage
fūrŏr, -ōrĭs (m.), *rage*
fūrĭae, -ārŭm (f. pl.), *fury*
Fūrĭae, -ārŭm (f. pl.), *the*
Furies
fūrĭbundŭs, -ă, -ŭm } *raging*
fūrĭōsŭs, -ă, -ŭm }

fĕrō, tŭlī, lātŭm, ferrĕ, *to bear,*
carry
fĕrĕtrŭm, -ī (n.), *a bier*
fercŭlŭm, -ī (n.), *a litter*
fĕrax, -ācĭs } *fruitful*
fertĭlĭs, -ĕ }
fertĭlĭtās, -ātĭs (f.), *fertility*
affĕrō, attŭlī, allātŭm, affer-
rĕ, *to bring to*
aufĕrō, abstŭlī, ablātŭm, aufer-
rĕ, *to carry off*
ablātīvŭs, -ī (m.), *the ablative*
case
confĕrō, contŭlī, collātŭm, con-
ferrĕ, *to bring together*
collātĭŏ, -ōnĭs (f.), *a collecting*
dĕfĕrō, dĕtŭlī, dēlātŭm, defer-
rĕ, *to bring*
dēlātĭŏ, -ōnĭs (f.), *a denunci-*
ation

dēlătŏr, -ōrĭs (m.), *an informer*

differō, distŭlĭ, dīlătŭm, differrĕ, *to put off, to differ*

dīlātĭŏ, -ōnĭs (f.), *a delaying*

diffĕrentĭă, -ae (f.), *a difference*

dīlătărĕ, *to spread out*

effĕrō, extŭlĭ, ēlātŭm, efferrĕ, *to bring out*

ēlātŭs, -ă, -ŭm, *exalted*

infĕrō, intŭlĭ, illătŭm, inferrĕ, *to bring into*

offĕrō, obtŭlĭ, oblătŭm, offerrĕ, *to present, offer*

perfĕrō, pertŭlĭ, perlătŭm, perferrĕ, *to carry through*

praefĕrō, praetŭlĭ, praelătŭm, praeferrĕ, *to carry before, prefer*

prōfĕrō, prōtŭlĭ, prōlătŭm, prōferrĕ, *to bring forth; to put off*

prōlātĭŏ, -ōnĭs (f.), *a putting off*

rĕfĕrō, rĕtŭlĭ, rĕlătŭm, rĕferrĕ, *to bring back; to report*

rĕlātĭŏ, -ōnĭs (f.), *a report*

rĕlātŏr, -ōrĭs (m.), *a reporter*

suffĕrō, (sustŭlĭ, sublătŭm), sufferrĕ, *to endure*

transfĕrō, transtŭlĭ, translătŭm, transferrĕ, *to bring over*

translātĭŏ, -ōnĭs (f.), *a transferring*

translātŏr, -ōrĭs (m.), *a transferrer*

translātīvŭs, -ă, -ŭm, *translative*

trălātīcĭŭs,-ă,-ŭm, *customary*

7. Verbs in sŏ, xŏ.

depsō, depsŭĭ, depstŭm, depsĕrĕ, *to knead*

pinsō, pinsŭĭ & pinsĭ, pinsĭtŭm & pistŭm, pinsĕrĕ, *to pound, grind*

pistŏr -ōrĭs, (m.), *a baker*

pistrīnŭm, -ī (n.), *a pounding-mill*

vīsō, vīsĭ, (without Sup.), vīsĕrĕ, *to visit*

invīsĕrĕ, *to go to see*

vīsĭtărĕ, *to visit*

texō, texŭĭ, textŭm, texĕrĕ, *to weave*

textŏr, -ōrĭs (m.), *a weaver*

textĭlĭs, -ĕ, *woven*

textĭlĕ, -ĭs (n.), *a fabric*

textrīnă, -ae (f.), *a weaver's shop*

praetexĕrĕ, *to fringe*

praetextă, -ae (f.), *a toga bordered with purple*

praetextătŭs,_-ī (m.), *a Roman boy*

praetextŭm,-ī (n.), *a pretence*

attexĕrĕ, *to weave to*

contexĕrĕ, *to weave together*

intexĕrĕ, *to weave into*

rĕtexĕrĕ, *to unweave*

contextŭs, -ŭs (m.), *connection*

According to the analogy of the Fourth Conjugation.

arcessō (accersō), arcessīvī, arcessītŭm, arcessĕrĕ, to summon

căpessō, căpessīvī, căpessītŭm, căpessĕrĕ, to lay hold of; to manage

făcessō, făcessīvī, făcessītŭm, făcessĕrĕ, to accomplish

lăcessō, lăcessīvī, lăcessītŭm, lăcessĕrĕ, to excite

incessō, incessīvī (incessī), (without Sup.), incessĕrĕ, to fall upon

8. Verbs in scō.

Verbal Inceptives from Obsolete Primitives.

crescō, crēvī, crētŭm, crescĕrĕ, to grow

accrescĕrĕ ⎱ to increase
increscĕrĕ ⎰

concrescĕrĕ, to grow together
concrētŭs, -ă, -ŭm, condensed
concrētiŏ, -ōnis (f.), matter
dēcrescĕrĕ, to decrease
succrescĕrĕ, to grow

noscō, nōvī, nōtŭm, noscĕrĕ, to become acquainted with

nōtŭs, -ă, -ŭm, known
ignōtŭs, -ă, -ŭm ⎱ un-
incognĭtŭs, -ă, -ŭm ⎰ known
nōtiŏ, -ōnis (f.), an idea
nōtĭtiă, -ae (f.), knowledge
nōtă, -ae (f.), a mark
nōtārĕ, to mark
nōtăbĭlis, -ĕ, remarkable
nōbĭlis, -ĕ, noble
nōbĭlĭtās, -ātis (f.), nobility
ignōbĭlis, -ĕ, of low birth
ignōbĭlĭtās, -ātis (f.), low birth
nōbĭlĭtārĕ, to render famous
nōmĕn, -ĭnis (n.), a name
nōmĭnārĕ, to call by name
nōmĭnātĭm, by name

cognōmĕn, -ĭnis (n.), a surname
praenōmĕn, -ĭnis (n.), the first name
ignōmĭniă, -ae (f.), dishonor
ignōmĭniōsŭs, -ă, -ŭm, shameful
ignoscĕrĕ, (without Sup.), to pardon
dignoscĕrĕ ⎱ (without Sup.),
internoscĕrĕ ⎰ to distinguish
agnoscō, agnōvī, agnĭtŭm, agnoscĕrĕ, to acknowledge
cognoscō, cognōvī, cognĭtŭm, cognoscĕrĕ, to know
rĕcognoscō, rĕcognōvī, rĕcognĭtŭm, rĕcognoscĕrĕ, to know again
cognĭtiŏ, -ōnis (f.), an inquiry
cognĭtŏr, -ōris (m.), an advocate

pascō, pāvī, pastŭm, pascĕrĕ, to drive to pasture, to feed

pastŭs, -ūs (m.), pasture
pastŏr, -ōris (m.), a herdsman
pascŭă, -ōrŭm (n. pl.), a pasture
dēpascĕrĕ, to feed upon

quĭescŏ, quĭēvĭ, quĭētŭm, quĭe-
scĕrĕ, *to rest*

quĭētŭs, -ă, -ŭm, *quiet*
inquĭētŭs, -ă, -ŭm, *restless*
quĭēs, -ētĭs (f.), *rest*
rĕquĭēs,-ētĭs & -ĕĭ (f.), *repose*
acquĭescĕrĕ, *to become quiet*
conquĭescĕrĕ, *to take rest*
rĕquĭescĕrĕ, *to repose*

suescŏ, suēvĭ, suētŭm, suescĕrĕ,
to become used

assuescĕrĕ ⎰ *to be accustom-*
consuescĕrĕ ⎱   *ed to*
assuētŭs, -ă,-ŭm, *accustomed*
insuētŭs, -ă, -ŭm, *unaccus-
tomed*
assuĕfăcĕrĕ (ĭō), *to accustom*
dĕsuĕfactŭs, -ă, -ŭm, *disused*
consuētŭdŏ, -ĭnĭs (f.), *custom*

compescŏ, compescŭĭ, **(without
Sup.)**, compescĕrĕ, *to restrain*
compēs, -ĕdĭs (f.), *a fetter*

discŏ, dĭdĭcĭ, **(without Sup.)**, di-
scĕrĕ, *to learn*

discĭpŭlŭs, -ĭ (m.), *a scholar*
condiscĭpŭlŭs, -ĭ (m.), *a schoolmate*
discĭplīnă,-ae (f.), *instruction*
addiscĕrĕ, *to learn further*
dĕdiscĕrĕ, *to unlearn*
ĕdiscĕrĕ, *to learn by heart*
perdiscĕrĕ, *to learn thoroughly*

poscŏ, pŏposcĭ, **(without Sup.)**,
poscĕrĕ, *to demand*

dĕposcĕrĕ, *to request*
exposcĕrĕ, *tò request earnestly*
rĕposcĕrĕ, **(without Perf. and
Sup.)**, *to demand back*
postŭlārĕ, *to demand*
postŭlātĭŏ,-ōnĭs (f.), *a demand*
expostŭlārĕ, *to complain*

gliscŏ, **(without Perf. and Sup.)**,
gliscĕrĕ, *to grow up*

Verbal Inceptives with the Perfect and Supine of their Primitives.

ăbŏlescŏ – ăbŏlĕŏ – ăbŏlēvĭ, ăbŏlĭtŭm, ăbŏlescĕrĕ, *to disap-
pear*

exŏlescŏ – exŏlĕŏ – exŏlēvĭ, exŏlētŭm, exŏlescĕrĕ, *to grow
out of use*

ădŏlescŏ – ădŏlĕŏ – ădŏlēvĭ, ădultŭm, ădŏlescĕrĕ, *to grow
up*

obsŏlescŏ – obsŏlĕŏ – obsŏlēvĭ,
obsŏlētŭm, obsŏlescĕrĕ, *to
become obsolete*

cŏălescŏ – ălŏ – cŏălŭĭ, cŏălĭtŭm,
cŏălescĕrĕ, *to grow together*

concŭpiscŏ – cŭpĭŏ – concŭpīvĭ,
concŭpītŭm, concŭpiscĕrĕ,
to covet

convălescŏ – vălĕŏ – convălŭĭ,
convălĭtŭm, convălescĕrĕ,
to recover

exardescŏ – ardĕŏ – exarsĭ, exar-
sŭm, exardescĕrĕ, *to take fire*

indŏlescŏ – dŏlĕŏ – indŏlŭĭ, indŏlĭ-
tŭm, indŏlescĕrĕ, *to feel pain*

invĕtĕrascō – invĕtĕrō – invĕtĕrāvī, invĕtĕrātŭm, invĕtĕrascĕrĕ, to grow old

obdormiscō – dormīō – obdormīvī, obdormītŭm, obdormiscĕrĕ, to fall asleep
ēdormiscĕrĕ, to sleep out

rĕvīviscō – vīvō – rĕvixī, rĕvictŭm, rĕvīviscĕrĕ, to come to life again

sciscō – scīō – scīvī, scītŭm, sciscĕrĕ, to enact, decree
plēbiscītŭm,-ī (n.)) a decree of
pŏpŭliscītŭm,-ī(n.)) the people

Verbal Inceptives with the Perfect of their Primitives.

ăcescō – ăcĕō – ăcŭī, ăcescĕrĕ, to turn sour
ăcīdŭs, -ă, -ŭm, sour
ăcētŭm, -ī (n.), vinegar

albescō, exalbescō – albĕō – exalbŭī, exalbescĕrĕ, to become white
albŭs, -ă, -ŭm, white

ārescō – ārĕō – ārŭī, ārescĕrĕ, to become dry
ārīdŭs, -ă, -ŭm, dry

călescō – călĕō – călŭī, călescĕrĕ, to become warm

cănescō – cănĕō – cănŭī, cănescĕrĕ, to become gray

contĭcescō – tăcĕō – contĭcŭī, contĭcescĕrĕ, to become still

contrĕmiscō – trĕmō – contrĕmŭī, contrĕmiscĕrĕ, to tremble

dēfervescō – fervĕō – dēfervī & dēferbŭī, dēfervescĕrĕ, to cease boiling

dēlĭtescō – lătĕō – dēlĭtŭī, dēlĭtescĕrĕ, to hide away

effervescō – fervĕō – effervī & efferbŭī, effervescĕrĕ, to boil up

excandescō – candĕō – excandŭī, excandescĕrĕ, to take fire

expăvescō – păvĕō – expăvī, expăvescĕrĕ, to become terrified

extĭmescō, pertĭmescō – tĭmĕō – extĭmŭī, extĭmescĕrĕ, to fear greatly

flōrescō – flōrĕō – flōrŭī, flōrescĕrĕ, to begin to blossom
dēflōrescĕrĕ, to fade
efflōrescĕrĕ, to bloom

haerescō – haerĕō – haesī, haerescĕrĕ, to stick
ădhaerescĕrĕ, to cleave to
ĭnhaerescĕrĕ, to stick fast

horrescŏ – horrĕŏ – horrŭī, hor-
rescĕre, *to become frightened*

exhorrescĕrĕ, *to tremble*

pĕrhorrescĕrĕ, *to tremble great-*
[*ly*

illŭcescŏ – lŭcĕŏ – luxī, illŭce-
scĕrĕ, *to grow light*

ingĕmiscŏ – gĕmŏ – ingĕmŭī, in-
gĕmīscĕrĕ, *to groan*

intŭmescŏ – tŭmĕŏ – intŭmŭī, in-
tŭmescĕrĕ, *to swell up*

languescŏ, ēlanguescŏ, rĕlan-
guescŏ – languĕŏ – langŭī,
languescĕrĕ, *to become faint*

līquescŏ –līquĕt, *it appears*– lī-
quī, līqaescĕrĕ, *to melt*

līquŏr, –ŏrīs (m.), *a fluid*
līquĭdŭs, –ă, –ŭm, *liquid*

mădescŏ – mădĕŏ – mădŭī, mă-
descĕrĕ, *to become wet*

mădĭdŭs, –ă, –ŭm, *wet*

marcescŏ – marcĕŏ – marcŭī,
marcescĕrĕ, *to wither*

ēmarcescĕrĕ, *to dwindle away*

obtorpescŏ – torpĕŏ – obtorpŭī,
obtorpescĕrĕ, *to become stiff*

occallescŏ – callĕŏ – occallŭī, oc-
callescĕrĕ, *to grow callous*

pallescŏ – pallĕŏ – pallŭī, palle-
scĕrĕ, *to turn pale*

pŭtescŏ –pŭtĕŏ– pŭtŭī, pŭte-
scĕrĕ, *to rot*

pŭtĭdŭs, –ă, –ŭm, *rotten*

pŭtrescŏ– pŭtrĕŏ– pŭtrŭī, pŭtre-
scĕrĕ, *to rot*

pŭtrĭdŭs, –ă, –ŭm, *rotten*

rĕfrĭgescŏ – frĭgĕŏ – rĕfrixī, rĕfrīgescĕrĕ, *to grow cold*

rĕsĭpiscŏ –săpĭŏ – rĕsĭpŭī, rĕsĭpi-
scĕrĕ, *to come to one's self*
again

rŭbescŏ, – rŭbĕŏ – rŭbŭī, rŭbe-
scĕrĕ, *to turn red*

ērŭbescĕrĕ, *to turn red*

sĕnescŏ, – sĕnĕŏ – sĕnŭī, sĕne-
scĕrĕ, *to grow old*

consĕnescĕrĕ, *to grow old to-*
gether

sĕnex, sĕnĭs (m.), *an old man*
sĕnectŭs, –ūtĭs (f.), *old age*

stŭpescŏ – stŭpĕŏ – stŭpŭī, stŭ-
pescĕrĕ, *to startle*

obstŭpescĕrĕ, *to be amazed*

tābescŏ – tābĕŏ – tābŭī, tābe-
scĕrĕ, *to waste away*

tābēs, –ĭs (f.), *consumption*

tĕpescŏ – tĕpĕŏ – tĕpŭī, tĕpĕ-
scĕrĕ, *to become lukewarm*

tĕpŏr, –ŏrĭs (m.), *a gentle*
warmth

tĕpĭdŭs, –ă, –ŭm, *lukewarm*

tŭmescŏ – tŭmĕŏ – tŭmŭī, tŭmescĕrĕ, *to swell up*

vĭrescŏ – vĭrĕŏ – vĭrŭī, vĭrescĕrĕ,
to grow strong, recover

Verbal Inceptives without Perfect and Supine.

hiscō – hiō – hiscĕrĕ, *to yawn*
hĭārĕ, *to gape*
hĭātŭs, – ūs (m.), *a cleft*

augescō – augēō – augescĕrĕ, *to augment*

flăvescō – flăvēō – flăvescĕrĕ, *to become yellow*

hĕbescō –hĕbĕō– hĕbescĕrĕ, *to grow dull*

Denominative Inceptives.

A. Without a Perfect.

aegrescō (aegĕr, *sick*), aegrescĕrĕ, *to fall sick*
aegrōtŭs, -ă, -ŭm, *sick*
aegrōtārĕ, *to be sick*
aegrĭtŭdŏ, -ĭnĭs (f.), *sorrow*

dĭtescō (dĭvĕs, *rich*), dĭtescĕrĕ, *to grow rich*
dĭvĭtĭae, -ārŭm (f. pl.), *riches*

dulcescō (dulcĭs, *sweet*), dulcescĕrĕ, *to become sweet*
dulcĕdŏ, -ĭnĭs (f.), *sweetness*

grandescō (grandĭs, *large*), grandescĕrĕ, *to grow large*

grăvescō, ingrăvescō (grăvĭs, *heavy*), grăvescĕrĕ, *to grow heavy*
grăvĭtās, -ātĭs (f.), *gravity*
grăvārĕ, *to load*

hĕbescō (hĕbĕs, *blunt*), hĕbĕscĕrĕ, *to grow blunt*

incurvescō (curvŭs, *crooked*), incurvescĕrĕ, *to become crooked*
curvārĕ, *to crook*

intĕgrascō (intĕgĕr, *fresh*), intĕgrascĕrĕ, *to break out afresh*

jŭvĕnescō (jŭvĕnĭs, *young*), jŭvĕnescĕrĕ, *to grow young*
jŭventŭs, -ūtĭs (f.), *youth*
jŭvĕnĭlĭs, -ĕ, *youthful*

mītescō (mītĭs, *mild*), mītescĕrĕ, *to become mild*
immītĭs, -ĕ, *hard*

mollescō (mollĭs, *soft*), mollescĕrĕ, *to grow soft*

pinguescō (pinguĭs, *fat*), pinguescĕrĕ, *to grow fat*

plŭmescō (plŭmă, *a feather*), plŭmescĕrĕ, *to get feathers*

pŭĕrascō, rĕpŭĕrascō (pŭĕr, *a child*), pŭĕrascĕrĕ, *to become a child*
pŭĕrĭlĭs, -ĕ, *childish*
pŭĕrĭtĭă, -ae (f.), *childhood*

stĕrĭlescō (stĕrĭlĭs, *unfruitful*), stĕrĭlescĕrĕ, *to become barren*
stĕrĭlĭtās, -ātĭs (f.), *sterility*

tĕnĕrescō, tĕnĕrascō (tĕnĕr, *tender*), tĕnĕrescĕrĕ, tĕnĕrascĕrĕ, *to grow tender*
tĕnĕrĭtās,-ātĭs (f.), *tenderness*

B. With a Perfect.

crēbrescō, incrēbrescō (crēber, frequent), crēbrŭĭ, crēbrescĕrĕ, to become frequent

percrēbrescĕrĕ, to be spread abroad

crēbrō, frequently

crēbrĭtās, -ātĭs (f.), frequency

dūrescō, obdūrescō (dūrŭs, hard), dūrŭĭ, dūrescĕrĕ, to grow hard

dūrārĕ, to harden

dūrĭtĭă, -ae (f.), hardness

ēvānescō (vānŭs, empty), ēvānŭĭ, ēvānescĕrĕ, to vanish, pass away

vānĭtās, -ātĭs (f.), vanity

innōtescō (nōtŭs, known), innōtŭĭ, innōtescĕrĕ, to become known

măcrescō (măcĕr, meager), măcrŭĭ, măcrescĕrĕ, to grow meager

măcĭēs, -ēī (f.), meagerness

mansuescō (mansuētŭs, tame), mansuēvī, mansuētŭm, mansuescĕrĕ, to grow tame

mansuētūdō, -ĭnĭs (f.), gentleness

mātūrescō (mātūrŭs, ripe), mātūrŭĭ, mātūrescĕrĕ, to ripen

mātūrĭtās, -ātĭs (f.), ripeness

mātūrārĕ, to make ripe

nĭgrescō (nĭgĕr, black), nĭgrŭĭ, nĭgrescĕrĕ, to become black

nĭgrŏr, -ōrĭs (m.), blackness

nĭgrārĕ, to blacken

obmūtescō (mūtŭs, dumb), obmūtŭĭ, obmūtescĕrĕ, to become dumb

obsurdescō (surdŭs, deaf), obsurdŭĭ, obsurdescĕrĕ, to become deaf

surdŭs, -ă, -ŭm, deaf

surdĭtās, -ātĭs (f.), deafness

rĕcrūdescō (crūdŭs, raw), rĕcrūdŭĭ, rĕcrūdescĕrĕ, to break open afresh

crūdŭs, -ă, -ŭm, bloody, raw

crūdĭtās, -ātĭs (f.), indigestion

crŭŏr, -ōrĭs (m.), blood

crŭentŭs, -ă, -ŭm, stained with blood

crŭentārĕ, to spot with blood

crūdēlĭs, -ĕ, cruel

crūdēlĭtās, -ātĭs (f.), cruelty

sānescō, consānescō (sānŭs, sound), sānŭĭ, sānescĕrĕ, to get well

vīlescō, ēvīlescō (vīlĭs, vile), vīlŭĭ, vīlescĕrĕ, to become vile

vīlĭtās, -ātĭs (f.), cheapness

IV. Fourth Conjugation.

Regular Verbs.

audīrĕ, *to hear*

  audītĭŏ, -ŏnĭs (f.) ⎱ *a hearing*
  audĭentĭă, -ae (f.) ⎰
  audītŭs, -ŭs (m.), *the hearing*
  audītŏr, -ŏrĭs (m.), *a hearer*
  audītōrĭŭm, -ī (n.), *a lecture-room*
  exaudīrĕ, *to hear clearly*
  ŏboedīrĕ, *to obey*
  ŏboedĭentĭă,-ae (f.), *obedience*

condīrĕ, *to season*
  condīmentŭm, -Ĭ (n.), *spice*

dormīrĕ, *to sleep*
  dormītărĕ, *to fall asleep*
  ēdormīrĕ, *to sleep out*

ērŭdīrĕ, *to educate*
  ērŭdītĭŏ, -ŏnĭs (f.), *learning*
  rŭdĭs, -ĕ, *rude*

fīnīrĕ, *to put an end to*
  fīnĭs, - (m.), *an end*
  dēfīnīrĕ, *to define* [*tion*
  dēfīnītĭŏ, -ŏnĭs (f.), *a defini-*
  fīnĭtĭmŭs, -ă, -ŭm, *neighboring*
  infīnītŭs, -ă, -ŭm, *without end, indefinite*
  affĭnĭs, -ĕ, *related by marriage*
  affīnĭtăs,-ătĭs (f.),*relationship by m rriage*
  confīr⸗ ⸗ĕ, *adjoining*

garrīrĕ, *to chatter*
  garrŭlĭtăs, -ă, -ŭm, *chattering*
  garrŭlĭtăs, -ătĭs (f.), *talkativeness*

mollīrĕ, *to make soft*
  mollĭs, -ĕ, *soft*
  mollĭtĕr, *softly*
  mollĭtĭă, -ae (f.), *effeminacy*
  mollĭtūdŏ, -ĭnĭs (f.), *softness*

mūgīrĕ, *to low*
  mūgĭtŭs, -ŭs (m.), *a lowing*

mūnīrĕ, *to fortify*
  mūnĭtĭŏ, -ŏnĭs (f.) ⎱ *a forti-*
  mūnĭmentŭm, -Ĭ (n.) ⎰ *fication*
  moenĭă, -ĭŭm (n. pl.),*city walls*
  praemūnīrĕ, *to fortify*

nūtrīrĕ, *to nourish*
  nūtrĭx, -ĭcĭs (f.), *a nurse*
  nūtrīmentŭm, -Ĭ (n.), *nourishment*

pōlīrĕ, *to smooth, polish*
  expōlīrĕ ⎱ *to refine*
  perpōlīrĕ ⎰
  expōlītĭŏ,-ŏnĭs (f.),*a polishing*
  interpōlărĕ, *to dress up*

pūnīrĕ, *to punish*
  pūnītŏr, -ŏrĭs (m.), *an avenger*
  poenă, -ae (f.), *punishment*
  impūnītŭs, -ă, -ŭm, *unpunished*
  impūnītĕ ⎱ *with impunity*
  impūnĕ ⎰
  impūnĭtăs, -ătĭs (f.), *impunity*

săgīrĕ, *to perceive quickly*
  săgă, -ae (f.), *a fortune-teller*

sāgax, -ācīs, *of quick percep-
ception*
sāgācītās, -ātīs (f.), *sagacity*
praesāgīrĕ, *to forebode*
praesāgītīŏ, -ŏnīs (f.), *a foreboding*

scīrĕ, *to know*

insciens, -tīs, *unaware*
scītŭs, -ă, -ŭm, *skilful*
scītĕ, *skilfully*
inscītŭs, -ă, -ŭm, *unskilful*
scientiă, -ae (f.), *knowledge*
inscientiă, -ae (f.), *want of
knowledge*
inscītiă, -ae (f.), *unskilfulness*
conscientiă,-ae (f.),*conscience*
nescīrĕ, *not to know*
nesciŭs, -ă, -ŭm }
insciŭs, -ă, -ŭm } *unaware*

servīrĕ, *to serve*

servŭs, -ī (m.), *a slave*
servītŭs, -ūtīs (f.), *slavery*

servīlīs, -ĕ, *slavish*
servītīŭm, -ī (n.), *service*
inservīrĕ, *to be submissive to*

sītīrĕ, *to be thirsty*
sītīs, -- (f.), *thirst*

sōpīrĕ, *to lull to sleep*

sōpŏr, -ŏrīs (m.), *a heavy
sleep*
sōpōrŭs, -ă, -ŭm, *heavy with
sleep*
sōpōrārĕ, *to cast into sleep*

tinnīrĕ, *to ring*

tinnītŭs, -ūs (m.), *a ringing*
tintinnābŭlŭm, -ī (n.), *a bell*

vestīrĕ, *to clothe*

vestīs - (f.), *a garment*
vestītŭs, -ūs (m.), *clothing*
vestīmentŭm, -ī (n.), *a garment*

Irregular Verbs.

ĕŏ, īvī, ītŭm, īrĕ, *to go*

ītārĕ, *to go*
ītŭs, -ūs (m.), *a going*
ītĕr, ītīnĕrīs (n.), *a going, a
way*
ăbĕŏ, ăbīī, ăbītŭm, ăbīrĕ, *to
go away*
ăbītŭs, -ūs (m.), *a going away*
ădĕŏ, ădīī, ădītŭm, ădīrĕ, *to
go to*
ădītŭs, -ūs (m.), *access*
ambīŏ, ambīvī, ambītŭm, am-
bīrĕ, *to go around, solicit*

ambītŭs, -ūs (m.), *a suing for
office by unlawful means*
ambītīŏ, -ŏnīs (f.), *ambition*
ambītīōsŭs, -ă, -ŭm, *ambi-
tious*
ambŭlārĕ, *to take a walk*
antĕĕŏ, antĕīī, antĕītŭm, an-
tĕīrĕ, *to go before*
circŭmĕŏ,circŭmīī, cīrcŭītŭm,
circŭmīrĕ, *to go around*
circŭītŭs, -ūs (m.), *a circuit*
cŏĕŏ, cŏīī, cŏītŭm, cŏīrĕ, *to
come together*

coetŭs, -ŭs (m.), an assemblage

exĕŏ, exĭī, exĭtŭm, exĭrĕ, to go out

exĭtŭs, -ŭs (m.), a departure

exĭtĭŭm, -ī (n.), destruction

ĭnĕŏ, ĭnĭī, ĭnĭtŭm, ĭnĭrĕ, to enter

ĭnĭtĭŭm, -ī (n.), a beginning

ĭnĭtĭārĕ, to initiate

ĭntĕrĕŏ, ĭntĕrĭī, ĭntĕrĭtŭm, ĭntĕrĭrĕ, to perish

ĭntĕrĭtŭs, -ŭs (m.), destruction

ĭntrŏĕŏ, ĭntrŏĭī, ĭntrŏĭtŭm, ĭntrŏĭrĕ, to enter

ĭntrŏĭtŭs, -ŭs (m.), entrance

ŏbĕŏ, ŏbĭī, ŏbĭtŭm, ŏbĭrĕ, to enter upon

pĕrĕŏ, pĕrĭī, pĕrĭtŭm, pĕrĭrĕ, to perish

praeĕŏ, praeĭī, praeĭtŭm, praeĭrĕ, to go before

praetŏr, -ŏrĭs = prae-ĭtŏr (m.), a leader

praetĕrĕŏ, praetĕrĭī, praetĕrĭtŭm, praetĕrĭrĕ, to go past

praetĕrĭtŭs, -ă, -ŭm, past

prŏdĕŏ, prŏdĭī, prŏdĭtŭm, prŏdĭrĕ, to come out

rĕdĕŏ, rĕdĭī, rĕdĭtŭm, rĕdĭrĕ, to return

rĕdĭtŭs, -ŭs (m.), a return

sŭbĕŏ, sŭbĭī, sŭbĭtŭm, sŭbĭrĕ, to come up to

sŭbĭtŭs, -ă, -ŭm, sudden

sŭbĭtŏ, suddenly

transĕŏ, transĭī, transĭtŭm, transĭrĕ, to go across

transĭtĭŏ, -ŏnĭs (f.) } a passing
transĭtŭs, -ŭs (m.) } over

vēnĕŏ, vēnĭī, vēnĭtŭm, vēnĭrĕ, to go to sale

farcĭŏ, farsī, fartŭm, farcĭrĕ, to stuff

confercĭŏ, confersī, confertŭm, confercĭrĕ, to stuff together

effercĭŏ, effersī, effertŭm, effercĭrĕ, to stuff out

rĕfercĭŏ, rĕfersī, rĕfertŭm, rĕfercĭrĕ, to stuff

infercĭŏ, infersī, infertŭm, infercĭrĕ, to stuff into

farcĭmĕn, -ĭnĭs (n.), a sausage

confertim, closely

fulcĭŏ, fulsī, fultŭm, fulcĭrĕ, to prop up

fulcrŭm, -ī (n.), a support

haurĭŏ, hausī, haustŭm, haurĭrĕ, to draw

haustŭs, -ŭs (m.), a draught

exhaurĭrĕ, to draw out

ĭnexhaustŭs, -ă, -ŭm, unexhausted

saepĭŏ, saepsī, saeptŭm, saepĭrĕ, to fence in

obsaepĭrĕ, to fence in

praesaepĭrĕ, to block up

praesaepĕ, -ĭs (n.), a manger

saeptă, -ŏrŭm (n. pl.), a fence

sălĭŏ, sălŭī, (saltŭm), sălĭrĕ, to leap

saltŭs, -ŭs (m.), a leap

saltārĕ, to dance

saltātĭŏ, -ŏnĭs (f.), a dance

saltātŏr, -ŏrĭs (m.), a dancer

assĭlĭŏ, assĭlŭī, (assultŭm), assĭlĭrĕ, to spring at

assultārĕ, to attack

insĭlĭŏ, insĭlŭī, (insultŭm), insĭlĭrĕ, to spring at

insultărĕ, to insult
prōsĭlĭŏ, prōsĭlŭī, (prōsultŭm),
prōsĭlīrĕ, to spring up
rĕsĭlĭŏ, rĕsĭlŭī, (rĕsultŭm), rĕ-
sĭlīrĕ, to spring back
rĕsultārĕ, to spring back, resound
dēsĭlĭŏ, dēsĭlŭī, (dēsultŭm), dē-
sĭlīrĕ, to leap down
exsĭlĭŏ, exsĭlŭī, (exsultŭm),
exsĭlīrĕ, to spring out
exsultārĕ, to jump up

sancĭŏ, sanxī, sanctŭm & sancī-
tŭm, sancīrĕ, to establish,
sanction
sanctŭs, -ă, -ŭm, sacred
sanctĭtās, -ātĭs (f.), sacredness
sanctĭŏ, -ōnĭs (f.), a decree

sarcĭŏ, sarsī, sartŭm, sarcīrĕ,
to mend
sartŏr, -ōrĭs (m.), a botcher
sarcĭnae, -ārŭm (f. pl.), baggage

sentĭŏ, sensī, sensŭm, sentīrĕ,
to feel, think
sensŭs, -ŭs (m.), sense
sensĭm, gradually
sententĭă, -ae (f.), an opinion
consentīrĕ, to agree
consensĭŏ, -ōnĭs (f.) ⎱ agree-
consensŭs, -ŭs (m.) ⎰ ment
consentănĕŭs, -ă, -ŭm, agree-
ing
dissentīrĕ, to disagree
dissensĭŏ, -ōnĭs (f.), disagree-
ment
praesentīrĕ, to presage
praesensĭŏ, -ōnĭs (f.), a foreboding

sĕpĕlĭŏ, sĕpĕlīvī, sĕpultŭm, sĕ-
pĕlīrĕ, to bury
insĕpultŭs, -ă, -ŭm, unburied
sĕpultūră, -ae (f.), a burial
sĕpulcrŭm, -ī (n.), a grave

vĕnĭŏ, vēnī, ventŭm, vĕnīrĕ, to
come
ventĭtārĕ, to come often
advĕnīrĕ, to arrive
adventŭs, -ŭs (m.), an arrival
advĕnă, -ae (m.), a stranger
circumvĕnīrĕ, to surround
convĕnīrĕ, to come together
contĭŏ, -ōnĭs (f.), a meeting
called together
conventŭs, -ŭs (m.), an assembly
conventŭm, -ī (n.), an agreement
convĕnĭentĭă, -ae (f.), an ac-
convĕnĭentĕr, fitly   [cord
dēvĕnīrĕ, to go to
pervĕnīrĕ, to arrive at
ēvĕnīrĕ, to come out   [rence
ēventŭs, -ŭs (m.), an occur-
invĕnīre, to invent
inventŭm, -ī (n.) ⎱ an inven-
inventĭŏ, -ōnĭs (f.) ⎰ tion
inventŏr, -ōrĭs (m.), an in-
ventor
intervĕnīrĕ, to come between
interventĭŏ, -ōnĭs (f.), the act
of intervening
obvĕnīrĕ, to fall to one
praevĕnīrĕ, to come before,
prevent
rĕvĕnīrĕ, to come back
subvĕnīrĕ, to come to one's
assistance
sŭpervĕnīrĕ, to come in addition to

vĭnclŏ, vinxī, vĭnctŭm, vĭncīrĕ,
 to bind

vincŭlŭm, -ī (n.), *a bond*
dēvincīrĕ, *to oblige*
rĕvincīrĕ, *to bind fast*

ămĭclŏ, (without Perf.), ămictŭm,
 ămĭcīrĕ, *to clothe*
ămictŭs, -ŭs (m.), *a garment*
ămĭcŭlŭm, -ī (n.), *a mantle*

Compounds of
päriŏ (pĕriŏ), *bring forth* (p. 60)

ăpĕriŏ, ăpĕrŭī, ăpĕrtŭm, ăpĕ-
 rīrĕ, *to open*
ŏpĕriŏ, ŏpĕrŭī, ŏpertŭm, ŏpĕ-
 rīrĕ, *to cover*
cŏŏpĕriŏ, cŏŏpĕrŭī, cŏŏpertŭm,
 cŏŏpĕrīrĕ, *to cover over*
compĕriŏ, compĕrī, comper-
 tŭm, compĕrīrĕ, *to ascer-
 tain, learn*

rĕpĕriŏ, rĕpĕrī (reppĕrī), rĕ-
 pĕrtŭm, rĕpĕrīrĕ, *to find*

fĕrĭŏ, (without Perf. & Sup.), fĕrīrĕ,
 to strike. In the Active per-
 cussī is used as a Perfect and
 in the Passive ictŭs sŭm.

fĕrŏcĭŏ, (without Perf. & Sup.), fĕrŏ-
 cīrĕ, *to be unruly*

fĕrox, -ōcĭs, *bold, brave*
fĕrōcĭă, -ae (f.) } *boldness,*
fĕrōcĭtās, -ātĭs (f.) } *courage*
fĕrŭs, -ă, -ŭm, *wild*
fĕrĭtās, -ātĭs (f.), *wildness*
fĕră, -ae (f.), *a wild beast*
effĕrătŭs, -ă, -ŭm, *fierce*

sŭperbĭŏ, (without Perf. & Sup.), sŭ-
 perbīrĕ, *to be haughty*
sŭperbŭs, -ă, -ŭm, *haughty*
sŭperbĭă, -ae (f.), *haughtiness*

V. Deponent Verbs.
First Conjugation.

admĭnĭcŭlārī, *to aid, prop*
 admĭnĭcŭlŭm, -ī (n.), *a prop,
 support*

adversārī, *to oppose*
 adversārĭŭs, -ī (m.), *an opponent*

ădūlārī, *to fawn upon*
 ădūlătĭŏ, -ōnĭs (f.), *flattery*
 ădūlătŏr, -ōrĭs (m.), *a flatterer*

aemŭlārī, *to rival*
 aemŭlŭs, -ī (m.), *a rival*
 aemŭlătĭŏ, -ōnĭs (f.), *emulation*

altercārī, *to quarrel*
 altercătĭŏ, -ōnĭs (f.), *a dispute*

ălūcĭnārī, *to talk idly*

amplexārī, *to embrace*

ancillārī, *to serve as a handmaid*
 ancillă, -ae (f.), *a maid-servant*

āprĭcārĭ, *to sun one's self*
āprĭcŭs, -ā, -ŭm, *sunny*

āquārĭ, *to fetch water*
āquātĭŏ, -ōnĭs (f.), *a fetching of water*

arbĭtrārĭ, *to think, consider*
arbĭtĕr, -rĭ (m.), *an arbiter*
arbĭtrĭŭm, -ĭ (n.), *a judgment*

archĭtectārĭ, *to build*
archĭtectŭs, -ĭ (m.), *a builder*

argŭmentārĭ, *to adduce proof*
argŭmentātĭŏ, -ōnĭs (f.), *argumentation*

argŭtārĭ, *to prattle*

aspernārĭ, *to despise*

assentārĭ, *to agree, flatter*
assentātĭŏ, -ōnĭs (f.), *flattery*
assentātŏr, -ōrĭs (m.), *a flatterer*

auctĭōnārĭ, *to sell at auction*

aucŭpārĭ, *to catch birds*
auceps, -ŭpĭs (m.), *a bird-catcher*

augŭrārĭ, *to foretell*
augŭr, -ĭs (m.), *a soothsayer*
augŭrĭŭm, -ĭ (n.), *an augury*

auspĭcārĭ, *to auspicate*
auspex, -ĭcĭs (m.), *a bird seer*
auspĭcĭŭm, -ĭ (n.), *augury from birds*

auxĭlĭārĭ, *to help*
auxĭlĭŭm, -ĭ (n.), *help*

āversārĭ, *to turn away*

bacchārĭ, *to revel (like the Bacchae)*

călumnĭārĭ, *to accuse falsely*
călumnĭā, -ae (f.), *a false accusation*
călumnĭātŏr, -ōrĭs (m.), *a slanderer*

căvillārĭ, *to jest*
căvillātĭŏ, -ōnĭs (f.), *irony*
căvillātŏr, -ōrĭs (m.), *a jester*

caupōnārĭ, *to trade*
caupŏ, -ōnĭs (m.), *an innkeeper*
caupōnă, -ae (f.), *a tavern*

causārĭ, *to plead*
causă, -ae (f.), *a cause*

circŭlārĭ, *to form a circle about one's self*

cōmissārĭ, *to revel*
cōmissātĭŏ,-ōnĭs(f.),*a reveling*
cōmissātŏr, -ōrĭs (m.), *a reveler*

cōmĭtārĭ, *to accompany*
cōmĕs, -ĭtĭs (m. & f.), *a companion*
cōmĭtātŭs, -ŭs (m.), *an escort*

commentārĭ, *to meditate*
commentātĭŏ, -ōnĭs (f.), *a meditation, treatise*

commentārĭ, –ōrŭm (m. pl.),
a commentary

contĭōnārĭ, to hold a speech

conflictārĭ, to contend

cōnārĭ, to undertake
cōnātŭs, –ūs (m.), an attempt

consĭlĭārĭ, to consult, advise

conspĭcārĭ, to behold

contemplārĭ, to contemplate
contemplātĭŏ, –ōnĭs (f.), con-
templation

convīcĭārĭ, to revile
convīcĭŭm, –ī (n.), reviling

convīvārĭ, to banquet with others
convīvă, –ae (m. & f.), a guest
convīvĭŭm, –ī (n.), a banquet

cornīcārĭ, to caw like a crow
cornĭx, –īcĭs (f.), a crow

crīmĭnārĭ, to accuse
crīmĕn, –ĭnĭs (n.), a crime
crīmĭnātĭŏ, –ōnĭs (f.), an accusation

cunctārĭ, to delay, tarry
cunctātĭŏ,–ōnĭs (f.), a delaying
cunctātŏr,–ōrĭs (m.), a delayer

dēpēcūlārĭ, to despoil

despĭcārĭ, to despise
despĭcātŭs, –ă, –ŭm, despised

dēversārĭ, to lodge, to put up

dīglădĭārĭ, to fight fiercely

dignārĭ, to deem worthy
dignŭs, –ă, –ŭm, worthy
dēdignārĭ, to disdain

dŏmĭnārĭ, to be lord and master
dŏmĭnŭs, –ī (m.), a master
dŏmĭnă, –ae (f.), a mistress
dŏmĭnātĭŏ, –ōnĭs (f.) ⎱ rule
dŏmĭnātŭs, –ūs (m.) ⎰
dŏmĭnĭŭm, –ī (n.), property
dŏmĭnātŏr, –ōrĭs (m.), a ruler,
lord

ēlŭcūbrārĭ, to compose by lamp-
light

ĕpŭlārĭ, to feast, banquet
ĕpŭlŭm, –ī (n.), a banquet
ĕpŭlae, –ārŭm (f. pl.), sumptuous dishes

exsēcrārĭ, to curse, execrate
exsēcrātĭŏ, –ōnĭs (f.), execration

făbrĭcārĭ, to form, fashion
făbĕr, –rī (m.), a worker in
hard materials
făbrĭcă, –ae (f.), a fabric
făbrĭcātŏr,–ōrĭs (m.), a framer
făbrĭcātĭŏ,–ōnĭs (f.), a framing

fābŭlārĭ, to converse
confābŭlārĭ, to converse together
fābŭlă, –ae (f.), a story

faenĕrārī, *to lend on interest*
faenŭs, –ŏrĭs (n.), *interest*
faenĕrātŏr, –ŏrĭs (m.), *a capitalist*

fērĭārī, *to keep holiday*
fērĭae, –ārŭm (f. pl.), *holidays*

frūmentārī, *to fetch corn*
frūmentŭm, –ī (n.), *corn*
frūmentātĭŏ, –ŏnĭs (f.), *a foraging*

frustrārī, *to deceive*
frustrā, *in vain*

fūrārī, *to take by stealth*
suffūrārī, *to steal*
fūr, –ĭs (m.), *a thief*

glōrĭārī, *to boast*
glōrĭă, –ae (f.), *glory* ·

graecārī, *to live in the Greek style (luxuriously)*

grassārī, *to go about, proceed*

grātārī }
grātŭlārī } *to wish joy*
grātŭlātĭŏ, –ŏnĭs (f.), *a wishing joy*
grātŭlābŭndŭs, –ă, –ŭm, *congratulating*

grātĭfĭcārī, *to do a favor*

hărĭŏlārī, *to prophesy*
hărĭŏlŭs, –ī (m.), *a prophet*
hărĭŏlă, –ae (f.), *a prophetess*

hellŭārī, *to gormandise*
hellŭŏ, –ŏnĭs (m.), *a glutton*

hortārī, *to exhort*
ădhortārī }
exhortārī } *to exhort*
dēhortārī, *to advise to the contrary*
hortātŏr, –ŏrĭs (m.), *an exhorter*
hortātĭŏ, –ŏnĭs (f.), *an exhortation*
hortāmĕn, –ĭnĭs (n.) } *an in*
hortāmentŭm, –ī (n.) } *citement*
hortātū, *on advice*

hospĭtārī, *to be a guest, to put up*
hospĭtĭŭm, –ī (n.), *an inn*
hospĕs, –ĭtĭs (m.), *a guest*
hospĭtālĭs, –ĕ, *hospitable*
hospĭtālĭtās, –ātĭs (f.), *hospitality*

ĭmāgĭnārī, *to fancy*
ĭmāgŏ, –ĭnĭs (f.), *a likeness*

ĭmĭtārī, *to imitate*
ĭmĭtātŏr, –ŏrĭs (m.), *an imitator*
ĭmĭtātĭŏ, –ŏnĭs (f.), *imitation*

indignārī, *to deem unworthy; to be displeased*
indignātĭŏ, –ŏnĭs (f.), *displeasure*
indignābŭndŭs, –ă, –ŭm, *full of indignation*
indignŭs, –ă, –ŭm, *unworthy*
indignĭtās, –ātĭs (f.), *unworthiness, indignation*

infĭtĭārī, to deny

infĭtĭae, -ārŭm (f. pl.), denial

infĭtĭālĭs, -ĕ, negative

infĭtĭātĭŏ, -ōnĭs (f.), a denial

infĭtĭātŏr, -ōrĭs (m.), one who denies a debt

insĭdĭārī, to lie in wait

interprĕtārī, to be an interpreter

interprĕs, -ĕtĭs (m. & f.), an interpreter

interprĕtātĭŏ, -ōnĭs (f.), an explanation

jăcŭlārī, to throw

jŏcārī, to jest

jŏcŭs, -ī (m.), a jest, joke

laetārī, to rejoice

laetŭs, -ă, -ŭm, joyful

laetĭtĭă, -ae (f.), joy

lāmentārī, to wail

lāmentātĭŏ, -ōnĭs (f.), a wailing

lātrōcĭnārī, to rob on the highway

lātrŏ, -ōnĭs (m.), a highwayman

lātrōcĭnĭŭm, -ī (n.), a highway robbery

lēnōcĭnārī, to flatter

lĭbīdĭnārī, to be voluptuous

lĭbīdŏ, -ĭnĭs (f.), lust

lĭbīdĭnōsŭs, -ă, -ŭm, voluptuous

lĭcĭtārī, to bid, offer a price

lĭcĭtātĭŏ, -ōnĭs (f.), a bidding

lignārī, to fetch wood

lignŭm, -ī (n.), wood

lŭcrārī, to gain

lŭcrŭm, -ī (n.), gain

luctārī, to wrestle

ŏbluctārī } to struggle against
rēluctārī }

luctātĭŏ, -ōnĭs (f.), wrestling

lūdĭfĭcārī, to make sport of

lūdĭfĭcātĭŏ, -ōnĭs (f.), a mocking

māchĭnārī, to devise

māchĭnă, -ae (f.), a machine

māchĭnātĭŏ, -ōnĭs (f.), a contrivance

māchĭnātŏr, -ōrĭs (m.), a contriver

mătĕrĭārī, to fell wood

mătĕrĭă, -ae (f.), timber

mĕdĭcārī, to heal

mĕdĭcŭs, -ī (m.), a physician

mĕdĭcāmentŭm, -ī(n.) } a rem-
mĕdĭcīnă, -ae (f.) } edy

mĕdĭtārī, to meditate

mĕdĭtātĭŏ, -ōnĭs (f.), meditation

mercārī, to trade

merx, -cĭs (f.), ware [chant
mercātŏr, -ōrĭs (m.), a mer-
mercātŭs, -ūs (m.), a market

mercātūră, -ae (f.), traffic

commercĭŭm, -ī (n.), commerce

mĕrĭdĭārĭ, *to take a nap at noon*

mĕrĭdĭēs, -ēĭ (m.), *noon*

mētārĭ, *to measure*

mētă, -ae (f.), *a goal*

mētătŏr, -ōrĭs (m.), *a land-surveyor*

mĭnārĭ ⎫
mĭnĭtārĭ ⎭ *to threaten*

mĭnae, -ārŭm (f. pl.), *a threat*

mīrārĭ, *to wonder*

dēmīrārĭ, *to wonder at*
admīrārĭ, *to admire*
admīrătĭŏ, -ōnĭs (f.), *admiration*

mĭsĕrārĭ, *to pity*

commĭsĕrārĭ, *to bewail*
mĭsĕr, -ă, -ŭm, *wretched*
mĭsĕrătĭŏ, -ōnĭs (f.) ⎫ *a pi-*
commĭsĕrătĭŏ,-ōnĭs(f.) ⎭ *tying*

mŏdĕrārĭ, *to moderate*

mŏdĕrătŭs, -ă, -ŭm, *moderate*
mŏdĕrătē, *with moderation*
mŏdĕrătĭŏ, -ōnĭs (f.), *moder-ateness*
mŏdŭs, -ī (m.), *measure*

mŏdŭlārĭ, *to modulate*

mōrĭgĕrārĭ, *to gratify*

mōrĭgĕrŭs, -ă, -ŭm, *obsequi-ous*

mŏrārĭ, *to delay, stay*

commŏrārĭ, *to stop somewhere*

mūnĕrārĭ, *to bestow*

mūnŭs, -ĕrĭs (n.), *a gift*
rĕmūnĕrārĭ, *to reward*
rĕmūnĕrătĭŏ, -ōnĭs (f.), *a re-ward*

mūtŭārĭ, *to borrow*

nĕgōtĭārĭ, *to carry on business*

nĕgōtĭŭm, -ī (n.), *a business*
nĕgōtĭātŏr, -ōrĭs (m.), *a trader*

nīdŭlārĭ, *to build a nest*

nīdŭs, -ī (m.), *a nest*

nūgārĭ, *to trifle*

nūgae, -ārŭm (f. pl.), *trifles*

nundĭnārĭ, *to hold market*

nundĭnae, -ārŭm (f. pl.), *a market day*

nūtrīcārĭ, *to bring up*

nūtrix, -īcĭs (f.), *a nurse*

ŏdōrārĭ, *to smell at, to scent*

ōmĭnārĭ, *to forebode*

ăbōmĭnārĭ, *to abhor*
ōmĕn, -ĭnĭs (n.), *a foreboding*

ŏpĕrārĭ, *to take pains*

ŏpĕră, -ae (f.), *pains*
ŏpŭs, -ĕrĭs (n.), *work*

ŏpīnārĭ, *to be of opinion*

ŏpīnĭŏ, -ōnĭs (f.), *an opinion*

ŏpĭtŭlārĭ, *to bring aid*

[ops], ŏpĭs, *aid*

oscĭtārī, *to yawn*

ōs, ōrĭs (n.), *the mouth*

oscŭlārī, *to kiss*

oscŭlŭm, -ī (n.), *a kiss*
oscŭlātĭŏ, -ōnĭs (f.), *a kissing*

ōtĭārī, *to be at leisure*

ōtĭŭm, -ī (n.), *leisure*
ōtĭōsŭs, -ă, -ŭm, *at leisure*

pābŭlārī, *to forage*

pābŭlŭm, -ī (n.), *fodder*
pābŭlātĭŏ, -ōnĭs (f.), *a foraging*
pābŭlātŏr, -ōrĭs (m.), *a forager*

pācĭfĭcārī, *to make a peace*

pācĭfĭcŭs, -ă, -ŭm, *peaceable*
pācĭfĭcātĭŏ, -ōnĭs (f.), *a peacemaking*
pācĭfĭcātŏr,-ōrĭs (m.), *a peacemaker*

pālārī, *to stroll about*

palpārī, *to stroke*

părăsītārī, *to play the parasite, to sponge*

părăsītŭs, -ī (m.), *a sponger*

pătrōcĭnārī, *to protect*

pătrōnŭs, -ī (m.), *a protector, patron*
pătrōcĭnĭŭm, -ī (n.), *protection, patronage*

percontārī, *to inquire*

pĕrĕgrīnārī, *to go abroad, to sojourn abroad*

pĕrĕgrē, *abroad*
pĕrĕgrīnŭs, -ă, -ŭm, *foreign*
pĕrĕgrīnātĭŏ, -ōnĭs (f.), *a being abroad*
pĕrĕgrīnātŏr, -ōrĭs (m.), *he who travels about*

pĕrīclĭtārī, *to put to the test*

pĕrīcŭlŭm,-ī (n.), *a trial; danger*
pĕrīcŭlōsŭs, -ă, -ŭm, *perilous*

phĭlŏsŏphārī, *to philosophize*

phĭlŏsŏphĭă, -ae (f.), *philosophy*
phĭlŏsŏphŭs, -ī (m.), *a philosopher*

pignĕrārī, *to take as a pledge*

pignŭs, -ōrĭs (n.), *a pledge*

pĭgrārī, *to be slow*

pĭgĕr, -ră, -ŭm, *slow*

piscārī, *to fish*

piscĭs, - (m.), *a fish*
piscătŏr, -ōrĭs (m.), *a fisherman*
piscătōrĭŭs, -ă, -ŭm, *of fishermen*
piscīnă, -ae (f.), *a fish-pond*

pŏpŭlārī, *to lay waste*

dēpŏpŭlārī, *to plunder*
dēpŏpŭlātĭŏ, -ōnĭs (f.), *a pillaging*
pŏpŭlŭs, -ī (m.), *a people*

praedārī, *to plunder*

  praedătŏr, -ŏrĭs (m.), *a plunderer*

  praedătŏrĭŭs, -ă, -ŭm, *plundering*

  praedă, -ae (f.), *plunder*

praestŏlārī, *to wait for*

praevărĭcārī, *to walk crookedly; to make a sham accusation*

  praevărĭcătŏr, -ŏrĭs (m.), *a sham accuser*

prĕcārī, *to ask, pray*

  comprĕcārī, *to pray to*

  imprĕcārī, *to invoke*

  prĕcēs, -ŭm (f. pl.), *a prayer*

  dĕprĕcārī, *to deprecate*

  dĕprĕcătĭŏ, -ŏnĭs (f.), *a prayer for pardon*

proeliārī, *to join battle*

  proelĭŭm, -ī (n.), *a battle*

rătĭŏcĭnārī, *to reckon, to reason*

  rătĭŏcĭnătĭŏ, -ŏnĭs (f.), *reasoning*

rĕcordārī, *to remember*

  rĕcordătĭŏ, -ŏnĭs (f.) *a recollection*

rĕfrăgārī, *to oppose*

rīmārī, *to pry into*

rixārī, *to quarrel*

  rixă, -ae (f.), *a quarrel*

rustĭcārī, *to live in the country*

  rūs, rūrĭs (n.), *the country*

  rustĭcŭs, -ī (m.), *a country man*

scĭtārī   ⎱
sciscĭtārī ⎰ *to inquire*

scrūtārī, *to search*

sectārī, *to run after, attend*

  assectārī, *to accompany constantly*

  consectārī, *to pv ɪ sue, to strive after*

  insectārī, *to pursue*

  sectătŏr, -ŏrĭs (m.), *a follower*

sermōcĭnārī, *to converse*

sōlārī, *to comfort*

  sōlătĭŭm, -ī (n.), *a comfort*

  consōlārī, *to comfort* [lation

  consōlătĭŏ, -ŏnĭs (f.), *a consolation*

  consōlătŏr, -ŏrĭs (m.), *a comforter*

spătĭārī, *to take a walk*

  exspătĭārī, *to go out of the way*

spĕcŭlārī, *to spy out*

  spĕcŭlătŏr, -ŏrĭs (m.), *a spy*

stĭpŭlārī, *to stipulate*

  astĭpŭlārī, *to assent to*

stŏmăchārī, *to be irritated*

  stŏmăchŭs,-ī (m.), *the stomach*

suffrăgārī, *to assent to*

  suffrăgĭŭm, -ī (n.), *a vote*

suspĭcārī, *to suspect*

tergĭversārĭ, *to shuffle*

tergĭversātĭŏ, -ōnĭs (f.), *a shift*

testārĭ } *to bear witness*
testĭfĭcārĭ }

testĭs, - (m. & f.), *a witness*

testĭmōnĭŭm, -ĭ (n.), *witness*

trĭcārĭ, *to make difficulties; to play tricks*

trĭcae, -ārŭm (f. pl.), *vexations; tricks*

intrĭcārĕ, *to perplex*

tristārĭ, *to be sad*

tristĭs, -ĕ, *sad*

trŭtĭnārĭ, *to weigh*

trŭtĭnă, -ae (f.), *a pair of scales*

tŭmultŭārĭ, *to raise a tumult*

vădārĭ, *to summon to trial*

văs, vădĭs (m.), *a bail*

văgārĭ, *to stroll about*

văgŭs, -ă, -ŭm, *strolling about*
văgĕ, *far and wide*
pervăgārĭ, *to rove about*

vătĭcĭnārĭ, *to foretell*

vătĭcĭnātĭŏ, -ōnĭs (f.), *soothsaying*

vătēs, -ĭs (m.), *a prophet*

vēlĭfĭcārĭ, *to make sail*

vēlĭtārĭ, *to skirmish*

vēlĕs, -ĭtĭs (m.), *a skirmisher*

vĕnĕrārĭ, *to worship*

vĕnĕrātĭŏ,-ōnĭs(f.), *veneration*

vēnārĭ, *to hunt*

vēnātĭŏ, -ōnĭs (f.), *hunting*
vēnātŏr, -ōrĭs (m.), *a hunter*

vĕrēcundārĭ, *to feel bashful, be afraid*

vĕrēcundŭs, -ă, -ŭm, *bashful*
vĕrēcundĭă, -ae (f.), *bashfulness*

versārĭ, *to dwell, live; to be occupied in*
āversārĭ, *to scorn*
obversārĭ, *to appear to*

vōcĭfĕrārĭ, *to cry out*

vōcĭfĕrātĭŏ, -ōnĭs (f.), *an outcry*

Second Conjugation.

fătĕŏr, fassŭs sŭm, fătērĭ, *to confess*

confĭtĕŏr, confessŭs sŭm, confĭtērĭ, *to confess*

confessĭŏ, -ōnĭs (f.), *a confession*

prŏfĭtĕŏr, prŏfessŭs sŭm, prŏfĭtērĭ, *to profess*

prŏfessĭŏ, -ōnĭs (f.), *a profession*

lĭcĕŏr, lĭcĭtŭs sŭm, lĭcērĭ, *to bid at an auction*

pollĭcĕŏr, pollĭcĭtŭs sŭm, pollĭcērĭ, *to promise*

pollĭcĭtātĭŏ,-ōnĭs(f.),*a promise*

mĕdĕŏr, (without Perf.), mĕdērī, to heal

mĕrĕŏr, mĕrĭtŭs sŭm, mĕrērī, to deserve

prōmĕrērī, to deserve

mĭsĕrĕŏr, mĭsĕrĭtŭs & mĭsĕrtŭs sŭm, mĭsĕrērī, to pity

mĭsĕrĭă, -ae (f.), wretchedness
mĭsĕrĭcors, -dĭs, pitiful
mĭsĕrĭcordĭă, -ae (f.), pity

rĕŏr, rătŭs sŭm, rērī, to think

rătĭŏ, -ōnĭs (f.), reason
rătŭs, -ă, -ŭm, valid
irrĭtŭs, -ă, -ŭm, invalid

tŭĕŏr, tŭĭtŭs sŭm, tŭērī, to look upon; to defend

contŭērī ⎱ to look at
intŭērī ⎰

vĕrĕŏr, vĕrĭtŭs sŭm, vĕrērī, to fear

rĕvĕrērī, to respect
rĕvĕrentĭă, -ae (f.), reverence

Third Conjugation.

(ăpiscŏr, aptŭs sŭm, ăpiscī, to reach after)

ădĭpiscŏr, ădeptŭs sŭm, ădĭpiscī, to obtain

dēfĕtiscŏr, dēfessŭs sŭm, dēfĕtiscī, to become tired

dēfessŭs, -ă, -ŭm, tired

expergiscŏr, experrectŭs sŭm, expergiscī, to awake

frŭŏr, frŭĭtŭs & fructŭs sŭm, frŭī, to enjoy
  Part. Fut. frŭĭtūrŭs

perfrŭŏr, perfructŭs sŭm, perfrŭī, to enjoy fully
fructŭs, -ūs (m.), fruit
fructŭōsŭs, -ă, -ŭm, fruitful
frūgēs, -ŭm (f.), fruits
frūgĭ (indecl.), worthy
frūgălĭs, -ĕ, thrifty
frūgălĭtās, -ātĭs (f.), economy
frūgĭfĕr, -ă, -ŭm, fruitful

fungŏr, functŭs sŭm, fungī, to perform

functĭŏ, -ōnĭs (f.), a performance

dēfungī ⎱ to get through
perfungī ⎰

grădĭŏr, gressŭs sŭm, grădī, to step

grădŭs, -ūs (m.), a step
grădātĭm, step by step
gressŭs, -ūs (m.), a stepping
aggrĕdĭŏr, aggressŭs sŭm, aggrĕdī, to attack
congrĕdĭŏr, congressŭs sŭm, congrĕdī, to meet with one
congressĭŏ, -ōnĭs (f.) ⎱ a meet-
congressŭs, -ūs (m.) ⎰ ing
dĭgrĕdĭŏr, dĭgressŭs sŭm, dĭgrĕdī, to go aside
dĭgressĭŏ, -ōnĭs (f.), a deviation
ēgrĕdĭŏr, ēgressŭs sŭm, ēgrĕdī, to go out

ēgressūs, -ūs (m.), *a departure*
ingrēdĭŏr, ingressūs sŭm, in-
grēdĭ, *to enter*
ingressĭŏ, -ōnĭs (f.) \ *an en-*
ingressūs, -ūs (m.) / *trance*
praegrēdĭŏr, praegressūs sŭm,
praegrēdĭ, *to go before*
prōgrēdĭŏr, prōgressūs sŭm,
prōgrēdĭ, *to go on*
prōgressĭŏ, -ōnĭs (f.) \ *prog-*
prōgressūs, -ūs (m.) / *ress*
rĕgrēdĭŏr, rĕgressūs sŭm, rĕ-
grēdĭ, *to come back*
transgrēdĭŏr, transgressūs
sŭm, transgrēdĭ, *to step over*
transgressĭŏ, -ōnĭs (f.), *a passage*

Irascŏr, (withŏut Perf.), Irascĭ, *to
be angry*
Irātūs sŭm, *I am angry*
Iră, -ae (f.), *anger*
Irācundūs, -ă, -ŭm, *passion-
ate*
Irācundĭă, -ae (f.), *passion*

lābŏr, lapsūs sŭm, lābĭ, *to slide,
fall*
lapsūs, -ūs (m.), *a falling, a
fault*
collābĭ, *to fall in*
dēlābĭ, *to sink*
ēlābĭ, *to escape*
dīlābĭ, *to fall asunder*
prōlābĭ, *to slide forward*
rĕlābĭ, *to fall back*

lŏquŏr, lŏcūtūs sŭm, lŏquĭ, *to
speak*
lŏcūtĭŏ, -ōnĭs (f.), *a speaking*
ēlŏcūtĭŏ, -ōnĭs (f.), *utterance*

lŏquax, -ācĭs, *talkative*
lŏquācĭtās, -ātĭs (f.), *talkativeness*
collŏquĭŭm, -Ĭ (n.), *a conver-
sation*
ēlŏquens, -tĭs, *eloquent*
ēlŏquentĭă, -ae (f.), *eloquence*
allŏquĭ, *to salute*
collŏquĭ, *to converse*
ēlŏquĭ, *to speak out*
interlŏquĭ, *to interrupt in
speaking*
ŏblŏquĭ, *to gainsay*

[mĭniscŏr, *recollect*]
commĭniscŏr, commentūs sŭm,
commĭniscĭ, *to contrive*
rĕmĭniscŏr, (withŏut Perf.), rĕ-
mĭniscĭ, *to recollect* — Perf.
rĕcordātūs sŭm
mens, -tĭs (f.), *mind*
mĕmĭnĭ, *I remember*

mŏrĭŏr, mortūūs sŭm, mŏrĭ,
to die — Part. Fut. mŏrĭtūrŭs
mors, -tĭs (f.), *death*
mortālĭs, -ĕ, *mortal*
mortālĭtās, -ātĭs (f.), *mortality*
ēmŏrĭ \ *to depart, decease*
dēmŏrĭ /

nanciscŏr, nactūs (nanctūs) sŭm,
nanciscĭ, *to get*

nascŏr, nātūs sŭm, nascĭ, *to be
born* — Part. Fut. nascĭtūrŭs
nātĭŏ, -ōnĭs (f.), *a nation*
nātīvūs, -ă, -ŭm, *primitive*
nātālĭs, - (m.), *a birthday*
nātūră, -ae (f.), *nature*
nātūrālĭs, -ĕ, *natural*
innascĭ, *to be born in*

innātūs, -ă, -ŭm, *inborn*
cognātūs, -ī (m.), *a kinsman*
cognātīŏ, -ōnīs (f.), *blood relationship*
prognātūs,-ī (m.), *a descendant*

nītŏr, nīsūs & nixūs sūm, nītī, *to rest upon; to strive*

annītī }
cōnītī } *to take pains*
ēnītī, *to strive*
ēnixē, *strenuously*
innītī, *to lean upon*

ŏblīviscŏr, ŏblītūs sūm, ŏblīviscī, *to forget*

ŏblīvīŏ, -ōnīs (f.), *forgetfulness*

păciscŏr, pactūs sūm, păciscī, *to make a bargain*

pascŏr, pastūs sūm, pascī, *to feed* (intrans.)

pătīŏr, passūs sūm, pătī, *to suffer*

pătīens, -tīs, *bearing, patient*
pătīentēr, *patiently*
pătīentīă, -ae (f.), *patience*
pĕrpĕtīŏr, perpessūs sūm, perpĕtī, *to endure*
perpessīŏ, -ōnīs (f.), *a suffering*

[plectŏr, *entwine*]

amplectŏr, amplexūs sūm, ampiectī, *to embrace*
complectŏr, complexūs sūm, complectī, *to embrace*
amplexūs, -ūs (m.) } *an embrace*
complexūs, -ūs (m.) } *brace*

prŏfīciscŏr, prŏfectūs sūm, prŏfīciscī, *to travel*
prŏfectīŏ, -ōnīs (f.), *a voyage*

quĕrŏr, questūs sūm, quĕrī, *to complain*

conquĕrī, *to lament* [ing
questūs, -ūs (m.), *a complain-*
quĕrēlă, -ae (f.) } *a com-*
quĕrīmōnīă, -ae (f.) } *plaint*

ringŏr, (without Perf.), ringī, *to open wide the mouth, to grin*

rictūs, -ūs (m.), *the mouth wide open; a grin*

sĕquŏr, sĕcūtūs sūm, sĕquī, *to follow*

sĕcūs, *following, otherwise*
sĕcundūs, -ă, -ŭm, *following; second; favorable*
sĕcundŭm, *after*
assĕquī }
consĕquī } *to reach*
consĕcūtīŏ, -ōnīs (f.), *a consequence*
exsĕquī, *to go after; to execute*
exsĕquīae, -ārŭm (f. pl.), *a funeral procession*
insĕquī }
persĕquī } *to persecute*
insĕquens, -tīs, *following*
obsĕquī, *to yield to*
obsĕquīŭm, -ī (n.), *compliance*
prōsĕquī, *to accompany*
subsĕquī, *to follow close after*

ulciscŏr, ultūs sūm, ulciscī, *to avenge, punish*

ultŏr, -ōrīs (m.), *a punisher*
īnultūs, -ă, ˣm, *unrevenged*

ûtŏr, ûsûs sûm, ûtī, *to use*
ăbûtī, *to use up, to misuse*
ûsûs, -ûs (m.), *use, usefulness*
ăbûsûs, -ûs (m.), *misuse*
ûsītătûs, -ă, -ûm, *usual, wonted*
ûsûră, -ae (f.), *interest*
ûsûrpārě, *to make use of*
ûsûrpātīŏ, -ōnīs (f.), *a taking into use*
ûtīlīs, -ě, *useful*

ĭnûtīlīs, -ě, *useless*
ûtīlītās, -ātīs (f.), *usefulness*
ĭnûtīlītās, -ātīs (f.), *uselessness*

věhŏr, vectûs sûm, věhī, *to ride*
circumvěhī, *to ride around*
praetervěhī, *to drive by*
invěhī, *to inveigh*

vescŏr, (without Perf.), vescī, *to eat*

Fourth Conjugation.

assentĭŏr, assensûs sûm, assentīrī, *to assent*
assensĭŏ, -ōnīs (f.) ⎱ *assent*
assensûs, -ûs (m.) ⎰

blandĭŏr, blandītûs sûm, blandīrī, *to fawn upon*
blandûs, -ă, -ûm, *enticing*
blandīmentûm, -ī (n.), *a charm*
blandītĭae, -ārûm (f. pl.), *flatteries*

expěrĭŏr, expertûs sûm, expěrīrī, *to try; to know by experience*
expěrĭentĭă, -ae (f.), *experience*
expěrīmentûm, -ī (n.), *a trial*
compěrĭŏr, *am informed* (only in the Present)

largĭŏr, largītûs sûm, largīrī, *to give bountifully*
largītĭŏ, -ōnīs (f.), *a present*
largītŏr, -ōrīs (m.), *a briber*

largûs, -ă, -ûm, *abundant, liberal*
largītās, -ātīs (f.), *liberality*
dīlargīrī, *to give away*

mentĭŏr, mentītûs sûm, mentīrī, *to lie, feign*
mendax, -ācīs, *lying*
mendācĭûm, -ī (n.), *a lie*
ēmentīrī, *to feign*

mētĭŏr, mensûs sûm, mētīrī, *to measure*
mensŏr, -ōrīs (m.), *a measurer*
ăgrīmensŏr, -ōrīs (m.), *a land-surveyor*
mensûră, -ae (f.), *a measure*
admētīrī, *to measure out to*
dīmētīrī, *to measure out*
dimensĭŏ, -ōnīs (f.), *a measuring*
permētīrī, *to measure through*
immensûs, -ă, -ûm, *boundless*
immensītās, -ātīs (f.), *immensity*

mŏlĭŏr, mŏlītŭs sŭm, mŏlīrī, *to .set in motion; to undertake*

mŏlēs, -ĭs (f.), *a mass*
mŏlīmĕn, -ĭnĭs (n.), *an effort*
mŏlīmentŭm, -ī (n.), *an undertaking*
mŏlestŭs, -ă, -ŭm, *troublesome*
mŏlestĭă, -ae (f.), *trouble*
ămŏlīrī, *to carry away*
dēmŏlīrī, *to pull down, demolish*
ēmŏlīrī, *to move out*
ēmŏlŭmentŭm, -ī (n.), *gain*

oppĕrĭŏr, oppertŭs sŭm, oppĕrīrī, *to wait*

ordĭŏr, orsŭs sŭm, ordīrī, *to begin*
exordīrī, *to begin*
exordĭŭm, -ī (n.), *a beginning*

ŏrĭŏr, ortŭs sŭm, ŏrīrī, *to rise*
Part. Fut. ŏrĭtūrŭs
cŏŏrīrī, *to rise up*
exŏrīrī, *to spring up*
ŏbŏrīrī, *to arise*
ădŏrīrī, *to assail*
ŏrĭens, -tĭs (m.), *the east*
ortŭs, -ūs (m.), *a rising*
exortŭs, -ūs (m.), *a coming forth*
ŏrīgŏ, -ĭnĭs (f.), *origin*
ăbŏrīgĭnēs, -ŭm, (m. pl.), *original inhabitants*

partĭŏr, partītŭs sŭm, partīrī, *to share, part*

pars, -tĭs (f.), *a part*
partim, *partly*
partītĭŏ, -ōnĭs (f.), *a sharing*
partĭcŭlă, -ae (f.), *a little bit*
partĭceps, -ĭpĭs, *sharing*
partĭcĭpĭŭm, -ī (n.), *a participle*
expers, -tĭs, *without share*
bĭpartītŭs, -ă, -ŭm, *twofold*
bĭpartītŏ, *in two parts*
dispertīrī, *to distribute*
impertīrĕ ⎫ *to share with another*
impertīrī ⎭ *other*

pŏtĭŏr, pŏtītŭs sŭm, pŏtīrī, *to take possession of*

pŏtens, -tĭs, *mighty*
compŏs, -ŏtĭs, *master of*
pŏtentĭă, -ae, (f.), *might*
pŏtestās, -ātĭs (f.), *official power*
impŏtens, -tĭs, *powerless*
impŏtentĭă, -ae (f.), *want of moderation*
praepŏtens, -tĭs, *very powerful*
pŏtĭs, -ĕ, *able*
pŏtĭŏr, -ŭs, *preferable, better*
pŏtissĭmŭs, -ă, -ŭm, *the chief*

sŏrtĭŏr, sortītŭs sŭm, sortīrī, *to cast lots*

sortĭŏ, -ōnĭs (f.), *a casting of lots*
sors, -tĭs (f.), *a lot* [lots
consors, -tĭs, *sharing*
consortĭŏ, -ōnĭs (f.), *partnership*

VI. Deponent and Active Verbs

HAVING THE SAME MEANING.

admĭnĭcŭlārĭ	adjŭvārĕ, *to support*
arbĭtrārĭ	existĭmārĕ, *to be of opinion*
argŭmentārĭ	prŏbārĕ, *to prove*
argŭtārĭ	garrīrĕ, *to chatter*
aspernārĭ	spernĕrĕ, *to despise*
āversārĭ	rĕformĭdārĕ, *to shun*
auxĭlĭārĭ } ŏpĭtŭlārĭ }	jŭvārĕ, *to help*
căvillārĭ	illŭdĕrĕ, *to jest*
causārĭ	praetendĕrĕ, *to pretend*
commentārĭ	rĕpŭtārĕ, *to meditate*
contĭōnārĭ	ōrārĕ, *to hold a speech, plead*
cōnārĭ	suscĭpĕrĕ (ĭō), *to undertake*
consĭlĭārĭ	consŭlĕrĕ, *to consult*
conspĭcārĭ	conspĭcĕrĕ (ĭō), *to behold*
contemplārĭ	consĭdĕrārĕ, *to contemplate*
convĭcĭārĭ	mălĕdĭcĕrĕ, *to revile*
crīmĭnārĭ	argŭĕrĕ, *to accuse*
cunctārĭ	haesĭtārĕ, *to delay, tarry*
despĭcārĭ	despĭcĕrĕ (ĭō), *to despise*
dēversārĭ	dēvertĕrĕ, *to put up*
dĭglădĭārĭ	pugnārĕ, *to fight*
ĕpŭlārĭ	comĕdĕrĕ, *to feast upon*
exsĕcrārĭ	dēvŏvērĕ, *to execrate*
făbrĭcārĭ	confĭcĕrĕ (ĭō), *to make*
frustrārĭ	fallĕrĕ, *to deceive*
fūrārĭ	auferrĕ, *to purloin*
suffŭrārĭ	surrĭpĕrĕ (ĭō), *to steal*
hortārĭ	mŏnērĕ, *to incite*
ĭmĭtārĭ	assĭmŭlārĕ, *to imitate*
infĭtĭārĭ	nĕgārĕ, *to deny*
interprĕtārĭ	explĭcārĕ, *to explain*
jăcŭlārĭ	jăcĕrĕ (ĭō), *to throw*
jŏcārĭ	lŭdĕrĕ, *to jest, joke*
lŭcrārĭ	acquīrĕrĕ, *to gain*
măchĭnārĭ	excōgĭtārĕ, *to devise*
mĕdĕrĭ } mĕdĭcārĭ }	sānārĕ, *to heal*

mĕdĭtārī	cōgĭtārĕ, *to meditate*
mercārī	ĕmĕrĕ, *to buy*
mĭnārī mĭnĭtārī	dēnuntĭārĕ, *to threaten*
mĭsĕrārī	maerērĕ, *to bewail*
mŏdĕrārī	tempĕrārĕ, *to moderate*
mŏrārī	rĕtardārĕ, *to delay*
ŏdōrārī	săgīrĕ, *to scent*
ōmĭnārī	praesăgīrĕ, *to forebode*
ŏpĭnārī	pŭtārĕ, *to be of opinion*
oppĕrīrī	exspectārĕ, *to wait for*
pătrōcĭnārī	dēfendĕrĕ, *to protect*
percontārī	pervestĭgārĕ, *to inquire*
praedārī	dīrĭpĕrĕ (ĭō), *to plunder*
praestŏlārī	exspectārĕ, *to wait for*
prĕcārī	rŏgārĕ, *to ask, pray*
proelĭārī	pugnārĕ, *to fight*
rīmārī	indăgārĕ, *to pry into*
scĭtārī sciscĭtārī	investĭgārĕ, *to inquire*
scrūtārī perscrūtārī	perquīrĕrĕ, *to search*
sōlārī consōlārī	lēnīrĕ, *to comfort*
spĕcŭlārī	explōrārĕ, *to spy out*
suspĭcārī·	suspectārĕ, *to suspect*
tūtārī	mūnīrĕ, *to defend*
vĕnĕrārī	cōlĕrĕ, *to worship*
vĕrēcundārī	tĭmērĕ, *to be afraid*
vōcĭfĕrārī	clămārĕ, *to cry out*

fătērī	concēdĕrĕ, *to concede*
pollĭcērī	prōmittĕrĕ, *to promise*
rērī	censērĕ, *to think*
tŭērī	mūnīrĕ, *to defend*
vĕrērī	mĕtŭĕrĕ, *to fear*

ădĭpiscī	acquīrĕrĕ, *to reach*
ăggrĕdī (ĭŏr)	pĕtĕrĕ, *to attack*
lŏquī	dīcĕrĕ, *to speak*

nanciscĭ	părĕrĕ (ĭŏ), *to get*
pătĭ (ĭŏr)	tŏlĕrārĕ, *to endure*
assĕquĭ	impĕtrārĕ, *to obtain*
consĕquĭ	compărārĕ, *to get*
exsĕquĭ	efficĕrĕ (ĭŏ), *to perform*
persĕquĭ	exăgĭtārĕ } *to pursue* vexārĕ }
vescĭ	ĕdĕrĕ, *to eat*
ulciscĭ	vindĭcārĕ, *to avenge*
ûtĭ	ûsurpārĕ } *to use* ădhĭbĕrĕ }

ădŏrīrĭ	{ suscĭpĕrĕ (ĭŏ), *to undertake* { oppugnārĕ, *to assail*
blandīrĭ	mulcĕrĕ, *to flatter*
largīrĭ	prŏfundĕrĕ, *to squander*
mentīrĭ	fingĕrĕ, *to feign*
mŏlīrĭ	mŏvĕrĕ, *to set in motion*
ordīrĭ	incĭpĕrĕ (ĭŏ), *to begin*
partīrĭ	dīvĭdĕrĕ, *to share*
pŏtīrĭ	occŭpārĕ, *to take possession of*

LATIN PROVERBS and QUOTATIONS.

A bonis bona disce. — *Profit by good example.*

A bove majōri discit arāre minor. — *From the old ox the young one learns to plow.*

Ab equīnis pedĭbus procul recēde. — *Trust not a horse's heels.*

Ab inopĭa ad virtūtem obsaepta est via. — *Hard is the path from poverty to renown.*

Abĕunt studĭa in mores. — *Habit becomes second nature.*

Absens heres non erit. — *The absent one will not be the heir.*

Absentem laedit, cum ebrĭo qui litīgat. — *He who quarrels with a drunken man, injures one who is absent.*

Absentem qui rodit amīcum, qui non defendit, alĭo culpante, hic niger est. — *He who speaks ill of an absent friend, or fails to take his part if attacked by another, is a scoundrel.*

Abundans cautēla non nocet. — *An excess of caution does no harm.*

Acerrīma proximōrum odĭa. — *The hatred of relations is the most bitter.*

Actum ne agas. — *Do nothing twice over.*

Ad astra per aspĕra. — *To the stars through difficulties.* (The motto of Kansas.)

Ad finem ubi pervenĕris, ne velis reverti. — *Having achieved your purpose, seek not to undo what has been done.*

Ad laetitĭam datum est vinum, non ad ebrietātem. — *Wine is given to bring mirth, not drunkenness.*

Ad nova omnes concurrunt. — *All concur to novelties.*

Ad perdĭtam secūrim manubrĭum adjicĕre. — *To throw the helve after the hatchet.*

Ad unguem factus homo. — *A man perfect to the finger tips.*

Adhibenda est in jocando moderatio.	*Joking must have its proper limit.*
Adhuc sub judice lis est.	*The question is yet before the court.*
Adulescentem verecundum esse decet.	*Modesty should accompany youth.*
Aedificant domos et non habitabunt.	*They build houses, but shall not inhabit them.*
Aegroto, dum anima est, spes est.	*While there is life, there is hope.*
Aemulatio aemulationem parit.	*Emulation begets emulation.*
Aemulatio alit ingenia.	*Emulation is the whetstone of wit.*
Aequalis aequalem delectat.	*Like likes like.*
Aequam memento rebus in arduis servare mentem, non secus in bonis.	*In hard times, no less than in prosperity, preserve equanimity.*
Aequitas sequitur legem.	*Equity follows law.*
Aestate paenulam deteris.	*Why wear out your overcoat in summer ?*
Aetate prudentiores reddimur.	*We become wiser as we grow older.*
Age, libertate Decembri, quando ita majores voluerunt, utere.	*Come, let us take a lesson from our forefathers, and enjoy the Christmas holiday.*
Age quod agis.	*What you are doing, do thoroughly.*
Agri non omnes frugiferi.	*Not all soils are fertile.*
Aleas fuge.	*Avoid gambling.*
Alia aliis placent.	*Different men like different things.*
Aliam aetatem alia decent.	*Different pursuits suit different ages.*
Alii sementem faciunt, alii messem.	*Some sow, others reap.*
Aliquid consuetudini dandum est.	*Something must be allowed to custom.*
Alitur vitium vivitque tegendo.	*A fault is fostered by concealment.*

Altissĭma quaeque flumĭna minĭmo sono labuntur.	*The deepest rivers flow with the least sound.*
Alĭud ex alĭo malo.	*Out of one evil another comes.*
Amīcus certus in re incerta cernĭtur.	*A true friend is tested in adversity.*
Amīcus omnĭum, amīcus nullōrum.	*Every man's friend is no man's friend.*
Amissum quod nescĭtur, non amittĭtur.	*A loss of which we are ignorant, is no loss.*
An dives sit, omnes quaerunt, nemo, an bonus.	*All ask if a man be rich, no one if he be good.*
An nescis longas regĭbus esse manus ?	*Know you not that kings have long arms?*
Anĭmis opĭbusque parăti.	*Prepared in mind and resources.* (The motto of South Carolina.)
Anĭmum rege, qui nisi paret, impĕrat.	*Govern your temper, which will rule you unless kept in subjection.*
Anĭmus homĭnis semper appĕtit agĕre alĭquid.	*The human mind ever longs for occupation.*
Annōsa vulpes non capĭtur laquĕo.	*An old fox is not caught in a snare.*
Annus prodūcit, non ager.	*It is the season, not the soil, that brings the crop.*
Ante Dei vultum nihil unquam restat inultum.	*Punishment awaits all offenses.*
Ante molam primus qui venit, non molat imus.	*He who has come to the mill first, does not grind last.*
Ante victorĭam ne canas triumphum.	*Sing not of triumph before the victory.*
Aquae furtĭvae dulciōres sunt.	*Stolen waters are the sweetest.*
Aquĭla non capit muscas.	*The eagle does not catch flies.*
Arcum intensĭo frangit, anĭmum remissĭo.	*Straining breaks the bow, relaxation the mind.*
Arcus nimis intentus rumpĭtur.	*A bow too much bent is broken.*
Argentĕis hastis pugna, et omnĭa expugnăbis.	*Fight with silver spears, and you will overcome every thing.*

Ars amat fortûnam et fortûna artem.
Fortune and the arts assist each other.

Ars compensâbit, quod vis tibi magna negâbit.
Skill will enable us to succeed in that which sheer force could not accomplish.

Ars longa, vita brevis.
Science is unlimited in its course, life is short.

Artem natûra supĕrat sine vi, sine cura.
Nature without an effort surpasses art.

Aspĕra vox "îte," sed vox est blanda "venîte."
Harsh is the voice which would dismiss us, but sweet is the sound of welcome.

Assidûa stilla saxum excăvat.
Constant dripping hollows out the rock.

Audâces fortûna juvat timĭdosque repellit.
Fortune smiles on the brave, and frowns upon the coward.

Audentes fortûna juvat.
Fortune favors the bold.

Audi, vide, tace.
Hear, see, and be silent.

Audiâtur et altĕra pars.
Hear both sides of a question.

Audîre est oboedîre.
To hear is to heed.

Audîto multa, sed loquĕre pauca.
Hear much, say little.

Aurĕa ne credas quaecunque nitescĕre cernis.
Believe not that all that shines, is gold.

Aurîbus lupum tenĕo.
I hold a wolf by the ears.

Aurîga virtûtum prudentîa.
Prudence is the charioteer of all virtues.

Auro loquente nihil pollet oratîo.
Eloquence avails nothing against the voice of gold.

Aurôra Musis amîca.
The early morn favors study.

Aut Caesar, aut nullus.
Either Cœsar, or nobody.

Avărus, nisi cum morîtur, nihil recte facit.
A covetous man does nothing that he should, till he dies.

Avîde audîmus, aures enim homĭnum novitâte laetantur.
We listen with deep interest to what we hear, for to man novelty is ever charming.

Balbus balbum rectĭus intellĕgit.	*To understand a stammerer, you ought to stammer yourself.*
Basis virtūtum constantĭa.	*Constancy is the basis of virtue.*
Beāti monocŭli in regiōne caecōrum.	*Happy are one-eyed men in the country of the blind.*
Beātus ille qui procul negotĭis, ut prisca gens mortalĭum, paterna rura bobus exercet suis, solūtus omni faenōre.	*Happy the man who, removed from all cares of business, after the manner of his forefathers cultivates with his own team his paternal acres, freed from all thought of usury.*
Bellum cum vitĭis, sed pax cum persōnis.	*War with vices, but peace with individuals.*
Benefacta male locāta, malefacta arbĭtror.	*Favors out of place I regard as positive injuries.*
Beneficĭi accepti memor esto.	*Be not unmindful of obligations conferred.*
Beneficĭum accipĕre, libertātem vendĕre.	*To receive a favor is to sell your liberty.*
Bis ac ter, quod pulchrum.	*A good thing can be twice, nay, even thrice spoken.*
Bis dat, qui cito dat.	*He giveth twice who giveth in a trice.*
Bis vincit, qui se vincit in victorĭa.	*He conquers a second time who controls himself in victory.*
Boni pastōris est tondĕre pecus, non deglubĕre.	*It is the duty of a good shepherd to shear, not to skin his sheep.*
Bonus dux bonum reddit comĭtem.	*A good leader makes a good follower.*

Caeca invidĭa est, nec quidquam alĭud scit quam detrectāre virtūtes.	*Envy is blind, and is only clever in depreciating the virtues of others.*
Caeci sunt ocŭli, cum anĭmus res alĭas agit.	*The eyes see not what is before them when the mind is intent on other matters.*
Caecus iter monstrāre vult.	*The blind man wishes to show the way.*

Caelum, non anÏmum mutant, qui trans mare currunt.	They change their sky, not their affections, who cross the sea.
Camēlus desidĕrans cornŭa etÏam aures perdÏdit.	The camel longing for horns lost also his ears.
Camēlus vel scabiōsus complurÏum asinōrum gestat onĕra.	Even a mangy camel will carry more than several asses.
Cancer lepōrem capit.	The crab would catch the hare!
CandÏda pax homÏnes, trux decet ira feras.	Honorable peace becomes men, fierce anger should belong to beasts.
Canis timÏdus vehementÏus latrat quam mordet.	A timid dog more eagerly barks than bites.
Cantābit vacŭus coram latrōne viātor.	A pauper traveler will sing before a highwayman.
Carpe diem quam minÏmum credŭlus postĕro.	Catch the opportunity while it lasts, and rely not on what the morrow may bring.
Casus dementis correctÏo fit sapientis.	The misfortune of the foolish is a warning to the wise.
Cave a cane muto et ab aqua silenti.	Beware of a silent dog and of still water.
Cavĕat emptor.	Let the buyer be on his guard.
Cedant arma togae.	Let the arms yield to the gown.
Cede Deo.	Yield to divine power.
Celsae graviōre casu decÏdunt turres.	The higher the tower, the greater its fall.
Certa amittÏmus, dum incerta petÏmus.	In grasping at uncertainties, we lose that which is certain.
Certe ignoratÏo futurōrum malōrum utilÏor est quam scientÏa.	Ignorance of impending evil is far better than a knowledge of its approach.
Certis rebus certa signa praecurrunt.	Certain signs are the forerunners of certain events.
Cito matūrum, cito putrÏdum.	Soon ripe, soon rotten.
Cito pede praetĕrit aetas.	Time flies with hasty wings.
Cochlĕa consillÏs, in factis esto volŭcris.	Be a snail in deliberation, a bird in execution.

Coena brevis juvat.

A light supper is beneficial.

Cogitáto, quam longa sit hiems.

Consider how long the winter will last.

Collíge, non omni tempóre messis erit.

Fill your garners, harvest lasts not forever.

Comes jucundus in via pro vehículo est.

A pleasant traveling companion helps us on our journey as much as a carriage.

Commúne naufragíum omníbus est consolatío.

A common shipwreck is a consolation to all.

Communía sunt amicórum inter se omnía.

Friends have all things in common.

Conciliant homínes mala.

Misfortunes make friends.

Conciliat anímos comítas affabilítasque sermónis.

Politeness and an affable address are our best introduction.

Concordía res parvae crescunt, discordía maxímae dilabuntur.

Small endeavors obtain strength by unity of action: the most powerful are broken down by discord.

Conscientía crimen prodit.

Conscience betrays guilt.

Consilíum senum est sanum.

The counsel of the aged is sound.

Consuetúdo est altéra natúra.

Custom is second nature.

Contra vim mortis non herbúla crescit in hortis.

There grows not the herb which can protect against the power of death.

Cor unum, via una.

One heart, one way.

Corrumpunt bonos mores colloquía prava.

Evil communications corrupt good manners.

Crambe bis cocta.

Colewort twice cooked.

Crede, quod habes, et habes.

Believe that you have it, and it is yours.

Crescit amor nummi, quantum ipsa pecunía crescit.

The love of money grows as money grows.

Crescíte et multiplicamíni.

Grow and multiply.
(The motto of Maryland.)

Crevérunt et opes, et opum furiósa cupído, ut, quo possidéant pluríma, plura petant.

Riches increase, and the maddening craving for gold, so that men ever seek for more, that they may have the most.

Crimĭna qui cernunt aliōrum, non sua cernunt, hi sapĭunt allĭis, desipĭuntque sibi.

Those who see the faults of others, and see not their own, are wise for others and fools for themselves.

Crimĭne nemo caret.

No man is faultless.

Cuĭvis dolōri remedĭum est patientĭa.

Patience is the remedy for every misfortune.

Cujusvis homĭnis est errăre, nullĭus nisi insipientis in errōre perseverăre.

To err is human, but to persevere in error is only the act of a fool.

Culpam poena premit comes.

Punishment follows close on the heels of crime.

Cum fortūna perit, nullus amĭcus erit.

When fortune deserts us, our friends are nowhere.

Cunĕus cunĕum trudit.

One wedge drives another.

Currus bovem trahit.

The carriage draws the ox.

Cutem gerit lacerătam canis mordax.

A biting cur wears a torn skin.

———

Dat Deus immĭti cornŭa curta bovi.

Providence provides but short horns for the fierce ox.

De duŏbus malis minus est semper eligendum.

Of two evils the least is always to be chosen.

De gustĭbus non est disputandum.

There is no disputing about tastes.

De male quaesĭtis vix gaudet tertĭus heres.

A third heir seldom profits by ill-gotten wealth.

De mortŭis nil nisi bonum.

Say nothing but good of the dead.

De parva scintilla magnum saepe excitătur incendĭum.

From a little spark there will often be produced a great conflagration.

Dejecta arbŏre, quivis ligna collĭgit.

When the tree is felled, every one runs to it with his axe.

Deliberando saepe perit occasĭo.

By hesitation the opportunity is often lost.

Desunt inopĭae multa, avaritĭae omnĭa.	Poverty needs much, avarice every thing.
Deus, quos dilĭgit, castĭgat.	Whom the Lord loveth he chasteneth.
Dii laborĭbus omnĭa vendunt.	The gods sell all things for labor.
Dii lanĕos habent pedes.	The avenging gods have their feet clothed in wool.
Dilucŭlo surgĕre saluberrĭmum est.	Early rising is most conducive to health.
Dimidĭum facti, qui coepit, habet.	Well begun is half done.
Dirĭgo.	I guide. (The motto of Maine.)
Discipŭlus est priŏris posterĭor dies.	To-morrow is the pupil of to-day.
Divĭde et impĕra.	Divide and rule.
Divitĭae non semper optĭmis contingunt.	Riches fall not always to the lot of the most deserving.
Docendo disces.	You will learn by teaching.
Domi suae quilĭbet rex.	A man is a king in his own house.
Donec eris felix, multos numerăbis amīcos : tempŏra si fuĕrint nubĭla, solus eris.	In prosperity you may count on many friends: if the sky becomes overcast, you will be alone.
Ducit amor patrĭae.	The love of country leads.
Dulce "domum."	Sweet home.
Dulce et decōrum est pro patrĭa mori.	It is sweet and meritorious to die for one's country.
Dulce pomum, quum abest custos.	Stolen fruit is sweet.
Dum Aurōra fulget, flores colligĭte.	Gather flowers while the morning sun lasts.
Dum caput infestat, labor omnĭa membra molestat.	When the head aches, all the members suffer with it.
Dum deliberămus, quando incipiendum, incipĕre jam serum est.	While we are making up our minds as to when we shall begin, the opportunity is lost.

Dum loquor, hora fugit.

While I am speaking, the opportunity is lost.

Dum spiro, spero.

While there's life, there's hope.

Dum vires annique sinunt, tolerăte labōrem: jam veniet tacĭto curva senecta pede.

Work while your strength and years permit you; crooked age will by and by come upon you with silent foot.

Dum vitant stulti vitĭa, in contrarĭa currunt.

In avoiding one vice, fools rush into the opposite extreme.

Dum vivĭmus, vivămus.

While life lasts, let us enjoy it.

Duos qui sequĭtur lepŏres, neutrum capit.

He who follows two hares, loses both.

Duro flagello mens docētur rectĭus.

The mind is best taught with a a sharp whip.

Durum et durum non facĭunt murum.

Hard things alone will not make a wall.

Durum telum necessĭtas.

Necessity is a strong weapon.

E cantu dignoscĭtur avis.

A bird is distinguished by its note.

E plurĭbus unum.

One out of many.
(The motto of the United States.)

E scilla non nascĭtur rosa.

An onion will not produce a rose.

Edĕre oportet, ut vivas, non vivĕre, ut edas.

We should eat to live, not live to eat.

Eheu! fugăces labuntur anni.

Alas! the fleeting years, how they roll on!

Elephantum ex mure facis.

You make an elephant of a mouse.

Elephantus non capit murem.

An elephant does not catch mice.

Emĕre malo quam rogăre.

I would rather buy than beg.

Empta dolōre docet experientĭa.

Experience purchased by suffering teaches wisdom.

Ense petit placĭdam sub libertăte quiētem.

With the sword she seeks quiet peace under liberty.
(The motto of Massachusetts.)

Eripĭte isti gladĭum, qui sui est impos anĭmi.

Leave not a sword in the hand of an idiot.

Eripŭit caelo fulmen, sceptrumque tyrannis.

He snatched the thunderbolt from heaven, and the scepter from tyrants (said of Franklin).

Est modus in rebus: sunt certi denĭque fines, quos ultra citrăque nequit consistĕre rectum.

There is a medium in all things: there are certain limits on both sides of which, that which is right, cannot exist.

Est natūra homĭnum novitătis avĭda.

Man naturally yearns for novelty.

Est proprĭum stultitĭae aliōrum vitĭa cernĕre, oblivisci suōrum.

It is peculiarly a fool's habit to discern the faults of others, and to forget his own.

Esto quod esse vidēris.

Be what you appear to be.

Et mihi res, non me rebus submittĕre conor.

I strive to mold circumstances to myself, not myself to circumstances.

Etĭam mendĭcus mendĭco invĭdet.

Even the beggar envies the beggar.

Etĭam sanăto vulnĕre cicătrix manet.

Even when the wound is healed, the scar remains.

Ex arēna funicŭlum nectis.

You would weave a rope of sand.

Ex aurĭbus cognoscĭtur asĭnus.

A donkey is known by his ears.

Ex inimĭco cogĭta posse fiĕri amĭcum.

Consider that an enemy may become a friend.

Ex lingua stulta venĭunt incommŏda multa.

Many an injury comes from a fool's speech.

Ex uno disce omnes.

From one you may judge of the whole.

Excelsĭor.

Higher. (The motto of New York.)

Excusatĭo non petĭta fit accusatĭo manifesta.

An uncalled for defense becomes a positive accusation.

Excūde mihi ignem, et allucēbo tibi.

Strike me a light, and I will light you.

Exemplo plus quam ratiōne vivĭmus.

We live more by fashion than by common sense.

Experientĭa docet.	*Experience teaches.*
Experto crede.	*Believe him who speaks from experience.*
Expressĭo unĭus est exclusĭo alterĭus.	*The naming of one person amounts to the exclusion of another.*
Extrēmis malis extrēma remedĭa.	*Desperate maladies require desperate remedies.*

Fabas indulcat fames.	*Hunger gives a relish even to raw beans.*
Faber est quisque fortūnae suae.	*Every man is the architect of his own fortune.*
Fabrĭcando fabri sumus.	*Work makes the workman.*
Fac de necessĭtāte virtūtem.	*Make a virtue of necessity.*
Fac nidum unum una in arbŏre.	*Build but one nest in one tree.*
Facĭle consilĭum damus alĭis.	*We easily give advice to others.*
Facile, cum valēmus, recta consilĭa aegrōtis damus.	*When in good health, we easily give good advice to the sick.*
Fama nihil est celerĭus.	*Nothing moves more quickly than scandal.*
Fames est optĭma coqua.	*Hunger is the best cook.*
Fames optĭmum condimentum.	*Hunger is the best sauce.*
Fas est et ab hoste docēri.	*It is good to be taught even by an enemy.*
Favōre et benevolentĭa etĭam immānis anĭmus mansuescit.	*By good nature and kindness even fierce spirits become tractable.*
Felicĭter sapit, qui alĭēno pericŭlo sapit.	*He gets his wisdom cheaply who gets it at another's cost.*
Felix, quem facĭunt alĭēna pericŭla cautum.	*Fortunate is he whom the dangers of others have rendered cautious.*
Felix, qui nihil debet.	*Happy is the man who is out of debt.*

Fere libenter homĭnes id, quod volunt, credunt.	*Men freely believe that which they wish to be the truth.*
Ferĭunt summos fulmĭna montes.	*Lightning strikes the tops of the mountains.*
Ferrĕus assidŭo consumĭtur anŭlus usu.	*Even a ring of iron is worn away by constant use.*
Ferrum, cum igni candet, tundendum.	*Strike while the iron is hot.*
Ferrum ferro acuĭtur.	*Steel whets steel.*
Fervet olla, vivit amicitĭa.	*Friendship lasts as long as the pot boils.*
Festīna lente.	*Hasten gently.*
Festinäre nocet, nocet et cunctatĭo saepe, tempŏre quaeque suo qui facit, ille sapit.	*Haste is productive of injury, and so is too much hesitation; he is the wisest man who does every thing at the proper time.*
Fiat justitĭa, ruat caelum!	*Let justice be done, though the heavens fall !*
Fide, sed cui vide.	*Have confidence, but beware in whom.*
Figŭlus figŭlo invĭdet, faber fabro.	*Potter envies potter, and smith smith.*
Finis corōnat opus.	*The end crowns the work.*
Flamma fumo est proxĭma.	*Where there is smoke, there is fire.*
Formōsa facĭes muta commendatĭo est.	*Handsome features are a silent recommendation.*
Fortes creantur fortĭbus et bonis.	*The brave are born from the brave and good.*
Fortes fortūna adjŭvat.	*Fortune helps the brave.*
Fortis cadĕre, cedĕre non potest.	*The brave man may die, but he will never say "die."*
Fortĭter ferendo vincĭtur malum, quod evitāri non potest.	*By a brave endurance of unavoidable evils, we conquer them.*
Fortūna multis dat nimĭum, nulli satis.	*Fortune gives too much to many, to no one enough.*

Fortūna nimĭum quem fovet, stultum facit.

Fortune, by being too lavish of her favors on a man, makes a fool of him.

Fortūna opes auferre, non anĭmum potest.

Fortune may rob us of our wealth, not of our courage.

Fortūna, quod dedit, erĭpit.

Fortune gives, Fortune takes away.

Fortūna vitrĕa est; tum, cum splendet, frangĭtur.

Fortune is like glass; she breaks when she is brightest.

Frangĭtur ira gravis, cum fit responsĭo suāvis.

The force of anger is broken by a soft answer.

Fructu, non folĭis arbŏrem aestĭma.

Judge of a tree by its fruit, not by its leaves.

Frustra labōrat qui omnĭbus placēre studet.

He labors in vain who attempts to please every body.

Fugit irrevocabĭle tempus.

Time flies never to be recalled.

Fumum fugĭens in ignem incĭdi.

While avoiding the smoke, I have fallen into the flame.

Fundum aliēnum arat, suum incultum desĕrit.

He plows the land of others, and leaves his own untilled.

Funicŭlus triplex non facĭle rumpĭtur. .

A triple rope is not easily broken.

Furem fur cognoscit, et lupum lupus.

Thief knows thief, and wolf knows wolf.

Furor arma ministrat.

Fury itself supplies arms.

Furor irǎque mentem praecipĭtant.

Passion and strife carry away the mind.

Furtīvus potus plenus dulcedĭne totus.

Stolen waters are sweetest.

Gaudĭa principĭum nostri sunt saepe dolōris.

Pleasure is often the introduction to pain.

Genĭtrix virtūtum frugalĭtas.

Frugality is the mother of all virtues.

Gratĭa gratĭam parit.

One good turn deserves another.

Gravĭōra quaedam sunt remedĭa pericŭlis.

Some remedies are worse than the disease itself.

Gravissĭmum est imperĭum consuetudĭnis.	*All -powerful is the rule of fashion.*
Gutta cavat lapĭdem, non vi, sed saepe cadendo.	*Dropping water makes the rock hollow, not by its force, but by constant action.*
Gutta fortūnae prae dolĭo sapientĭae.	*A drop of luck is worth a cask of wisdom.*

Habent insidĭas homĭnis blanditĭae mali.	*The soft speeches of the wicked are full of deceit.*
Habet et musca splenem.	*Even a fly can show temper.*
Haud semper errat fama.	*Common report is not always wrong.*
Heus! proxĭmus sum egŏmet mihi.	*Look you! I myself am nearest to myself.*
Hic est, aut nusquam, quod quaerĭmus.	*Here, or nowhere, is the thing we seek.*
Hoc retĭne verbum, frangit Deus omne superbum.	*Providence crushes pride.*
Hodĭe mihi, cras tibi.	*To-day to me, to-morrow it belongs to you.*
Homĭnes ad deos nulla re propĭus accēdunt quam salūtem homĭnibus dando.	*In nothing do men so much resemble the gods as in giving help to their fellow-creatures.*
Homĭnes nihil agendo discunt male agĕre.	*In doing nothing men learn to do evil.*
Homĭnis est errāre, insipientis perseverāre.	*To err is human, to persevere in error is the act of a fool.*
Homo homĭni aut deus aut lupus.	*Man is to man a god or a wolf.*
Homo propōnit, sed Deus dispōnit.	*Man proposeth, God disposeth.*
Homo sum: humāni nihil a me aliēnum puto.	*I am myself a man, and deem nothing that relates to man foreign to my feelings.*
Homo totĭes morĭtur, quotĭes amittit suos.	*A man suffers death himself as often as he loses those dear to him.*

Homo trium litterārum : FUR.	*A man of three letters : Thief.*
Honōres mutant mores.	*Success alters our manners.*
Honos alit artes, et virtus laudāta crescit.	*Honorable mention encourages science, and merit is fostered by praise.*
Honos habet onus.	*Honor brings responsibility.*
Horrĕa formīcae tendunt ad inanīa nunquam, nullus ad amissas ibit amīcus opes.	*Ants will not go to an empty granary, and friends will not visit us when our wealth is gone.*

Idem velle idemque nolle, ea demum firma amicitīa est.	*To have the same likes and dislikes, therein consists the firmest bond of friendship.*
Ignāvis semper ferīae sunt.	*With the idle it is always holiday time.*
Ignem igni ne addas.	*Add not fire to fire.*
Ignis aurum probat.	*Fire tries gold.*
Ignis cinerībus alītur suis.	*A fire is nourished by its own ashes.*
Ignis non exstinguītur igni.	*Fire will not put out fire.*
Ignorantīa legis nemīnem excūsat.	*Ignorance of the law excuses no one.*
Ignosce saepīus altĕri, numquam tibi.	*Pardon another often, thyself never.*
Illa dolet vere, quae sine teste dolet.	*Her grief is real who grieves when no one is by.*
Illa mihi patrīa est, ubi pascor, non ubi nascor.	*That country will I call mine which supports me, not that which gave me birth.*
Illiberāle est mentīri, ingenŭum verītas decet.	*It is ungentlemanly to lie; truthfulness becomes the gentleman.*
Imperāre sibi maxīmum imperīum est.	*The greatest power of ruling consists in the exercise of self-control.*
Impĕrat aut servit collecta pecunīa cuīque.	*Money, as it increases, becomes either the master or the slave of its owner.*

Impröbe Neptūnum accūsat, qui naufragĭum itĕrum facit.

He blames Neptune unjustly who twice suffers shipwreck.

In capĭte orphăni discit chirur- gus.

A surgeon tries his experiments on the head of orphans.

In mari magno pisces capiuntur.

In the great sea fish is always to be caught.

In morbo recollĭgit se anĭmus.

In time of sickness the soul col- lects itself anew.

In sudōre vultus tui comĕdes pa- nem tuum.

In the sweat of thy face shalt thou eat thy bread.

In trivĭo sum.

I am in a fix. (In a place where three ways meet.)

In vestimentis non stat sapientĭa mentis.

Wisdom does not consist in dress.

In vili veste nemo tractătur ho- neste.

No one in a shabby coat is treated with respect.

Incĭdit in Scyllam cupĭens vităre Charybdim.

In avoiding Charybdis, he drives against Scylla.

Incus maxĭma non metŭit strepĭ- tum.

A great anvil fears not noise.

Infirmi est anĭmi exiguĭque vo- luptas ultĭo.

It is but the weak and little mind that rejoices in revenge.

Infra tuam pellicŭlam te contĭne.

Live according to your means.

Ingeniōrum cos aemulatĭo.

Emulation is the whetstone of talent.

Ingens telum necessĭtas.

Necessity is a strong weapon.

Ingrătus est, qui remōtis testĭbus agit gratĭas.

He may as well not thank at all, who thanks when none are by.

Ingrătus unus misĕris omnĭbus nocet.

One ungrateful man injures all who need assistance.

Ingrătus vir dolĭum est perforā- tum.

An ungrateful man is a tub full of holes.

Injurĭam qui factūrus est, jam facit.

To meditate an injury is to com- mit one.

Inter arma silent leges.

When war is raging, the laws are dumb.

Inter caecos regnat luscus.	*Among the blind a one-eyed man is a king.*
Inter mallĕum et incūdem.	*Between the hammer and the anvil.*
Interdum lacrǐmae pondĕra vocis habent.	*Tears are at times as eloquent as words.*
Interdum stultus bene loquǐtur.	*Even a fool sometimes speaks to the purpose.*
Interdum vulgus rectum videt.	*The mob will now and then see things in a right light.*
Invĕni portum, Spes et Fortūna, valēte, sat me lusistis, ludǐte nunc alǐos.	*I've reach'd the harbor, Hope and Chance, adieu! You've play'd with me, now play with others too.*
Invidǐa festos dies non habet.	*Envy never has a holiday.*
Invǐtat culpam, qui peccātum praetĕrit.	*He who leaves a fault unpunished, invites crime.*
Ipsa scientǐa potestas est.	*Knowledge is power.*
Ipsa senectus morbus est.	*Old age is in itself a disease.*
Ira furor brevis est.	*Anger is a transient madness.*
Iracundǐam qui vincit, hostem supĕrat maxǐmum.	*He who gets the better of an irascible temperament, conquers his worst enemy.*
Irătus cum ad se redit, sibi tum irascǐtur.	*An angry man, when he returns to reason, will then be angry with himself.*
Is minǐmo eget mortālis, qui minǐmum cupit.	*He is the least in want who is the least covetous.*
Iter pigrōrum quasi saepes spinărum.	*The way of a slothful man is as a hedge of thorns.*

Jactantǐae comes invidǐa.	*Envy waits on boasting.*
Jejūnus raro stomăchus vulgarǐa temnit.	*A hungry stomach rarely despises rough food.*
Jucunda est memorǐa praeteritōrum malōrum.	*Pleasant is the recollection of dangers past.*

Jucundi acti labōres.	*Sweet is the recollection of difficulties overcome.*
Jucundissĭma navigatĭo juxta terram, ambulatĭo juxta mare.	*The most pleasant cruise is near the land, the most inviting walk near the sea.*
Judex damnătur, cum nocens absolvĭtur.	*The judge is condemned when the guilty are acquitted.*
Juniōres ad labōres.	*Young men for labors.*
Juxta fluvĭum putĕum fodit.	*Hard by a river he digs a well.*

Labor ipse voluptas.	*The labor is in itself a pleasure.*
Labor omnĭa vincit.	*Labor conquers all things.*
Lacrĭma nihil citĭus arescit.	*Nothing dries up more quickly than a tear.*
Laudāta virtus crescit, et immensum glorĭa calcar habet.	*Virtue is increased by the smile of approval, and the love of renown is the greatest incentive to honorable acts.*
Laus proprĭa sordet.	*Praise of one's own self defiles.*
Lavant lacrĭmae delictum.	*Repentant tears wash out the stain of guilt.*
Lepŏrem frondĭum crepĭtus terret.	*Even the rustling of leaves will alarm the hare.*
Leve fit, quod bene fertur onus.	*A burden cheerfully borne becomes light.*
Levis est dolor, qui capĕre consilĭum potest.	*Light is that grief which counsel can allay.*
Levĭus fit patientĭa, quicquid corrigĕre est nefas.	*Patience lightens the burden we cannot avert.*
Lingua lapsa verum dicit.	*An unguarded speech reveals the truth.*
Linguam frenāre plus est quam castra domāre.	*It is more difficult to bridle the tongue than to conquer an army.*
Lis litem genĕrat.	*One lawsuit begets another.*
Littĕra scripta manet.	*A letter once written can not be recalled.*

Litterārum radīces amārae, frūctus dulces.

Learning has bitter roots, but sweet fruits.

Longo in itinēre etīam palěa onēri est.

On a long voyage even a straw becomes a burden.

Longum est iter per praecepta, breve et effīcax per exempla.

Long is the road to learning by precepts, but short and successful by examples.

Lupus pilum mutat, non mentem.

The wolf changes his hair, but not his nature.

Magistrātus indīcat virum.

Office tests the man.

Magna civītas, magna solitūdo.

A great city, a great desert.

Magnum est vectīgal parsimonīa.

Frugality is a great revenue.

Mala gallīna, malum ovum.

Bad fowl, bad egg.

Male parta male dilabuntur.

Evil gotten, evil spent.

Malum vas non frangītur.

A useless pitcher does not get broken.

Manus manum lavat.

One hand washes the other.

Mater artīum necessītas.

Necessity is the mother of invention.

Medīo tutissīmus ibis.

A middle course is the safest.

Melīus est cavēre semper, quam pati semel.

It is better to be always prepared than to suffer once.

Memento mori.

Remember death.

Memento quod es homo.

Forget not that you are a man.

Mendācem memōrem esse oportet.

A liar should have a good memory.

Mendāci homīni, ne verum quidem dicenti, credēre solēmus.

We believe not a liar, even when he is speaking the truth.

Mens sana in corpōre sano.

A sound mind in a sound body.

Metǔe senectam, non enim sola advěnit.

Fear increasing age, for it does not come without companions.

Metus enim mortis musīca depellītur.

Even the fear of death is dispelled by music.

Minĭma possunt, qui plurĭma jactant.	*They can do least who boast loudest.*
Miserrĭma est fortûna, quae caret inimĭco.	*That is a most miserable lot which is without an enemy.*
Monĭti meliōra sequâmur.	*Being warned, let us pursue a better course.*
Montâni semper libĕri.	*Mountaineers are always free men.* (The motto of West Virginia.)
Mors malōrum finis est.	*Death is the end of evils.*
Mors omnĭbus commûnis.	*Death is common to all.*
Mors optĭma rapit, deterrĭma relinquit.	*Death snatches away the best and leaves the wicked.*
Mors sceptra ligonĭbus aequat.	*Death brings to a level spades and scepters.*
Mortŭi non mordent.	*Dead men do not bite.*
Mortŭo leōni et lepōres insultant.	*Even hares jump on a dead lion.*
Multa cadunt inter calĭcem supremâque labra.	*There is many a slip 'twixt the cup and the lip.*
Multa docet fames.	*Hunger teaches us many a lesson.*
Multa petentĭbus desunt multa.	*The covetous are always in want.*
Multa senem circumvenĭunt incommŏda.	*Many annoyances surround an aged man.*
Multa verba, modĭca fides.	*Many words, little credit.*
Multae manus onus levĭus facĭunt.	*Many hands make light work.*
Multae regum aures atque ocŭli.	*Kings have many ears and many eyes too.*
Multi morbi curantur abstinentĭa.	*Many diseases may be cured by abstinence.*
Multis ictĭbus dejicĭtur quercus.	*By repeated blows even the oak is felled.*
Multōrum manĭbus grande levâtur onus.	*By the hands of many a great work is made light.*
Murus aerĕus conscientĭa sana.	*A clear conscience is a wall of brass.*

Mus non uni fidit antro.	*A mouse relies not solely on one hole.*
Musica est mentis medicina maestae.	*Music is the best cure for a sorrowing mind.*
Mutum est pictūra poēma.	*A picture is a poem wanting words.*

Nam ut quisque est vir optĭmus, ita difficillĭme esse alĭos imprŏbos suspicātur.	*The more virtuous a man himself is, the less does he suspect baseness in others.*
Natūra dedit agros, ars humāna aedificăvit urbes.	*Nature made the fields, and man the cities.*
Natūram expellas furca, tamen usque recurret.	*Though you drive out Nature with a club, yet will she always return.*
Ne puĕro gladĭum.	*Intrust not a sword to a boy.*
Ne quid nimis.	*Too much of any thing is bad.*
Ne sutor supra crepĭdam.	*The cobbler should not go beyond his last.*
Nec obŏlum habet, unde restim emat.	*He has not a farthing left wherewith to buy a rope to hang himself.*
Nec piĕtas moram rugis et instanti senectae afferet, indomĭtaeque morti.	*Not even piety will stay wrinkles, nor the encroachments of age, nor the advance of death, which can not be resisted.*
Nec, quae praeterĭit, itĕrum revocabĭtur unda; nec, quae praeterĭit, hora redīre potest.	*Neither shall the wave, which has passed on, ever be recalled; nor can the hour, which has once fled by, return again.*
Nec scire fas est omnĭa.	*It is not permitted, that we should know every thing.*
Necesse est multos timĕat, quem multi timent.	*He must of necessity fear many whom many fear.*
Necessĭtas non habet legem.	*Necessity recognizes no law.*
Necessităti qui se accommŏdat, sapit.	*He is wise, who suits himself to the occasion.*

Neglecta solent incendĭa sumĕre vires.

Fire, if neglected, will soon gain strength.

Nemĭni fidas, nisi cum quo prius modĭum salis absumpsĕris.

Trust no one, until you have eaten a peck of salt with him.

Nemo bene impĕrat, nisi qui paruĕrit impĕrio.

No man orders well unless he has himself learnt to obey orders.

Nemo bis vexāri debet pro eādem causa.

No man ought to be twice tried for the same offense.

Nemo mortalĭum omnĭbus horis sapit.

No mortal man is wise at all times.

Nemo potest nudo vestimenta detrahĕre.

You can not take a shirt from a naked man.

Nemo prudens punit, quia peccātum est, sed ne peccētur.

Prudence will punish to prevent crime, not to avenge it.

Nemo repente fit optĭmus.

No man acquires perfection all at once.

Nemo sua sorte contentus.

No man is contented with his lot in this life.

Nescĭat manus dextra, quid facĭat sinistra.

Let not your right hand know what your left hand doeth.

Nescĭo qua natāle solum dulcedĭne mentem tangit, et immemŏrem non sinit esse sui.

Our native land attracts us with some mysterious charm, never to be forgotten.

Nescis, quid serus vesper vehat.

You know not what the evening may bring with it.

Nihil agendo homĭnes male agĕre discunt.

By doing nothing men learn to do evil.

Nihil est ab omni parte beātum.

There is no such thing as perfect happiness.

Nihil est tam volŭcre quam maledictum, nihil facilĭus emittĭtur, nihil citĭus excipĭtur, nihil latĭus dissipātur.

Nothing is so swift as calumny, nothing is more easily propagated, nothing more readily credited, nothing more widely circulated.

Nihil prodest imprŏbam mercem emĕre.

There is nothing to be gained by buying inferior goods.

Nihil semper floret; aetas succēdit aetāti.

Summer lasts not forever; seasons succeed each other.

Nihil sub sole novi.	*There is nothing new under the sun.*
Nihil tam firmum est, quod non expugnāri pecunīa possit.	*Nothing is so secure that money will not defeat it.*
Nihil mortalĭbus ardŭum est.	*Nothing is so difficult but that man will accomplish it.*
Nil prodest, quod non laedĕre possit idem.	*There is no useful thing which may not be turned to an injurious purpose.*
Nil sine labōre.	*Nothing is achieved without toil.*
Nil sine numĭne.	*Nothing without God.* (The motto of Colorado.)
Nimĭa cura detĕrit magis quam emendat.	*Too much care does more harm than good.*
Nimĭa familiarītas parit contemptum.	*Too much familiarity breeds contempt.*
Nitĭmur in vetĭtum semper, cupĭmusque negāta.	*We always strive for that which is forbidden, and desire that which is denied us.*
Nobilītas morum plus ornat quam genitōrum.	*Nobility of conduct is a greater recommendation than nobility of birth.*
Nocet empta dolōre voluptas.	*Pleasure bought with pain does harm.*
Nomĭna stultōrum semper parietĭbus haerent.	*The names of fools are always written on walls.*
Non deĕrat voluntas, sed facultas.	*The means were wanting, not the will.*
Non esse cupĭdum pecunīa est.	*To have no wants is money.*
Non est de sacco tanta farīna tuo.	*All that meal comes not from your own sack.*
Non est in mundo dives, qui dicit: "abundo !"	*No man is so rich as to say: "I have enough !"*
Non est ratĭo, ubi vis impĕrat.	*Reason is absent, when impulse rules.*
Non est tritĭcum sine palĕis.	*There is no wheat without chaff.*
Non nobis solum nati sumus.	*We are not born for ourselves alone.*

Non omne, quod nitet, aurum est.	*All is not gold that glitters.*
Non omnem molĭtor, quae fluit unda, videt.	*The miller sees not every wave that flows.*
Non omnĭa possŭmus omnes.	*We can not all of us do every thing.*
Non semper erit aestas.	*Summer will not last forever.·*
Non, si male nunc, et olim sic erit.	*If things look badly to-day, they may look better to-morrow.*
Non si te rupĕris, par eris.	*Not if you burst yourself, will you equal him.*
Non sunt amĭci, qui degunt procul.	*They cease to be friends who dwell afar off.*
Non venit ad silvam, qui cuncta rubēta verētur.	*He who fears every bramble, should not go to the woods.*
Non verbis, at facto opus est.	*Deeds, not words are required.*
Non volat in buccas assa columba tuas.	*Birds fly not into our mouths ready roasted.*
Nondum omnĭum diērum sol occĭdit.	*My sun has not yet set forever.*
Nosce tempus.	*Catch the opportunity.*
Nulla aetas ad perdiscendum sera est.	*It is never too late to learn.*
Nulla certĭor custodĭa innocentĭa.	*No protection is so sure as that of innocence.*
Nulla dies sine linĕa.	*Not a day should pass without something being done.*
Nullĭus hospĭtis grata est mora longa.	*The prolonged visit of no guest is pleasant.*
Nullus dies omnīno malus.	*No day is wholly unproductive of good.*
Num tibi, cum fauces urit sitis, aurĕa quaeris pocŭla ?	*When your throat is parched with thirst, do you desire a cup of gold ?*
Nunquam alĭud natūra, alĭud sapientĭa dicit.	*Nature never says one thing, science another.*
Nunquam minus solus, quam cum solus.	*Never less alone, than when alone.*

O praeclārum custōdem ovĭum, lupum!
O rare protector of the sheep, a wolf!

O tempŏra! O mores!
O these degenerate days!

Oboedientĭa felicitātis mater.
Obedience is the mother of happiness.

Occasĭo aegre offertur, facĭle amittĭtur.
An opportunity is found with difficulty and easily lost.

Occasĭo facit furem.
Opportunity makes the thief.

Ocŭlis magis habenda fides quam aurĭbus.
We should trust more to our eyesight than to our ears.

Ocŭlus domĭni sagĭnat equum.
The master's eye makes the horse fat.

Odi profānum vulgus et arcĕo.
I abhor the profane rabble and keep them at a distance.

Odĭmus accipĭtrem, quia semper vivit in armis.
We hate the hawk, because he ever lives in battle.

Omne anĭmal se ipsum dilĭgit.
Every living being loves itself.

Omne solum forti patrĭa.
To a brave man every soil is his country.

Omnĭa tempus habent.
Every thing has its season.

Omnis ars imitatĭo est natūrae.
Every thing in art is but a copy of nature.

Oportet remum ducĕre qui didĭcit.
Let him take the oars who has learned to row.

Optĭma medicĭna temperantĭa est.
Temperance is the best medicine.

Optĭmum est aliĕna frui experientĭa.
It is best to learn wisdom by the experience of others.

Optĭmum est pati, quod emendāre non possis.
What can't be cured, must be endured.

Opus opifĭcem probat.
The work tests the workman.

Orĭmur, morĭmur.
We are born; we die.

Ornat spina rosas, mella tegunt apes.
Roses grow on thorns, and honey wears a sting.

Otĭa corpus alunt, anĭmus quoque pascĭtur illis; immodĭcus contra carpit utrumque labor.
Rest strengthens the body, the mind too is thus supported; but unremitting toil destroys both.

Otĭum sine littĕris mors est, et homĭnis vivi sepultūra.   *Retirement without literary occupation is death itself, and a living tomb.*

Paenitentĭa sera raro vera.   *Late repentance is rarely sincere.*

Par pari refĕro.   *That which I receive, that I return.*

Pardus macŭlas non depōnit.   *A leopard does not change his spots.*

Pares cum parĭbus facillĭme congregantur.   *Two of a kind, whate'er they be, are forthwith certain to agree.*

Parĭtur pax bello.   *Peace is obtained by war.*

Parvum parva decent.   *Small things become the small.*

Patrĭae fumus igne aliēno luculentĭor.   *The smoke of our own country is brighter than fire abroad.*

Paucis carĭor est fides quam pecunĭa.   *But few prize honesty more than money.*

Paupertas mors altĕra.   *Poverty is death in another form.*

Per angusta ad augusta.   *Through dangers to distinction.*

Per risum multum possis cognoscĕre stultum.   *By much laughter you may know the fool.*

Permitte divis cetĕra.   *Trust the rest to the gods.*

Pessĭmum genus inimicōrum laudantes.   *The most detestable race of enemies are flatterers.*

Pisces magni parvŭlos comĕdunt.   *Great fish feed on the lesser.*

Plures adōrant solem orientem quam occidentem.   *Men worship the rising, not the setting sun.*

Pluris est oculātus testis unus quam aurĭti decem.   *One eye-witness is better than ten hearsays.*

Plus a medĭco quam a morbo pericŭli.   *There is more to be feared from the doctor than from the disease.*

Plus dolet quam necesse est, qui ante dolet, quam necesse est.   *He grieves more than is necessary who grieves before any cause for sorrow has arisen.*

Plus vident ocŭli quam ocŭlus.	*Four eyes can see more than two.*
Post malam segĕtem serendum est.	*After a bad harvest sow again.*
Post tenĕbras lux.	*After darkness comes light.*
Prima carĭtas incĭpit a se ipso.	*Charity begins at home.*
Principĭis obsta; sero medicĭna parâtur, cum mala per longas convaluĕre moras.	*Check the beginning of evil; the remedy is too late when the disease by delay has gained strength.*
Principĭum dimidĭum totĭus.	*The beginning is half of the whole.*
Priusquam incipĭas, consulto, et ubi consuluĕris matûre, facto opus est.	*Deliberate before you begin; but, having carefully done so, execute with vigor.*
Proba merx facĭle emptŏrem repĕrit.	*Good wares soon find a purchaser.*
Probĭtas laudâtur et alget.	*Integrity is praised and starves.*
Procellae, quanto plus habent virĭum, tanto minus tempŏris.	*The more violent the storm, the sooner it is over.*
Prohibenda est ira in puniendo.	*Anger should never appear in awarding punishment.*
Proprĭa domus omnĭum optĭma.	*Our own house surpasses every other.*
Proprĭo laus sordet in ore.	*Self-praise is odious.*
Prudens futûri tempŏris exĭtum caliginôsa nocte premit Deus.	*Designedly God covers in dark night the issue of futurity.*
Pugna suum finem, cum jacet hostis, habet.	*The battle is over, when the foe has fallen.*
Puras Deus, non plenas adspĭcit manus.	*Clean hands are better than full ones in the sight of God.*

Quaerenda pecunĭa primum est, virtus post nummos.	*Riches are first to be sought for; after wealth, virtue.*
Qualis vir, talis oratĭo.	*You may judge of a man by his remarks.*
Quam quisque novit artem, in hac se exercĕat.	*Let every man practice the trade which he best understands.*

Quanto superĭōres sumus, tanto nos gerāmus submissĭus.

The higher our position, the more modestly should we behave.

Quem di dilĭgunt, adulescens morĭtur.

He whom the gods love, dies young.

Qui amat me, amat et canem meum.

Love me, love my dog.

Qui dedit benefĭcium, tacĕat; narret, qui accēpit.

Let him who has granted a favor, not speak of it; let him who has received one, proclaim it.

Qui e nuce nuclĕum esse vult, frangat nucem.

He who would have the kernel, must crack the shell.

Qui facit per altĕrum, facit per se.

What a man does by the agency of another, is his own act.

Qui fert malis auxilĭum, post tempus dolet.

He who assists the wicked, will in time rue it.

Qui fugit molam, fugit farīnam.

Shirk work, and you will want bread.

Qui jacet in terra, non habet, unde cadat.

He who lies on the ground, can not fall.

Qui nihil debet, lictōres non timet.

He who owes nothing, fears not the sheriff's officer.

Qui nocēre potest, et idem prodesse.

One who can do you a deal of good, can also do you a deal of harm.

Qui non profĭcit, defĭcit.

He who does not advance, recedes.

Qui parcit virgae, odit filĭum.

He who spares the rod, hates his son.

Qui peccat ebrĭus, luat sobrĭus.

He who offends when drunk, will have to atone for it when sober.

Qui pingit florem, non pingit floris odōrem.

He who paints the flower, does not paint its fragrance.

Qui prior est tempŏre, potĭor est jure.

He who is first in time, has the prior right.

Qui se ipsum laudat, cito derisōrem invenĭet.

He who sounds his own trumpet, will soon find plenty to laugh at him.

Qui semel est laesus fallāci piscis ab hamo, omnĭbus unca cibis aera subesse putat.

The fish which has once felt the hook, suspects the crooked metal in every food which offers.

Qui sitĭunt, silentĭo bibunt.

They who are thirsty, drink in silence.

Qui spe aluntur, pendént, non vivunt.

Those who are nourished by hope, live ever in suspense, and enjoy not life.

Qui tacet, consentĭre vidētur.

From his·silence a man's consent is inferred.

Qui totum vult, totum perdit.

Want all, lose all.

Qui transtŭlit, sustĭnet.

He who transplanted, still sustains. (The motto of Connecticut.)

Qui vult caedĕre canem, facĭle invĕnit fustem.

He who has a mind to beat a dog, will easily find a stick.

Quid caeco cum specŭlo ?

What need has a blind man of a looking-glass?

Quid est dignĭtas indigno, nisi circŭlus aurĕus in narĭbus suis?

What is an exalted position to a low fellow but a golden ring in a swine's snout ?

Quid magis est durum saxo? Quid mollĭus unda? Dura tamen molli saxa cavantur aqua.

What is harder than stone? What more soft than water? Nevertheless, hard though the rock be, it is hollowed by the wave.

Quid sit futūrum cras, fuge quaerĕre.

Seek not to inquire what the morrow will bring with it.

Quid te exempta juvat spinis de plurĭbus una ?

Wherein is the use of getting rid of one thorn out of many?

Quis famŭlus amantĭor domĭni quam canis ?

By what servant is his master better loved than by his dog?

Quo plus habent, eo plus cupĭunt.

The more they have, the more they want.

Quo semel est imbūta recens, servābit odōrem testa diu.

The cask will long retain the flavor of the wine with which it was first seasoned.

Quod cibus est alĭis, alĭis est acre venēnum.

What's one man's meat, 's another man's poison.

Quod contemnĭtur, saepe utilissĭmum est.	*That which is despised, is often most useful.*
Quod factum est, infectum fiĕri non potest.	*What's done, can't be made undone.*
Quod nova testa capit, inveterăta sapĭt.	*The old cask tastes of what the new cask held.*
Quod quisque sperat, facĭle credit.	*We easily believe that which we hope for.*
Quod tibi fiĕri non vis, altĕri ne fecĕris.	*Do not unto another that which you would not he should do unto you.*
Quot homĭnes, tot sententĭae.	*As many men, so many opinions.*

Rarum carum.	*Scarce things are prized.*
Reddĭte cuĭque suum.	*Give to each man that which is his due.*
Regĭa, crede mihi, res est succurrĕre lapsis.	*Believe me, it is a kingly act to help the fallen.*
Regnant popŭli.	*The people rule.* (The motto of Arkansas.)
Religĭo docenda, non coërcenda.	*Religion must be taught, not forced.*
Reluctante natūra irrĭtus labor est.	*Labor against the voice of nature is labor in vain.*
Rem acu tetigisti.	*You have hit the point exactly.*
Res ad restim redĭit.	*It is all over: I may as well go and hang myself.*
Respĭce finem.	*Keep your eye upon the goal.*
Rete non tendĭtur accipĭtri neque milŭo.	*The net is not spread for the hawk or the kite.*
Rex eris, si recte facĭes.	*If your conduct be noble, you will be a king.*
Risus abundat in ore stultōrum.	*Laughter abounds in the mouths of fools.*
Rosam, quae praeterĭit, ne quaeras itĕrum.	*Seek not the rose which has passed away.*

Rota plaustri male uncta stridet.	*A wheel not greased will creak.*
Rustĭcus exspectat, dum deflŭat amnis.	*The clown waits for the river to run itself dry.*

Saepe est sub sordĭdo palliŏlo sapientĭa.	*Wisdom often exists under a shabby coat.*
Saevĭus ventis agitătur ingens pinus, et çelsae graviŏre casu decĭdunt turres.	*The lofty pine is more furiously shaken by the force of the wind, and the higher the tower, the greater its fall.*
Salus popŭli suprēma lex est.	*The welfare of the people is the supreme law.* (The motto of Missouri.)
Sapĭens nihil facit invĭtus.	*A wise man does nothing by constraint.*
Saxum volūtum musco non obducĭtur.	*A rolling stone gathers no moss.*
Scintilla etĭam exigŭa in tenĕbris micat.	*Even the smallest spark shines brightly in darkness.*
Semel in omni vita cuĭque arrīdet fortūna.	*Once in each man's life Fortune smiles upon him.*
Semper avărus eget.	*The miser is ever in want.*
Semper bonus homo tiro est.	*A novice always behaves with propriety.*
Semper tibi pendĕat hamus; quo minĭme credis gurgĭte, piscis erit.	*Always keep your hook in the water: where you least expect one, the fish will be found.*
Semper timĭdum scelus.	*Guilt is always timid.*
Senem juventus pigra mendīcum creat.	*An idle youth becomes in age a beggar.*
Sensim, sine sensu aetas senescit.	*Slowly and imperceptibly old age comes creeping on.*
Septem horas dormisse sat est juvenīque senīque.	*Seven hours of sleep is enough for the young and the aged.*
Sepulcri immĕmor struis domos.	*Forgetful of thy tomb thou buildest houses.*

Sequĭtur ver hiĕmem.	*Spring succeeds to winter.*
Sera nunquam est ad bonos mores via.	*The way to good conduct is never too late.*
Si possis, suavĭter; si non, quocunque modo.	*Quietly, if you can; if not, by any means.*
Si qua sede sedes, atque est tibi commŏda sedes, illa sede sede, si nova tuta minus.	*If you sit on a seat, and that seat is a comfortable seat, remain sitting on that seat, if another one is less easy.*
Si quaeris peninsŭlam amoenam, circumspĭce.	*If thou seekest a beautiful peninsula, behold it here.* (The motto of Michigan.)
Si Romae fuĕris, Romăno vivĭto more.	*When you are at Rome, live as Romans live.*
Si vis pacem, para bellum.	*If you desire peace, be ever prepared for war.*
Sibi non cavēre, et alīis consilĭum dare stultum est.	*To counsel others, and to disregard one's own safety, is folly.*
Sic semper tyrannis.	*Ever so to tyrants.* (The motto of Virginia.)
Sic timet insidĭas, qui scit se ferre viător, cur timĕat; tutum carpit inānis iter.	*A wealthy traveler fears an ambush, while one with empty pockets journeys on in safety.*
Sic transit glorĭa mundi.	*So ends all earthly glory.*
Simĭles simĭli gaudent.	*Like likes like.*
Sincērum est nisi vas, quodcunque infundis, acescit.	*Unless the vessel be pure, every thing which is poured into it, will turn sour.*
Sine ope divīna nihil valēmus.	*Without divine assistance we can achieve nothing.*
Sine pennis volāre haud facĭle est.	*It is difficult to fly without wings.*
Solāmen misĕris socĭos habuisse malōrum.	*It is a solace to the miserable to have a companion in their grief.*
Spem pretĭo non emo.	*I give not gold for mere expectations.*
Spes est vigĭlantis somnĭum.	*He is a waking dream.*

Spirĭtus promptus, caro autem infirma.	*The spirit is willing, but the flesh is weak.*
Stultum est in luctu capillum sibi evellěre, quasi calvitĭo maeror levětur.	*It is sheer folly to tear out the hair in grief, as if sorrow could be relieved by baldness.*
Stultum est timěre, quod vitāri non potest.	*It is folly to fear what can not be avoided.*
Stultus stulta loquĭtur.	*A fool talks of folly*
Sublāta causa tollĭtur effectus.	*The cause at an end, the effect is removed.*
Summa sedes non capit duos.	*The highest seat will not hold more than one.*
Summum jus, summa injurĭa.	*Strict law is often great injustice.*
Sunt asĭni multi solum bino pede fulti.	*Many asses have only two legs.*
Suum cuīque.	*Let every man have his due.*
Suus cuīque mos.	*Every man has his peculiar habit.*

Talis hominĭbus est oratĭo, qualis vita.	*Men's language is as their lives.*
Tam deest avāro quod habet, quam quod non habet.	*What he has is of no more use to the miser than that which he has not.*
Tempestas minātur, antěquam surgat; crepant aedificĭa, antě- quam corrŭant.	*The tempest threatens before it comes; houses creak before they fall.*
Tempŏra labuntur, tacĭtisque se- nescĭmus annis.	*Time rolls on, and we grow old with silent years.*
Tempŏra mutantur, nos et mutā- mur in illis.	*The times are changing; we too are changing with them.*
Tempŏre pacis cogitandum de bello.	*In times of peace we should think of war.*
Tempus erit, quo vos specŭlum vidisse pigěbit.	*The time will come when you will hate the sight of a mirror.*
Tempus fugit.	*Time flies.*

Testis nemo in sua causa esse debet.	*No man should be a witness in his own cause.*
Timor mortis morte pejor.	*The fear of death is worse than death itself.*
Totus mundus agit histriōnem.	*All the world 's a stage.*
Tres muliĕres nundĭnas faciunt.	*Three women will make as much noise as a market.*
Tu ne cede malis, sed contra audentĭor ito.	*Yield not to calamity, but face her boldly.*
Tunĭca pallĭo propĭor.	*The shirt is nearer than the coat.*

Ubi cadāver, ibi erunt et aquĭlae.	*Where the carcass is, there will the vultures be.*
Ubi libertas, ibi patrĭa.	*Where freedom is, there shall my country be.*
Una domus non alit duos canes.	*One house can not keep two dogs.*
Una hirundo non facit ver.	*One swallow does not make spring.*
Unde habĕas, quaerit nemo; sed oportet habēre.	*How you come by it no one asks; but wealth you must have.*
Unus lanĭus non timet multas oves.	*One butcher fears not many sheep.*
Urtĭcae proxĭma saepe rosa est.	*The rose is often found near the nettle.*
Usus est altĕra natūra.	*Habit is second nature.*
Usus est tyrannus.	*Custom is a tyrant.*
Ut desint vires, tamen est laudanda voluntas.	*Though the power be wanting, the will deserves praise.*
Ut sementem fecĕris, ita metes.	*As you sow, so shall you reap.*
Utrumque vitĭum est, et omnĭbus credĕre et nulli.	*It is equally a fault to believe all or to believe none.*

Vacŭum vas altĭus pleno vase resōnat.	*An empty vessel makes the most sound.*
Vel capillus habet umbram suam.	*Even a hair has its shadow.*
Velox consilĭum sequĭtur paenitentĭa.	*Repentance follows hasty counsel.*

Verba ligant homĭnes, taurōrum cornŭa fŭnes.	*Men are bound by words, bulls' horns by ropes.*
Verbum sapienti sat.	*A word is sufficient for the wise.*
Verĭtas premĭtur, non opprimĭtur.	*Truth may be suppressed, but not strangled.*
Verĭtas vel mendacĭo corrumpĭtur vel silentĭo.	*Truth is violated either by a lie or by silence.*
Veritātis simplex oratĭo est.	*Simple is the language of truth.*
Vestis virum facit.	*A man is judged by his clothes.*
Via trita, via tuta.	*A beaten track is a safe one.*
Vilĭus argentum est auro, virtutĭbus aurum.	*Silver is of less value than gold, gold than virtue.*
Vincit omnĭa verĭtas.	*Truth conquers all things.*
Vincit, qui se vincit.	*He is indeed a conqueror who conquers himself.*
Vir sapit, qui pauca loquĭtur.	*He acts wisely who says little.*
Virtus in actiōne consistit.	*Merit consists in action.*
Virtus vel in hoste laudātur.	*Valor even in an enemy is worthy of praise.*
Virtūte duce, comĭte fortūna.	*Virtue our leader, fortune our companion.*
Virtūtem primam esse puta compescĕre linguam.	*Consider it the greatest of all virtues to restrain the tongue.*
Visus fidelĭor audītu.	*We trust what we see rather than what we hear.*
Vita homĭnis peregrinatĭo.	*Man's life is a sojourn in a strange land.*
Volenti non fit injurĭa.	*No injury can be complained of by a consenting party.*
Volens et potens.	*Willing and able.* (The motto of Nevada.)
Vultus index anĭmi.	*The face is the index to the mind.*

Lightning Source UK Ltd.
Milton Keynes UK
UKHW021846140421
381978UK00005B/490